BOO!

SERIES IN AFFECTIVE SCIENCE

SERIES EDITORS

Richard J. Davidson

Paul Ekman

Klaus Scherer

Boo!

Culture, Experience, and the Startle Reflex

Ronald C. Simons

New York   Oxford
OXFORD UNIVERSITY PRESS
1996

Oxford University Press

Oxford   New York
Athens   Auckland   Bangkok   Bogota   Bombay
Buenos Aires   Calcutta   Cape Town   Dar es Salaam
Delhi   Florence   Hong Kong   Istanbul   Karachi
Kuala Lumpur   Madras   Madrid   Melbourne
Mexico City   Nairobi   Paris   Singapore
Taipei   Tokyo   Toronto

and associated companies in
Berlin   Ibadan

To protect privacy, informants' names and other potentially identifying information have been altered
throughout except where permission for their use was explicitly granted.

"Startle Neurosis" by F.C. Thorne, *American Journal of Psychiatry*, 101, 105–109.
    Copyright (c) 1944/45. the American Psychiatric Association. Reprinted by permission.
"*Lanti*, illness by fright among Bisayan Filipinos." In R.C. Simons and C.C. Hughes
    (Eds.), *The Culture-Bound Syndromes* (pp. 371–398). Copyright (c) D. Reidel. Reprinted
    by permission of Kluwer Academic Publishers.
An Introduction to Haiku by Harold G. Henderson. Copyright (c) 1958 by Harold G. Henderson.
    Used by permission of Doubleday, a division of Bantam Doubleday Dell Publishing Group, Inc.
On Love and Barley: Haiku of Basho, translated and edited by Lucien Stryke. Copyright
    University of Hawaii Press. Used with permission.

Library of Congress Cataloging-in-Publication Data
Simons, Ronald C.
    Boo! : culture, experience, and the startle reflex / Ronald C. Simons.
        p. cm.— (Series in affective science)
    Includes index.
    ISBN 0-19-509626-6
    1. Startle reaction—Social aspects.   2. Startle reactions—Cross-cultural studies.
    3. Latah (Disease)—Cross-cultural studies.   I. Title.   II. Series.
    QP372.6.S57   1995   95-11809
    304.5—dc20

9 8 7 6 5 4 3 2 1

Printed in the United States of America
on acid free paper

For Sherwood L. Washburn

PREFACE

An analysis of the biology of the actors is essential to the understanding of any human social system.

Sherwood Washburn & Elizabeth McCown, 1980,
Human Evolution: Biosocial Perspectives, p. 7

Accepting that humans are a product of evolution, we must endeavor to understand how the behavioral propensities with which human individuals have been endowed by natural selection can give rise to the complexities of human relationships and of societies, and how societal forces shape the nature of the individual. . . . Certainly it is here . . . that the really exciting challenge now lies.

Robert Hinde, 1989, *Animal Behavior*, 38, p. 732

The work that this book reports began in 1975, when I spent a sabbatical year in the anthropology department of the University of California at Berkeley as a graduate student in cultural anthropology and simultaneously as a postdoctoral student in physical anthropology with Professor Sherwood Washburn. It was at Berkeley that I began the study of the *latah* reaction, a "culture-bound syndrome" of Malaysia and Indonesia. As *latah* is discussed in some detail in the body of this book it is not necessary to describe it here, only to say that it is a set of rather peculiar behaviors performed by some individuals after they are startled.

What made studying *latah* so intriguing is the fact that, although it is generally regarded as merely a Malay and Indonesian custom, and therefore a cultural artifact, a similar set of behaviors occurs in a most improbable set of other places around the globe—Siberia, Maine, Yemen, and the Island of Hokkaido, to name a few. No one had suggested any plausible explanation why. I wondered if the answer might have anything to do with the biology of the startle reflex, but if so, why did it occur only in scattered locations and not ubiquitously? Much of the empirical work I was to do concerned itself with attempting to solve this puzzle. As P. M. Yap had suggested in his seminal 1952 paper on *latah*, the solution seemed to be the result of some interaction among the neurophysiology of startle, what people thought about startle, and how these ideas were reflected in social action. In the course of the work on *latah*, I became interested in what happens when people are startled in other contexts and in the larger question of how this simple evolved reflex enters into the private and social lives of people more generally. How is it that the same bit of neurophysiology is played out and experienced so similarly and yet so differently in different cultural contexts?

Thus startle, rather than *latah* per se, gradually became the focus of the work. The startle reflex—ubiquitous, discrete, and brief—presented itself as a Rosetta stone. I could look both at what people did with this simple reflex and also at what they said about it in a wide set of contexts, in both the popular and scholarly literatures. Just as Carlyle's *Sartor Resartus* had humorously examined human life as reflected in clothing, I could look at experience, interaction, and explanation as they were reflected in startle, using startle as a model system. Different disciplines developed different data, but data that could in this case be reconciled from one discipline to another along the dimensions of the startle reflex.

As I began to publish on this work, it was my good fortune to have an especially fluent and persuasive intellectual adversary, Michael Kenny, of Simon Fraser University. Professor Kenny took on the task of opposing the position I present here in a series of papers in which the relevant issues were argued back and forth between us. The opportunity to participate in this debate enormously clarified for me the line of thinking presented in this text. Much of the material in the second part of this book is an expansion of materials and ideas first developed in the course of that debate. The debate appeared in the pages of the *Journal of Nervous and Mental Disease*, which under the editorship of Professor Eugene Brody has long been a publication that encourages the thoughtful presentation of more than one side of any issue. To the *Journal* and to Professor Brody I am much indebted.

While this book was in press, Robert L. Winzeler published a work summarizing his long study of *latah*. In many ways our observations about the previous literature on *latah* and about the cultural and social setting in which contemporary *latah* is embedded are similar and mutually reinforcing. However, starting from rather disparate premises about the relationship of culture to biology, we arrive at quite different conclusions about the nature of *latah*, why *latah* has the form and cultural patterning we see. Our conclusions about *latah* differ in two important respects: the significance we find in the similarities among the family of culture-specific "*latah*" syndromes and, most importantly, the significance of neurophysiological factors in the syndrome's contemporary Malaysian presentations. To anyone interested in further pursuing the study of *latah*, Winzeler's book can be highly recommended.

Organizing and explaining the heterogenous assemblage of materials that have been collected over the years presented some major expository problems. Initially, I began with a discussion of *latah* which, after all, was the original subject of research. However, after wrestling with the material unprofitably for rather too long, I realized that most readers would find it easier to move from the familiar to the unfamiliar. Hence the organization of this book, with the section on *latah* and other non-Western manifestations of startle following material closer to the lives of most Western readers. The major problem proved to be that of sequentially presenting data and concepts linked by an intricate network of connections.

Of all the relevant disciplines, it is anthropology with its cultural, physical, linguistic, and archaeologic branches that makes the strongest claim to being a unified science of humankind. Yet in actuality, this is more of an idealized goal than a usual practice. Paul J. Bohannan once expressed the tension between this ethos and practice in an open letter to the membership of the American Anthropological Society published almost two decades ago on the front page of the *Anthropology Newsletter*:

> Anthropology covers a wider range than any other social science: from human biology to human language, from prehistory to civilization. That broad scope is not an accident or a mirror of vanity. To carry out our main job—determining the many ways that the many dimensions of human life can be fitted together—it has to be broad. Anthropology is an integrated and synthesizing discipline: it is within itself necessarily interdisciplinary. Its primary mode is one of comparison. . . .
>
> The need for precise monographic study of particular behavioral situations is obvious: without them we could not be comparative. . . . [However], the comparative task—which is, in my opinion, the primary one—seems far more difficult. Perhaps because it is farther removed from artifacts and from people. And as time goes on and a subject develops, it becomes increasingly difficult to make the leap to the comparative and the general.
>
> Yet, the fact of the broadness and the difficulty of making that leap gives anthropology the appearance of being constantly on the verge of shattering into its components. The unifying cement is something that must be constantly worked on if we are to preserve it. (Bohannan, 1978, pp. 1–2)

It is my hope that this book will function as a bit of the necessary cement. It is a book of connections. It is also my hope that it will be of use to those who hyperstartle and who find their hyperstartling problematic, and to those who will follow in the cross-cultural study of startle, hyperstartle, *latah*, and other culture-bound syndromes.

I am much indebted to the Harry Frank Guggenheim Foundation, which supplied the major portion of the costs of my fieldwork in Southeast Asia; to the University of California International Center for Medical Research (Grant AI 10051 from the National Institutes of Health, United States Public Health Service); and to the Institut Penyelidikan Perubatan, Kuala Lumpur, Malaysia, which provided office space and much logistic support during the time I was in the field.

This book was completed during a sabbatical year in London where Maurice Lipsedge at Guy's Hospital and Roland Littlewood at University College provided me with the time and freedom needed to bring this long-delayed project to completion. To their kindness and forbearance I owe a great deal. I would also like to register my appreciation to the inspired teachers, colleagues, and friends who, over the years, have so profoundly shaped my thought, most especially Eli and Pat Robins, George Engel, Franz Reichsman, Cornelus Bakker, Sherwood Washburn, Charles Hughes, and many friends and colleagues in the International Society for Human Ethology, the Society for the Study of Culture and Psychiatry, and the Departments of Psychiatry and Anthropology, Medical Anthropology Program, Institute for International Health, and Interaction Analysis Laboratory at Michigan State University. I would especially like to thank Paul Ekman and Brigitte Jordan, whose splendid studies of facial expressions and of human birthing practices showed that work such as this could be done.

I owe a special debt of gratitude to Joan Bossert, Executive Editor at Oxford University Press, who has been helpful and encouraging well above and beyond the line of duty.

I would also like to thank the many others who have helped with portions of this work, especially Ahmad bin Ngah and his family, James Anderson, Linda Spoerl Armstrong, Mary Buss, Mary Cameron, Jesus and Lolita Cortez, Polly Crisp, Frederic Erickson, Wallace Friesen, Brian Grant, Janice Harper, Nakagawa Hidezo, Sidang Hussein bin Dalip and his family, Leslie Lintern, Josefina Nazarea Gutmann, Donal O'Holohan, Jaafar Omar, Ogata Motoi, Gunter Pfaff, Arthur Rubel, Martha Salyers, Roya Sayadi, Betsy Shipley, Richard Schmidt, Maria Struck, Sandra Teel, Tanya Tremewan, Robert Wilks, Robert L. Winzeler, and the *latahs* of Kampung Padang Kemunting and its surrounding villages. To David J. Hufford I am especially indebted for his careful and insightful reading of an earlier draft of this work. Finally, I would like to thank my most patient and understanding wife, Mary Lynn Buss, for her support, never-failing encouragement, and wonderfully helpful editorial advice.

Vashon, Wash.   R.C.S.
May 1995

REFERENCES

Bohannan, P. (1978). Open letter. *Anthropology Newsletter, 19*, 1–2.

Hinde, R. A. (1989). *Animal Behavior, 38*; 732.

Washburn, S.L., & McCown, E.R. (1980). *Human evolution: Biosocial perspectives.* Menlo Park, CA: Benjamin/Cummings.

Winzeler, R. L. (1995). Latah *in Southeast Asia—the history and ethnography of a culture-bound syndrome.* Cambridge, U.K.: Cambridge University Press.

Yap, P.M. (1952). The *latah* reaction: Its pathodynamics and nosological position. *Journal of Mental Science, 98*, 515–564.

NOTE ON REFERENCE STYLE

Throughout this book, scholarly literature is cited in a way that will be familiar to most readers. In addition, the book contains many "exhibits," references to startle culled from newspapers, magazines, radio programs, films, and works of literature such as novels, short stories, poems, and plays. These exhibits are cited in the text by author, date of origin, source, and when relevant, page number, in the following format: (Jane Austen, 1818, *Persuasion*, p. 258.) To identify the cultural context in which the cited material was originally published, the date given is the date when the work was first published. The page number, however, is the page number in the edition consulted.

It is the edition consulted which is listed in the reference section that follows each chapter, with its publication date following that of the original publication, for example: "Austen, Jane. 1818/1971. *Persuasion*. In R. W. Chapman (Ed.), *The Oxford Illustrated Jane Austen*. Oxford: Oxford University Press."

Because there are so many editions of Shakespeare's plays which readers may choose to consult, references to Shakespeare are given by act and scene rather than by page number. Citations from newspapers and magazines are identified in the text by name and date of publication and are not repeated in the end-of-chapter bibliographies.

CONTENTS

Part I

STARTLE AND HYPERSTARTLE

Vera had not sensed my approach. . . .
I stole closer to her, and then I said, "Boo!"
She jerked her head away from the eyepiece.
"Hello," I said.
"You scared me half to death," she said.
"Sorry," I said, and I laughed.
These ancient games go on and on. It's nice they do.

Kurt Vonnegut, 1976, *Slapstick*,
London: J. Cape, p. 204

1

INTRODUCTION

The emotional behavior of man consists of a curious blending of innate reflex responses and acquired personal and social habits. In any gross observation of emotional behavior we find the two inextricably intermingled. Only by careful analytic techniques can they be separated.

Carney Landis & William A. Hunt, 1939, *The Startle Pattern*, p. 135

Everyone startles. Everyone knows the wrenching dislocation that lies alert and waiting just under the surface of the most ordinary experience. A foot slips, a car backfires, and wherever one is, like it or not, one finds oneself doing and thinking things quite unplanned. Startle is a reflex, something that happens in and to the body, but it is more than that. When one is startled one's soul is troubled, and one's mind finds itself, if only for a moment, in a strange and surprising place. Being startled changes, if ever so briefly, one's relationship with the entire experienced universe.

A strong startle is a memorable event that has phases. There is the perception of abruptly crossing some barrier, a brief and intense experience, often symbolized in cartoons by something like a lightning bolt or a hammer hitting the head. Then there is a stupefied afterstate in which one is either silent and motionless or acts in some way like an automaton, vulnerable in a special way to the influence of external stimuli.

If one is startled while interacting with others, all the give-and-take of ordinary social intercourse, the fine mutually adjusting dance of speech and body, is broken, and the awkward and disconcerting lapse in seemly social presence must be acknowledged and remedied. Yet in spite of this, or to be more precise, because of it, people everywhere delight in startling one another. Kurt Vonnegut called doing so "an ancient game." It probably is; certainly it is an old one, widespread among the peoples of the world. The fact that a startle is a set of experiences and events one person can induce in another, like laughing or crying or orgasm, makes possible its use as an interactional resource. Because the ease of its elicitation and its strength vary with circumstances and among individuals, the resource is a very rich one indeed.

Many English verbs signify the act of altering someone else's prior emotional state—for example, "frighten," "gladden," "comfort," "soothe," "terrify," "amuse," "excite," "intimidate." When used as a verb, "startle" is ambiguous in this regard. It may mean either that one has caused another person to experience and display a startle or that one has experienced and displayed a startle oneself; "startle" can be either a transitive or intransitive verb. In most contexts the presence or absence of an object makes the meaning clear: It's either "He startled" or "He startled John." English has only a few verbs that work in this way; "awaken" is another. Both are unambiguous in the passive. Like the variation in strength of response with person and with circumstance, the intransitive and transitive aspects of startle provide rich resources for cultural elaboration. The fact that people can and do make others jump and what happens in those jumps provide themes amenable to the most intricate and meaning-laden variations.

Because it is common to reflect on one's own startles, the subject of startle is of some intrinsic interest. But in addition, examining the ways people use and understand the startle reflex opens a window on a larger set of issues. Startle provides an especially revealing model for discovering how evolved neurophysiology shapes personal experience generally and also how it shapes patterns of recurrent interactions and the systems of meanings that people collectively create and transmit. This is because a host of experiences, interactions, meanings, and values are shaped in specific ways by the relatively small set of neurophysiologic events which comprise the startle reflex. In the most diverse social contexts, in cultures widely separated in time and space, the inescapable physiology of the reflex shapes the experience of startle and therefore biases the social usages to which the reflex is put.

THE UMWELT

It has long been known that, corresponding to differences in their anatomies and neurophysiologies, different animal species receive somewhat different sensory information about the world with which they must interact. Different species respond to different portions of the spectra of frequencies of sound and wavelengths of light, to different smells and tastes, and to different tactile, temperature, and kinesthetic sensations. In a now-classic book, Von Uexküll (1928) explored the significance of this fact, which is that members of each animal species eat, drink, breathe, reproduce, move, and, in short, live out their lives in a species-typical surrounding world different from those of members of other species. Things look, sound, smell, and feel different to me and to my dog. Von Uexküll called each such species-typical world an *Umwelt*. These species-typical worlds are not composed of mere sensations, but rather of perceptions, groups of sensations which have meanings.

That humans respond preferentially in specific ways to certain stimulus patterns has been known at least since the time of Pythagoras, who showed that the soul is mathematical. Pythagoras observed that when a vibrating string is divided exactly in half, the notes produced are heard as similar to, yet different from, the parent frequency in an unmistakable way. Dividing a vibrating string in thirds, quarters, or fifths generates sets of frequencies that are ubiquitously found pleasant in ways not true of less exact ratios. There is something special about those exact numerical ratios that is built into the human nervous system.

Like harmonies, colors are also not arbitrary. Although the spectrum of light is continuous, people in the most culturally diverse societies segment it in remarkably similar ways. When they name colors there is "red" and "yellow" and "blue" and "green," or less commonly, a single category of "blue-and-green" (Berlin & Kay, 1969; Rosch, 1975). This division of a continuous spectrum into discrete colors is determined in large part by known neuroanatomical and neurophysiological properties of the human visual system. Receptor systems in the eye and brain bias our perceptions of the physical universe in ways determined in part by their structure and mode of operation. In these ways neurophysiology provides both a resource and a constraint in the perception of and discourse about sound and about light.

Each species is characterized by a certain set or range of perceptual possibilities, and as one expands the population of individuals under consideration to genera, families, orders, and phyla, significant commonalities characterize the perceptual worlds of these larger groups as well. We live in a mammal's world, which shapes our specifically human world. As we are primates, we share with other primates a world in which visual stimuli can be exquisitely discriminated but also one in which many olfactory stimuli which signify much to most other mammals tell us little or nothing at all. The visual world is a highly salient resource for us, the olfactory world much less so.

The aspects of our world to which we can respond are those specific to the properties of our human senses, to human neurophysiology. Thus, it is not an undifferentiated biological substrate that shapes experience and meaning; it is specific and specifiable bits of evolved human neurophysiology. The raw material for cultural elaboration is the experience of individual persons, and the nature of that experience, while somewhat variable, is always species-typical.[1] Being startled and observing the startles of others are aspects of that species-typical individual and collectively experienced world.

CONCEPTUAL EMBODIMENT

A perennial subject of controversy in the literatures of the disciplines of anthropology, sociology, psychology, and psychiatry concerns what kind of resource and how much of a constraint innate, evolved, hard-wired neurophysiologic propensities provide. Must neurophysiology's evolved details be considered in explanations of personal experience and of culture or is it merely background, the mechanism by which the ship sails but irrelevant to its destination?

A particularly contentious difference among academic disciplines, especially prominent between physical and cultural anthropology, is the degree to which the implications of the fact that we humans are evolved and made of flesh and blood are considered relevant data in explanatory formulations. Though this was more the case 15 or 20 years ago than it is today, it remains a subject of controversy. There is still a strong voice in cultural anthropology that does not believe it reasonable or useful to consider bodily processes in accounting for culturally shaped behavior.

Cultural anthropologists have convincingly demonstrated that every aspect of human existence is shaped and colored by culturally transmitted systems of meanings and values. Nothing is experienced that is not so shaped and colored. Meanings and values also profoundly influence the interactions of any person with any other, and one's experience of reality is in large part the experience of these meanings and values. However, this book is intended to demonstrate that this system of meanings and values, the conceptual categories with which we reflect on our actions and those of others, is itself shaped in quite subtle and far-reaching ways by neurophysiological resources and constraints.

In a recent work, the sociolinguist George Lakoff presented a particularly clear formulation of the point at issue. Lakoff contrasted the widely held cultural relativist position with a concept he called "conceptual embodiment":

> *Conceptual embodiment:* The idea that the properties of certain [conceptual] categories are a consequence of the nature of human biological capacities and of the experience of functioning in a physical and social environment. It is contrasted with the idea that concepts exist independent of the bodily nature of any thinking beings and independent of their experience. (Lakoff, 1987, p. 12)

Lakoff pointed out that there is no argument with the relativist contention that "Human conceptual categories have properties that are a result of imaginative process (metaphor, metonymy, mental imagery) that do not mirror nature" (1987, p. 371).

This is not the point at issue. What is at issue is Lakoff's contention that, despite this psychological and cultural shaping,

> Conceptual categories are not merely characterized in terms of objective properties of category members. . . . Human conceptual categories have properties that are, at least in part, determined by the bodily nature of the people doing the categorizing rather than solely by the properties of the category members. (1987, p. 371)

Biology, Lakoff believes, does not influence human conceptual categorization in some general amorphous way. Rather, he contends (correctly, I believe) that specific aspects of human biology shape the world of human meanings.

In the scholarly literature on male/female relationships and other sex differences—aggression, aging, attachment, birth, childhood, development, and intelligence—the legitimacy of this sort of biologically informed approach is currently being hotly debated. For resolving many of the relevant issues, the numerous specific and readily identifiable properties of startle events make startle an especially useful model system.

TRACTABILITY OF THE STARTLE REFLEX AS A MODEL SYSTEM

The enormous literature on *Drosophila melanogaster* is not the result of an overwhelming scientific preoccupation with tiny flies. Instead, it is that these fruit flies' short intergenerational time, easy husbandry, and large chromosomes make *Drosophila* an especially useful experimental model for studies of genetics more generally. Because its visual system is highly regular and easily accessible for electrophysiological study, a second small fly, *Calliphora erythrocephala*, is widely used in research on neural information processing (Bialek, Rieke, de Ruyter van Steveninck, & Warland, 1991, p. 1761). Squid have a "giant" nerve axon that provides another widely used model system. A review of *Squid as Experimental Animals* (Gilbert, Adelman, & Arnold, 1990) noted that "Few life scientists, including squid specialists, however, are likely to appreciate the range and number of basic discoveries that also have stemmed from research on squid" (Gilly, 1991, p. 98).

A recent book, *Biological Systems* (Jasney & Koshland, 1990), discusses the model systems most widely used in contemporary experimental biology; there are many, each with specific advantages for specific classes of problems. Its review in the journal *Science* was titled "Hot Tools" (Anonymous, 1991).

For investigating how culture is shaped by biology, the startle reflex is a "hot tool," a particularly tractable model system. The neurophysiology of startle, the personal experience of startle, and the interactive uses of startle (both actual and symbolic) comprise a system unusually amenable to straightforward analysis. Single startles, and the events that precede and follow them, make convenient analytic units. Episodes of startle are brief, discrete, and of a high natural incidence. Because startles are visible (and often audible), they can be recorded and analyzed in detail. Because they are memorable discontinuities in the ongoing flow of experience, their phenomenology is often well remembered by those experiencing them. And because they are of high social salience, startles can often be described in detail by those witnessing them or participating in their elicitation.

Meanings and values associated with startles are often highly culturally elaborated, and although this set of meanings and values is large, it is of a size amenable to sorting and analysis. Parameters of interest can readily be sorted into analyzable sets such as "eliciting stimuli," "responses," and "social and cultural factors" (e.g., who may startle whom, how often, in what circumstances, and what the startle signifies). Startles can be elicited reliably on demand from willing subjects, and many of the reflex's parameters can be manipulated in controlled experiments. Because animals other than humans also startle, comparative data are available, and some relevant factors can be manipulated in ways not ethically permissible with humans.

A further attraction of startle as a model system is that it is a relatively apolitical subject. The dialectic on some evolved neurophysiologic aspects of human behavior and interaction (e.g., cognitive and behavioral differences between the sexes, the parent–child relationship, the whole field of sociobiology) has degenerated into such a battleground between competing ideologies that dispassionate empirical inquiry has become difficult. Startle, like any other human behavior, has its political dimensions, but these are less ubiquitously intrusive.

Therefore, this book is and is not about startle. There is nothing special about startle, only that it is easy to trace. Any set of experiences and behaviors in which one might be interested has both physiological and cultural determinants. The subject of the book is a more general one: (1) How one's experience of being in the world is shaped by neurophysiology and how it is shaped by prior experience, beliefs, values, and social condition, and (2) how these different types of shaping influences might be considered jointly in single explanatory formulations.

STARTLE IN EVOLUTIONARY PERSPECTIVE

The startle reflex is universal in mammals, reptiles, birds, and amphibians. It can be thought of as an override system, automatically activated when a sudden unexpected environmental event requires immediate first-priority attention. The essence of startle is that it is the mechanism designed to ensure that the startled organism responds to a potential danger as rapidly as possible, even before the eliciting stimulus is consciously classified and evaluated.

Most startles, of course, are false alarms. The startle reflex system is designed to be sensitive rather than selective: First respond, then assess. In this it is like the well-known spinal reflex, which removes a hand from a hot stove top long before the burned subject has time to think: "Hot. Too hot! Potentially injurious. Must move hand away. Hand, move away!" The stimulus that elicits a startle may turn out to have been a harmless snake or even a piece of vine. The unexpected suddenly appearing object may pose no actual danger, but when a rapid response is called for, there it is, as quickly as the body can produce it, without the lag preceding more usual responses to stimuli during their cognitive identification and assessment.

The startle produced by unexpectedly catching sight of a snake is a good example. Snakes are, cross-culturally, powerful elicitors of both phobic and startle responses.[2] This is functional; in many areas of the world, especially in both the Old and the New World tropics, a significant percentage of all snakes are venomous, and the morbidity from snakebite exceeds by an order of magnitude that from any other nonhuman vertebrate.[3] Danger from snakes would have been even greater during the time our species evolved, when the natural environment was less disturbed and shoes and leg covering were not worn.

The usual human startle response is precisely the set of behaviors that would be maximally effective in minimizing the chance of a fatal encounter. The response includes both physical events and alterations in attention, thought, and mood. Instantaneously and without reflection, forward motion is checked. The raised foot is arrested or drawn back and the upper limbs are drawn in to safety. Visual attention is locked onto the eliciting stimulus, whatever had been in consciousness is obliterated, and the mind is filled with one thought: "Snake!" Startling stimuli other than snakes elicit similar immediate patterned rapid-avoidance behaviors and similar redirection of attention.

FORM OF THE STARTLE REFLEX

Landis and Hunt (1939), who performed the pioneering laboratory investigations of startle in the 1930s using the then novel technology of high-speed photography, listed the most usual physical responses to startling stimuli. There is an eye blink, a forward movement of the head, a characteristic facial expression, a raising of the shoulders and moving them forward, a motion of the upper arms somewhat away from the body, a bending of the elbows so as to raise the forearms and hands, a rotation of the forearms inward so that the palms more or less face each other, a clenching of the fingers, a motion of the upper body forward from the hips, a tightening of the abdominal muscles, and a bending of the knees.

In the late 1970s and early 1980s, Paul Ekman, Wallace Friesen, and I replicated a portion of Landis and Hunt's work, concentrating especially on changes in the face in an attempt to specify them more precisely (Ekman, Friesen, & Simons, 1985). We used Ekman and Friesen's "Facial Action Coding System" (1975, 1978), which distinguishes 44 action units, the minimal units of facial activity visually distinguishable. The effects on the face of being unexpectedly startled by a .22-caliber blank fired from a few feet away

Table 1.1   Averaged Micromeasurements (in 20-msec blocks) of the Components of the Unanticipated Startle ($n=6$)

	Period				
Action	Movement latency	Movement onset	Movement apex	Movement offset	Total duration
Muscles around the eye	84.00	72.00	44.00	72.00	188.00
Horizontal lip stretch	104.00	72.00	36.00	88.00	196.00
Neck muscle activity	100.00	83.33	103.00	133.33	320.00
Eyes closed	73.33	53.33	123.33	103.33	280.00
Head movements	100.00	113.33	200.00	180.00	493.33
Trunk movements	120.00	110.00	673.33	210.00	993.33

Note: Table 1.1 presents the timing of six "Actions" which are components of a typical unanticipated startle. Because the film which we analyzed had been shot at 50 frames per second (roughly twice normal speed), each frame of the film is therefore the smallest available analytic unit. The table gives times in milliseconds (number of frames × 20) averaged for six subjects. Shown are the interval from the presentation of an unanticipated startling stimulus to the beginning of movement. ("Movement latency"), the time from the beginning of movement to maximum muscular contraction ("Movement onset"), the duration of maximum muscular contraction ("Movement apex"), the length of the period of muscular relaxation ("Movement offset), and the total duration of each of the six "Actions" ("Total duration").
From Ekman, Freisen, & Simons, 1985.

and out of sight are essentially as Landis and Hunt had described: The eyebrows lower, the eyes close and the lids tighten, the lips stretch horizontally, and both surface and deeper muscles of the neck tighten. All but the trunk movements are over in a half second or less, and the trunk movement in a second (Table 1.1). The rapidity of the response, 14 milliseconds (msec) in human jaw muscles, 6 msec in the forepaw of a rat, is quite extraordinary (Davis, 1984). Because transmission of an impulse from one neuron to another is mediated by chemical neurotransmitters and therefore takes some time, this rapid response means that only a few neuronal junctures (synapses) and hence neurons can be involved (Davis, 1984, pp. 287–288).

SUMMARY OF THE NEUROPHYSIOLOGY OF THE STARTLE REFLEX

As the literature on the neurophysiology and psychophysiology of startle is quite extensive, its comprehensive summary is beyond the scope of this book. A splendid review of the last several decades of work on mammalian startle can be found in the chapter by Michael Davis in *Neural Mechanisms of Startle Behavior* (1984), to which interested readers are referred. The brief summary that follows is largely based on Davis's review, which summarizes 214 papers, 32 of them by Davis himself and his co-workers. The summary also includes data from papers published in the years since Davis's review appeared.

Anatomy of the Startle Reflex

Although many of the structures involved have been tentatively or definitively identified, the complete neural path from stimulus to muscular response has not been definitively traced. Considerable evidence shows that the reticulospinal tract originating in the pontine reticular formation is required for the startle that is elicited by a sudden loud noise ("acoustic startle"). Lesions in this tract abolish acoustic startle; lesions above or below it do not. In addition, Davis and his co-workers have shown that in the brainstem of the rat, the neural pathway for acoustic startle consists of the auditory nerve, the ventricular cochlear nucleus, the paralemniscal zone, and the nucleus reticularis pontis caudalis. In the spinal cord there are multiple connections of several types between the nucleus reticularis pontis caudalis and motor neurons (Boulis, Kehpe, Miserendino, & Davis, 1990, p. 240).

Mediation and Modulation

Neurophysiologists make a distinction between the neurophysiology intrinsic to the reflex—that is, the systems that *mediate* startle—and the systems that modify the reflex as it is expressed on any given occasion, those which *modulate* it. Davis notes that even whether "flexion [bending] or extension [straightening out] occurs depends on the state of the nervous system at the time startle is elicited, since the probability of extension increases following voluntary extension or ongoing extension in the muscle being recorded" (Davis, 1984, p. 289). Although the neural circuitry that mediates acoustic startle is located entirely within the brainstem, this system is impinged on by modulating neural tracts from higher in the brain, so that many subjective states influence the expressed outflow of the startle system. The nucleus reticularis pontis caudalis in the brainstem may be the site on which brain structures mediating emotion, such as the amygdala, may act (Miserendino & Davis, 1993, p. 215). Direct connections between the amygdala and the nucleus reticularis pontis caudalis have been demonstrated. There are also connections between the amygdala and the locus coeruleus, whose activation results in increased vigilance and superior signal detection (Davis, 1992, p. 38).

Effect of Prior Fear Conditioning

In both humans and a number of experimental animals the startle response is increased when the experimental subject encounters a startling stimulus in the presence of a cue that has previously been paired with a fear-inducing stimulus, such as an electric shock. This has been called "the fear-potentiated startle effect" (Brown, Kalish, & Farber, 1951). Consistent with this finding is the observation that drugs which reduce fear or fear-related physiological responses (including antianxiety medications of various types) reduce both the likelihood and the magnitude of startle. This is true for sodium amytal, alcohol, several benzodiazapines, cloni- dine, and propranolol (a beta-blocker). Grillon and co-workers have shown that persons startle more readily and more violently to white noise when told to expect an electric shock, even when such a shock never arrives (1991, p. 588).

Effect of Prestimulation

A signal too weak to produce a measurable startle will reduce the amplitude of a startle to a subsequently presented sudden intense stimulus if the weak signal is presented, withdrawn, or altered approximately 100 msec before the stimulus that startles. If the weak signal is presented, withdrawn, or altered only 4 msec before an intense startle-eliciting stimulus, the latency of the startle in response to the intense stimulus will be shortened. The weak, modulating prestimulus does not have to be in the same modality as the subsequent startling stimulus—for example, the modulating pres- timulus could be a sound and the startling stimulus a sight (Hoffman, 1984, p. 275).

Neurotransmitters that Mediate Startle

The neurotransmitters that pass the impulse from one neuron to another across synapses, ultimately resulting in a startle, have not been identified. Davis notes that the most common neurotransmitters (serotonin, norepi- nephrine, dopamine, glycine, and acetylcholine) are almost certainly not involved, evidenced by the observation that their depletion or blockade does not prevent startle from occurring.

Neurotransmitters that Modulate Startle

More is known about neurotransmitters that modify the reflex. Serotonin probably inhibits startle, as its depletion is associated with increased star- tle; moreover, rats fed a diet lacking in tryptophan, the precursor of sero- tonin, startle with increased ease and violence. Davis believes that "depletion of serotonin seems to increase acoustic startle by increasing sensitization" to startle-inducing stimuli (1984, p. 307). However, the relationship between the level of serotonin and the magnitude of startle is a complex one. Although depletion of serotonin increases startle, markedly elevating sero- tonin also increases startle. It appears to depend on the site in the nervous system where the serotonin exerts its inhibitory effect.

Drugs that increase dopamine transmission increase the magnitude of the startle response, but this effect is probably indirect, because drugs that decrease dopamine transmission do not significantly reduce the magnitude of the response.

Norepinephrine may have an excitatory role in startle, for drugs that increase its availability augment the startle response and drugs that block norepinephrine release or reduce its availability decrease the response. Further evidence for an excitatory role for norepinephrine is the observation that "the drug clonidine, which decreases the firing rate of cells in the locus coeruleus and decreases norepinephrine release and turnover, markedly depresses acoustic and tactile startle at very low doses" (Davis, 1984, p. 314). Davis suggests there may be a significant interaction between norepinephrine and dopamine in modulating startle, with dopamine and norepinephrine acting in series "so that decreases in norepinephrine transmission prevent an expected dopamine-mediated activation of startle" (1984, p. 316). In addition, "increasing norepinephrine transmission augments the excitatory effect of dopamine transmission" (1984, p. 316).

Glycine appears to play an important role in dampening down or moderating the effect of startling stimuli. When its receptors are inhibited by strychnine or as occurs in hyperexplexia, a hereditary hyperstartling disease (see Chapter 11), startles are both easily elicited and massively exaggerated (Kehne, Gallagher, & Davis, 1981; Ivinson, 1993; Shiang, Ryan, Zhu, Hahn, et al., 1993, p. 351).

Whether acetylcholine, another important neurotransmitter, modulates the startle response is not known.

Sensitization and Habituation

Repetitive startling usually induces an increased readiness to startle and an increased violence of response, but under some circumstances the opposite is the case. The process by which being startled repetitively leads to more ready and violent startles is called "sensitization" and the process by which a person acclimates and begins to startle less readily and violently is called "habituation." Whether sensitization or habituation results from repetitive stimulation depends on the frequency of stimulation, the length of time between stimuli, the nature of the stimuli used, differences in the states of the subjects being tested, and probably also unknown individual variations in neurophysiology. The anatomical locations and neurophysiological mechanisms by which sensitization and habituation occur are almost certainly different. One is not merely the converse of the other, for it is possible to demonstrate both processes being induced simultaneously in experimental animals; the behavior observed results from which of the two mechanisms is evoked by the test stimulus. Davis believes that "taken together the data suggest that sensitization of startle is ultimately mediated in the spinal cord whereas habituation of startle occurs in supraspinal parts of the pathway" (1984, p. 332).

Variability of the Strength of the Response

Even when test conditions are controlled rigorously, the strength of any experimental animal's startle response varies considerably from one trial to another. Davis concludes from this that "startle is extremely sensitive to a variety of state changes" (1984, p. 333). People startle more readily and violently when watching slides of mutilated bodies or spiders than when watching slides of smiling children or nudes of the opposite sex. (Vrana, Spence, & Lang, 1988). Grillon and co-workers report studies by a number of authors in which persons startle more readily and more strongly when attending to startling stimuli than when their attention is directed away from them (1991, p. 593).

In life outside the laboratory, sometimes very little happens in a human startle and sometimes a great deal. It all depends on such factors as how loud, unexpected, terrifying, or improbable the stimulus is and how dark, frightening, or dangerous the setting. It also depends on how "jumpy" the subject is, either transiently because of factors such as preoccupation or vigilance (what psychologists refer to as a "state") or characteristically (a "trait"). Most important, what happens when a person is startled is determined by a host of social and cultural factors specific to the ongoing life of the individual affected. Startle, as Bennett concluded in the summary chapter of *Neural Mechanisms of Startle Behavior*, "may represent a way of using a single rapid warning system to trigger a variety of responses whose nature is based on prior experience" (1984, p. 361).

It is possible to enumerate the properties of startle events, the kinds of stimuli, responses, settings, states, and so forth that comprise or are associated with the reflex as it is experienced and played out in actual life. Table 1.2 summarizes and groups these properties. Subsequent chapters will discuss the ways in which they are experienced in the lives of individual persons and elaborated on in the beliefs and practices of various societies.

Table 1.2   Properties of Startle Events

I. Stimuli that startle
    A. Dangerous or appalling sights
        1. Snakes and creepy-crawlies
           a. Snakes and snakelike objects
           b. Creepy-crawlies (toads, lizards, scorpions, centipedes, wasps, spiders, etc.)
        2. Other dangers
        3. Appalling sights
    B. Loud noises, bright lights, and other intense stimulations
    C. The unexpected
        1. Sudden motion
           a. Motions in general
           b. Startles of other persons
        2. Unexpected occurrences
           a. Unexpected events
           b. Prohibited words (naughty talk)
           c. Significant, sometimes idiosyncratically significant, words
        3. Radical novelty (extreme unfamiliarity, mismatch of scale, etc.)

(*continued*)

Table 1.2 Properties of Startle Events (*continued*)

    D. Great beauty or value
       1. Great beauty
       2. Great prizes or treasures
    E. Cessation of a stimulus
II. Responses when startled
    A. Jumping, blinking, or vocalizing
    B. Striking out
    C. Dropping or flinging something that had been held
    D. Being stopped in thought or action
    E. Releasing an action that had been held in check
    F. Unintended speech
       1. Prohibited words (naughty talk)
       2. Improper reference to a deity
       3. Idiosyncratically stereotyped thought or utterance
       4. Secret or hidden thought
       5. Disorganized talk
    G. Matching
    H. Obedience
III. States in which persons startle especially readily and violently
    A. When ill or debilitated
    B. When wary
    C. When in a state of high anticipation
    D. When drowsy, dozing, or dropping off to sleep
    E. When asleep
    F. When lost in thought
IV. Settings in which startles are likely to occur
    A. Spooky and dangerous places
    B. Quiet places
V. Sensitization and habituation
    A. Being frequently startled may lead to hyperstartling
    B. Severe or prolonged trauma may lead to hyperstartling
    C. Familiarity with a stimulus may reduce the likelihood of startling to its
       presentation and may reduce the violence of the response when it occurs
VI. Miscellaneous other aspects of the startle reflex
    A. Stimuli in any modality may elicit startles
    B. Animals startle to equivalent stimuli in equivalent ways

THE DATA ON WHICH THIS BOOK IS BASED

Most of the data discussed in this book were collected over a period of about 10 years. The general strategy was inductive: Collect startles and examine them. Start not with a theory or even a hypothesis; instead, amass examples of startle and see what story they tell. Collect widely; if it pertains to startle, collect it. Thus, wherever I went, I looked for and at naturally occurring startles, and I collected representations and accounts of being startled and of startling others: startles in life, in plays, in books, in paintings, any startles. The collection now includes approximately a thousand such accounts and depictions of and references to startle events.

In addition to this unfocused collection, as certain patterns began to become more clear, a number of specific research projects were developed.

1. I identified a local (Michigan) population of persons who startle especially readily and especially strongly ("hyperstartlers") and interviewed them about the phenomenology of their experiences. I also filmed and measured their responses and those of a matched control population to a standard startling stimulus (Ekman et al., 1985; Simons, 1980).

2. I conducted a special study in Malaysia, a country in which being startled and startling others, especially hyperstartlers, holds a special culturally marked status. After a brief survey, I established residence with a local family in a small coastal fishing village, where I lived for approximately 8 months. There I observed and recorded in field notes the startles that formed such a salient part of the lives of these villagers. I collected film footage of startles, accounts of known hyperstartlers, descriptions of local attitudes about startle, and stories about the culture-typical interactive behavior complex, *latah*, which reflect perceptions of its cause and significance. I also collected experiential accounts and life history data from those who were filmed.

3. In the Portuguese community in Malacca, I collected additional film footage of *latah* episodes and comparable, though scantier, narrative data from Malaysians who are culturally Portuguese.

4. In the Philippines, I gathered comparable film and interview data on *mali-mali*, the behavior complex built around hyperstartling that is found there.

5. Though it would have been ideal to have a data sample from each of the culture areas from which hyperstartling and a *latah*-like syndrome has been reported, this was not possible for practical reasons. However, I was able to study two films that had been collected in 1936 and 1970 of Ainu subjects in Hokkaido, Japan, demonstrating *imu*, the Ainu behavior complex built around hyperstartling, as well as several hours of videotape of *bah-tche*, the Thai form of the syndrome.

6. As I learned of American subjects who not only were hyperstartlers but who also exhibited the special response phenomena usually alleged to be displayed only by Asian hyperstartlers, I collected their stories also.

In this book, none of these data are as exhaustively analyzed as might be the case in a discipline-centered investigation. Instead, they are discussed only as they bear on the work's central theme: how a simple reflex is experienced, how it is used socially, and how it is culturally elaborated. The text is divided into two parts. Part I deals with more familiar aspects of startle: what the experience of startle is like, how people of several cultures think about startle, and the especially revealing situation of those who startle readily and forcefully. Part II deals with *latah* and other "startle-matching syndromes," special elaborations of startle in the cultures and subcultures that prominently feature startle phenomena and interactions around the startle reflex.

NOTES

1. For an especially clear and persuasive exposition of this position, see *Being and Becoming Human* (Count, 1973).

2. The things about which people are phobic are not random but rather, as Martin Seligman has explained, "by and large, . . . comprise a relatively nonarbitrary and limited set of objects: agoraphobia, fear of specific animals, insect phobias, fear of heights, and fear of the dark, etc. All these are relatively common phobias. And only rarely, if ever, do we have pajama phobias, grass phobias, electric-outlet phobias, hammer phobias, even though these things are likely to be associated with trauma in our world. The set of potentially phobic events may be nonarbitrary: events related to the survival of the human species through the long course of evolution. . . ." (Seligman, 1971, p. 312).

3. For example, in Malaysia 428 people were admitted for treatment of snakebite to the General Hospital in Penang and 600 to hospitals in Kedah between 1965 and 1974. In the United States there are approximately 45,000 snakebites each year, and about 8,000 of these are by venomous snakes (Pottenger, 1993, p. 2).

REFERENCES

Anonymous. (1991). Hot Tools. *Science, 252,* 24 (special section).

Bennett, M.V.L. (1984). Escapism: Some startling revelations. In R.C. Eaton (Ed.), *Neural mechanisms of startle behavior* (p. 361). New York: Plenum.

Berlin, B., & Kay, P. (1969). *Basic color terms, their universality and evolution.* Berkeley: University of California Press.

Bialek, W., Rieke, F., de Ruyter van Steveninck, R.R., & Warland, D. (1991). Reading a neural code. *Science, 252,* 1761.

Boulis, N.M., Kehne, J.H., Miserendino, M.J.D., & Davis, M. (1990). Differential blockade of early and late components of acoustic startle following intrathecal infusion of CNQQX or AP-5. *Brain Research, 520,* 240–246.

Brown, J.S., Kalish, H.I., & Farber, I.E. (1951). Conditioned fear as revealed by the magnitude of startle response to an auditory stimulus. *Journal of Experimental Psychology, 41,* 317–327.

Count, E.W. (1973). *Being and becoming human: Essays on the biogram.* New York: Van Nostrand Reinhold.

Davis, M. (1984). The mammalian startle response. In R.C. Eaton (Ed.), *Neural mechanisms of startle behavior* (pp. 287–351). New York: Plenum.

Davis, M. (1992). The role of the amygdala in rear-potentiated startle: Implications for animal models of anxiety. *Trends in Pharmacological Sciences, 13,* 35–41.

Ekman, P., & Friesen, W.V. (1975). *Unmasking the face.* Englewood Cliffs, N.J.: Prentice-Hall.

Ekman, P., & Friesen, W.V. (1978). *The facial action coding manual.* Palo Alto, CA: Consulting Psychologists' Press.

Ekman, P., Friesen, W.V., & Simons, R.C. (1985). Is the startle reaction an emotion? *Journal of Personality and Social Psychology, 49,* 1416–1426.

Gilbert, D.L., Adelman, Jr., W.A., & Arnold, J.M. (Eds.). (1990). *Squid as experimental animals*. New York: Plenum.

Gilly, W.F. (1991). Review of "Squid as experimental animals." *Science, 251*, 98.

Grillon, C., Ameli, R., Woods, S.W., Merikangas, K., & Davis, M. (1991). Fear-potentiated startle in humans: Effects of anticipatory anxiety on the acoustic blink reflex. *Psychophysiology, 28*, 588–595.

Hoffman, H. (1984). Methodological factors in the behavioral analysis of startle. In R.C. Eaton (Ed.), *Neural mechanisms of startle behavior* (pp. 267–285). New York: Plenum.

Ivinson, A.J. (1993). Inhibition and over-reaction. *Nature, 366*, 488.

Jasney, B.R., & Koshland, D.E., Jr. (1990). *Biological systems*. Waldorf, MD: A.A.A.S. Books.

Kehne, J.H., Gallager, D.W. & Davis, M. (1981). Strychnine: Brainstem and spinal mediation of excitatory effects on acoustic startle. *European Journal of Pharmacology, 76*, 177–186.

Lakoff, G. (1987). *Women, fire, and dangerous things*. Chicago: University of Chicago Press.

Landis, C. & W.A., Hunt. (1939). *The startle pattern*. New York: Farrar & Rinehart.

Miserendino, M.J.D., & Davis, M. (1993). NMDA and non-NMDA antagonists infused into the nucleus reticularis pontis caudalis depress the acoustic startle reflex." *Brain Research, 623*, 215–222.

Pottenger, R.T., Jr. (1993, Nov./Dec.). A Nevada physician asks: "How would you treat venomous snakebite?" *Gratefully Yours* (National Library of Medicine), 1–2.

Rosch, E. (1975). Universals and specifics in cultural categorization. In R.W. Brislin, S. Bochner, & W.J. Lonner (Eds.), *Cross-cultural perspectives on learning* (pp. 177–206). New York: Halstead/Wiley.

Seligman, M.E.P. (1971). Phobias and preparedness. *Behavior Therapy, 2*, 307–320.

Shiang, R., Ryan, S.G., Zhu, Y.Z. (1993). Mutations in the Alpha 1 subunit of the inhibitory glycine receptor cause the dominant neurologic disorder, hyperekplexia. *Nature, 366*, 351–358.

Simons, R.C. (1980). The resolution of the latah paradox. *Journal of Nervous and Mental Disease, 168*, 195–206.

Von Uexküll, J.V. (1928). *Theoretische biologie*. Berlin: Springer.

Vrana, S.R., Spence, E.L., & Lang, P.J. (1988). The startle probe response: A new measure of emotion? *Journal of Abnormal Psychology, 97*, 487–491.

2

STARTLE AS A PERSONAL EXPERIENCE AND AS A SOCIAL RESOURCE

In an inner court Maya had set a pond of water clear and still as the air. A flight of stairs led into the pond, and on the bottom grew magic flowers, so that the pond looked empty. Duryodhana was walking there, and started down the steps without thinking, and when he got his feet wet he was so startled that he slipped and fell, splashing in the water.

And someone laughed at him—a devilish laugh.

Anonymous, 200 B.C.–A.D. 200, *Mahabharata*, pp. 53–54

When I grabbed it, there was a bat sitting on top of it. When I was expecting to hit the cold key, I hit something warm and furry instead, and I responded with a startle response. I screamed and screamed and could not stop. I sat down that time; I didn't fall to my knees. There were steps there, and as I was screaming I turned myself around and sat on the steps and just screamed and screamed and screamed, much to the delight of the people that I was with. You know they find this very funny.

Felicia Gould, 1977, interview

This chapter begins an examination of how startles are experienced and played out in real lives. Laboratory studies tell only some of the story, in part because a laboratory isolates a person from the social context in which he or she ordinarily operates. The physical responses that have been most studied account for only some of the existential reality. Because startles occur in settings in the real world, the variety of contexts in which startles occur is indefinitely large. Just before a person is startled he or she may be lying down, sitting, standing still, walking, or running. He or she may be alone or in company, and if in company, something social and interactive may have been happening. This is, of course, still rather abstract.

More specifically, just before being startled a person may be peeling vegetables, or watching a movie, or attending a funeral. Each startle is a unique event, happening once and only once to a specific individual who is at the time of the startle in a unique combination of physiological, psychological, social, and cultural circumstances. It is the simultaneous interaction of all these elements that accounts for the specifics of any startle experienced or observed. However, because there are certain kinds of stimuli that frequently startle, certain subjective states in which startles are especially likely, certain kinds of settings in which startles frequently occur, and certain recurrent responses, some kinds of startle events are encountered again and again.

ACCOUNTS THAT DESCRIBE BEING STARTLED

Even when they happen to one frequently, startles are memorable occurrences. People tend to remember startling events, and when asked, they can usually tell something about the circumstances, what happened physically, and the event's psychological and social consequences. Particular accounts may focus on any of these elements. What follows is a thoughtful and somewhat detailed description of some aspects of one person's startles:

> People who come up behind me or otherwise enter my space, when I think I'm alone, always elicit from me an involuntary shriek, and a simultaneous thoroughgoing shock-wave of momentary terror courses up and down (or vice versa) my spine (or more accurately radiates from some central source toward the periphery).
>
> I mentioned before my startle reaction to the sight of a large spider (or a picture or drawing of one); other large images of things with spindly legs, such as ants and other insects, produce a similar but less-violent startle reaction.
>
> A real snake (but not a picture of one) may induce a startle reaction if I come upon it unexpectedly. I recall (as a child of 6 years) having stepped on a small snake accidentally (a harmless garter snake, I later discovered)—and having run faster than I believed possible for a very long block, before calming down.
>
> As I told you, the unexpected sight of a human skull—of nearly life-sized or larger proportions, anyway—induces a shock in me . . . especially if it has dark eye-sockets.
>
> The sight of a larger-than-life human face looking directly at me (at the camera, in the case of a photo) has a similar shock value. I recall one instance of being quite unpleasantly startled by the

face of Sophia Loren on a magazine cover, and more than once by an ad in a magazine featuring eyes (larger than life) looking directly at the viewer. (Both eyes usually have to be present—one big eye doesn't have as much effect.) [T]hese reactions are involuntary and uncontrollable unless the sight in question is anticipated, and even then I am apt to experience an internal moment of panic. (Barbara Haldane, 1987, letter)

Accounts of startles like the one above can be analyzed by sorting what is reported. There are factors having to do with the nature and presentation of the stimulus, factors that are elements of the setting in which the startle takes place, factors that refer to a characteristic trait or transient state of the person being startled, factors that comprise the elements of the response, and social and cultural factors. Factors cited in accounts can be compared with those observed in both field and laboratory settings and can be compared among individuals both within and across cultural settings. Accounts are individually interesting, but en masse they are something more. By examining which elements sort together, it is possible to arrive at some conclusions about how this bit of human experience works.

Here is an account emphasizing a frequently occurring type of response and its social consequences. The narrator tells of being startled by unexpectedly hitting her head against a hard object:

At the end of a meeting with my colleagues at work I bent down to pick something up from the floor. Since I had been sitting fairly far from the table I wasn't alert to the possibility of hurting myself. But when I bent over, I hit my head against the corner of the table. Without stopping myself I said "Oh Shit!"

I found myself feeling kind of dazed, and then I realized that I'd hurt myself. But even though I was hurt and began to bleed I was more concerned with the embarrassment of the situation. First, hitting my head on the corner of the table and next that I had uttered "Oh Shit!" . . . The words seemed almost to have popped out of my mouth. (Karen Green, 1977, interview)

The point the narrator of this anecdote makes is that having been startled by an unexpected blow to the head she blurted out something she considered socially inappropriate and about which she was embarrassed. She notes that she had not planned to say what she said; the improper word seemed "almost" to have popped out of her mouth. Not only had she done something she believed would be seen by others as awkward, but without intending to do so, she had also uttered a word by tacit mutual understanding all understood to be inappropriate in that social context. (It would have been less of a violation to have said it in the presence of the same group of people if, for example, they were at a ballgame.) Why then did she do it?

Here is a second account of a similar response:

My little grandmother, she's so prim and proper from Virginia, and we were coming up the hill to her house, which scares the day-lights out of me because it's straight up. I was with my husband, and I begged him, "Let's leave the car at the bottom of the hill and we'll walk up." And he says, "Oh, we can make it, it'll be OK. You know we have a good car," and Grandma was in the car. Oh, he started up the hill, and then he pretended like it wouldn't go any more and pretended it was sliding backward—to tease. And it startled me, it really did. . . . So I said something. . . . I think it was something like "Shit!" or something. "Why, Elaine!" She couldn't believe that I had said that. I was extremely embarrassed. (Elaine Clark, 1977, interview)

Although the initiating events, the "stimuli," are very disparate in the two stories, in both a startled person says something unplanned and socially inappropriate and then experiences embarrassment about what she has just done. Many people can relate stories of similar experiences, so many that it is useful to consider saying something unplanned and socially inappropriate as a category of startle response in the same way that clos-ing the eyes is a category of response (Fig. 2.1).

The usual term for such improper speech is "coprolalia" ("dung-talk" in scientific Greek), quite exact in this case, though what is uttered after being startled may also be a term referring to sexual anatomy or activity or an improper reference to a deity. Although a startled person's uttering socially inappropriate words of this sort is evaluated negatively in most social contexts, in previous writing I have used the term "naughty talk" rather than any stronger negative descriptor to refer to this phenomenon because the startled person's doing so is usually understood to be involun-tary and is therefore usually accepted with amused tolerance.

Dropping or throwing something that had been held is also often part of the response to having been startled. Whether an object is dropped or thrown depends on the course of the arm movement when the object is released by the hand. Like "naughty talk," dropping and throwing may have social implications and social consequences. Here are descriptions from literary sources of one drop and one throw, examples of how skilled writers may incorporate elements of the reflex into their narratives:

There came a whistle in the air, and then a sounding smack, and the fragments of a broken arrow fell about their ears. Someone from the upper quarters of the wood, perhaps the very sentinel they saw posted in the fir, had shot an arrow at the chimney-top.

    Matcham could not restrain a little cry, which he instantly sti-

Figure 2.1　From *Glamour* (magazine), May 1982: "Sticky Situation of the Month: You use a swear word at the wrong time in the wrong place. Situation: You're having lunch with a business colleague and accidentally spill your wine. Without thinking you blurt out "Oh, s—!" It's the last thing you mean to say to a fellow professional, but it's too late now. What can you do to save face?" Cartoon by Durell Godfrey courtesy *Glamour*. Copyright 1982 by the Condé Nast Publications, Inc.

fled, and even Dick started with surprise, and dropped the windac from his fingers. (Robert Louis Stevenson, 1888 *The Black Arrow*, p. 62)

We crept up on the camp in a line, with Dana and Leon slightly forward on the wings. Poor James was peacefully reading, his back to us, in the shade of a large boulder. . . . I edged forward across the shingle until I crouched behind the rock and then, with what I imagined to be an Ukit-cum-Clouded leopard assassination howl, I lightly touched his neck. The Iban yodelled a particularly horrible battle cry. I can't say that James's hair stood on end, because the sample is not statistically significant, and he only emitted a smallish scream; but his legs went convulsively stiff and shot up in the air, and he threw his arms wildly over his head. His section of *Les Misérables* landed some yards away. (Redmond O'Hanlon, 1984, *Into the Heart of Borneo*, pp. 139–140)

Another frequent response to being startled is striking out with the hands. If someone has overlearned[1] a stylized defense posture, when startled he or she will often assume it without thought or prior planning. As is true of thrown objects, the defensive posture is usually not aimed at the eliciting stimulus.

I jump when startled and often assume a defense posture, especially if startled while sleeping. It is rather embarrassing to wake up and find myself in a full standing defense posture. It probably doesn't help that I've had some judo training, but it really shakes my husband up when it happens in the middle of the night if the phone should ring or there should be some other sudden noise. . . .

A typical situation in which I startle happened again last night—at 1:30 A.M. I walked into what I thought was an empty elevator and there was a person in the corner. I jumped and vocalized. There was really no reason to be scared of this person.

The other typical situation occurs when I'm working hard at a desk and someone comes up behind me or alongside me. I jump so much that people really react strangely. (Laura White, 1977, interview)

The first time I remember going into a standing alarm posture when startled while sleeping was my freshman year in college (1965). The posture consists of a stance with feet about 2 feet apart, almost straight legs, and elbows bent, arms at sides, fingers spread. This may well have occurred before then, but before then I didn't have an audience (roommate) to remark about how strange it was, so I don't remember. Seven years later, in 1972 (age 25) after I had a child, I took a judo class at an Air Force base just for the exercise—to get back in shape. To my astonishment, I was good at it. . . . I could always anticipate the moves of my opponents before they could put them into action. I stayed with it for a year, 3 nights a week, and got a brown belt. Part of the training involved going into appropriate balanced postures almost reflexively if threatened or even if touched on the shoulder.

The posture involved is not much different from the alarm posture I described earlier. It is modified in that the knees are bent, and elbows are bent but forearms and hands are facing forward and fingers aren't quite so spread apart. The hand is also rotated to be almost vertical.

At the time I was in training, I occasionally would go into the judo posture if startled from behind on a dark street, but not under normal daylight conditions — then I would just jump and vocalize.

I recently went into the posture when working late (after midnight) at the campus computer center when going down a stairwell and encountering a person who opened a door in front of me suddenly. There had been a couple of rapes in that building the week before so the posture probably was logically justified (even though I had no time to think before using it) but it sure scared the poor boy who had opened the door, particularly since the umbrella I was carrying was pointed straight at him.

Otherwise the posture has mostly been evoked when I've been sleeping and there's a sudden disturbance. It's not aimed toward anything. I think my using the judo posture when startled is probably just a learned modification of the initial startle response.

Most of the time I just jump and gasp. I wish I didn't — it scares the people who think they're scaring me. . . . If you ever develop a technique to teach people not to jump and gasp when startled, I'd really like to hear about it. (Sarah Unwin, 1977, interview)

Like the overlearned judo response, many other responses, especially those of people who startle readily and strongly, may become stereotyped. It is as though the startle sets off some sort of internal program, a program that combines both innate and acquired elements. In 1908, in *The Lancet*, an important British medical journal, William Fletcher described a man who

regardless of place or circumstances, would regularly shout out, "Go to hell," if startled by an unexpected stimulus, tactile or auditory. (Fletcher, 1908, p. 254)

Here is a second somewhat extreme example:

There was a man, white, a laborer or a farmer probably, somewhere in eastern Washington State during my relative's younger years who people called "Goosey" as a nickname, because if he was "goosed" (i.e., poked in the ribs),[2] he would dance off, skipping on his toes, raising and lowering his arms in something that resembled a modern ballet rendition of a bird's flight, singing "Spring is here! Spring is here! Spring is here!" My relative told me the story to illustrate how cruel people could be, that they would torment this man this way. Her impression, or attitude, as I remember it, was that there was nothing else wrong with this man, except this strange, unfortunate quirk, and that he would be quite all right if people would just leave him alone. (Vivian Garrison, 1986, letter)

HYPERSTARTLERS

It takes a powerful stimulus to startle some people, whereas others startle to minimal stimuli. Some people characteristically respond to startling stimuli with minimal startles; others with a considerable number of the possible response elements. Some persons startle rarely, others frequently. These factors do not sort randomly. Instead, those who startle readily not only find themselves startled frequently but also tend to respond strongly and elaborately. For the purposes of these studies I have called such people "hyperstartlers." Although no systematic epidemiological investigation of the distribution of readiness to startle, strength of startle, and frequency of being startled has ever been carried out, I believe it most likely that hyperstartlers are not a physiologically discrete group but instead are merely people who fall on the high end of a continuum of startle responsivity.[3] There is, however, at least one experimentally established qualitative difference between hyperstartlers and those who startle less frequently, readily, and forcefully.

In an experimental study of the responses of hyperstartlers to a standardized startling stimulus, Paul Ekman, Wallace Friesen, and I discovered that unlike normal control subjects, hyperstartlers did not respond with attenuated startles when they knew exactly when the startling stimuli would occur (Ekman, Friesen, & Simons, 1985). Telling control subjects that a blank pistol would fire immediately after a countdown[4] markedly reduced the strength of their responses, but this was not true of those who characteristically hyperstartled.

Hyperstartlers think a lot about how to manage their interactions with others around the theme of "startling." For this reason accounts of their experiences and interactions with others are especially revealing. They often told of experiences congruent with what we found experimentally:

> INTERVIEWER: What if you expect the noise? What happens when you expect a loud noise?
>
> TE: Even then sometimes I'll jump at it. Even though I'm expecting it, it just sort of happens anyway, sort of a nervous reflex. (Tom Eberhardt, 1977, interview)

> There are certain things, like for example, my husband does consistently that startle me every time, or my mother does. My mother's sneezing startles me. I can see her warming up to sneeze, but it's a loud noise, and it always makes me jump and blink. You know, it's quite obvious when she's going to do it, but it always makes me start like that. And [my husband] has a habit of clap-

ping, like, if we're watching a ball game or something, he'll start clapping really loud, you know. I can see he's going to do it, I can see he's excited about what's happening, and it still gives me that same kind of a lurching feeling. (Karen Ellis, 1977, interview)

Hyperstartlers often had many stories to tell of their vulnerability to startling stimuli, their stereotypic responses, and their unsuccessful attempts to repress them. For example:

I was trying to weed between the corn yesterday, and you know, it was kind of long. And every time I would brush against it, I would jump. [Even] knowing that I was standing right in the cornfield, that movement against it made me jump like there was an insect on me, and like, if bugs are on me, I go crazy. And that annoyed me. Every time I did it I would say "Shit!" or "Damn!" or whatever, you know. It annoyed me, because I thought it was ludicrous that I was acting that way. Nonetheless, every time I hit against it, it would sort of startle me. (Karen Ellis, 1977, interview)

To be this vulnerable to startling stimuli makes one especially vulnerable to being teased by being intentionally startled by others. This is a "predicament," a concept recently refined and used with great explanatory power by Taylor (1985): "Predicaments are painful social situations or circumstances, complex, unstable, morally charged and varying in their import in time and place" (p. 130). The condition of being a hyperstartler is a predicament with recurrent features. A number of army recruits with this predicament were described in a much referenced paper by Thorne published in the mid-1940s:

White selectee, age 21, college senior. An unusually intelligent, physically attractive young man with no objective evidences of nervous or mental disorder. Denies family history of mental deficiency, epilepsy, nervous or mental disease.

Past history essentially normal except for extreme sensitivity to loud startling noises. Cannot remember when this started. Has never handled a gun in his life or gone hunting because "couldn't stand the noise." Automobile backfiring startles him and "I nearly jump out of my skin." In his senior year in college was appointed to be manager of the basketball team but had to give up the position because he could not bear to shoot the blank cartridge pistol at the half and end of the games. Is able to stand noise better when warning is given but even then doesn't like it. No relative is similarly afflicted.

Psychiatric examination failed to elicit evidence of any other deviation from normality. The interview was conducted in a straightforward friendly manner with the selectee seemingly at ease and showing no evidences of tension or emotional instability. He seemed relatively well adjusted to his disability and had obtained work in a quiet atmosphere. During the middle of the interview the nature of the disability was inadvertently demonstrated when a swinging door slammed loudly behind his head. He involuntarily jumped from his chair but quickly regained control of himself and laughed. At the end of the interview the examiner suddenly slapped the selectee on the back without warning and the same excessive reaction occurred. The selectee said he was well adjusted in civilian life but did not think he would do well in the army where he would have to shoot guns. (Thorne, 1944/45, p. 106)

The recruit described above told of a socially comfortable personal adjustment, but for another potential soldier, hyperstartling was a considerable affliction:

White selectee, age 33, grammar school graduate, married, employed at arsenal making munitions. This man almost disrupted the induction procedure. Shortly after getting undressed one of the other selectees suddenly bumped him from behind and he gave a piercing yell, associated with an excessive startle reaction. This performance was repeated at least 8 times before he arrived at the psychiatric examination room. (Thorne, 1944/45, p. 107)

The site is the large room in which the young recruits are sitting about in their shorts with nothing to do, waiting for their physical examinations. This is a setting, of course, in which the much teased subject might be especially wary. Unfortunately for him, it is also a setting in which the usual societal constraints on teasing him are attenuated. And he can't leave. Thorne continues:

[The selectee] denies family history of nervous or mental disease. . . . The examiner got the impression that beneath [a variety of "minor" somatic complaints] lay a much more serious personality deviation. . . .
    Has always had difficulty adjusting in social groups or at work because of an excessive startle reaction on being "goosed" or suddenly startled. He jumps so violently when startled that he has long been the butt of practical jokers. Has given up several mill jobs because the boys wouldn't let him alone. On his present arsenal job, he has had to request the foreman and lieutenant in charge to intercede with the other workers on his behalf and forbid them to "goose me." He has become very touchy and irritable, losing his head easily, and fighting with his tormenters on at least three occasions. Last month he stayed away from work for one week because he couldn't stand the boys picking on him. The men stay away

from him now but still startle him by throwing fruit and other objects when he is not looking. . . .

The examiner requested him to step next door where another psychiatrist was working and slapped him from behind as he entered the other room. The selectee uttered a loud piercing scream and jerked around with arms raised in pugilistic position and would have launched a blow had not the examiner stepped quickly out of range. Subsequent tests revealed that almost any sudden unexpected stimulus was effective in producing the excessive startle reaction.

Physical examination within normal limits. (Thorne, 1944/45, p. 107)

A similar case was published in the *International Journal of Social Psychiatry* by a Dutch psychiatrist, J. A. Jenner:

A husband seeks help for his 40-year-old wife. They have had a near car accident as a result of her abnormal movements in reaction to the honking of another car. Both are lower middle class, white, and have no family ties with Indonesia (a former Dutch colony). For the last twenty years the woman has been overreactive to noise and other kinds of unexpected stimuli. . . . Several times a day she is startled by unexpected sounds or sudden movements of persons in her environment. In reaction she drops whatever she holds, stretches her arms, and becomes verbally abusive. Occasionally she behaves in an odd way or uses dirty language she is ashamed of later on. She has made a joke of it: "playing the clown," and she has caused much laughter at family feasts. Fear of teasing made her refuse to accompany her husband to festivities outside the family. (Jenner, 1990, p. 195)

As several of the accounts above make clear, startles in real lives, especially in the lives of persons who startle readily and strongly, may have quite elaborate ramifications. Indeed, the way one startles may significantly alter how one is perceived in many social contexts, and this fact shapes many of one's interactions, both behavioral and emotional, with others. Startling may, for example, be an element in the assertion or negotiation of status position. This theme shows up in several contexts including adolescent play, courtship (which may include assertive/submissive sequences and hence increased intimacy), and actual harassment.

People who lose their composure as a result of being startled are often perceived as incompetent and amusing. In *Interaction Ritual*, Erving Goffman explained why this is so.

The significant point here is that we find composure a concern and a value in many different cultures and across many different strata. There seem to be two major reasons for this.

First, whenever an individual is in the immediate presence of others, especially when he is cooperatively involved with them—as in, for example, the joint maintenance of a state of talk—his capacity as a competent interactant is important to them. The social order sustained in the gathering draws its ingredients, its substance, from disciplined small behaviors. His contribution of proper demeanor is melded in with the contribution of the others to produce socially organized co-presence. He will have to maintain command of himself if he is to make himself available to the affairs at hand and not disrupt them. Discomposure will disqualify him for these duties and threaten the jointly sustained world that the others feel they have a right to be in.

Second, whether or not the individual is in the presence of others, any task he performs involves the practiced easy use of human faculties—mind, limbs, and, especially, small muscles. Often this management must be acquired and sustained under very special circumstances: any temporary failure of control due to concern about the situation will itself provide a reason for still more self-consciousness and hence still further maladroitness and so on, until the individual is quite rattled and unable to handle the task. (Goffman, 1967, pp. 227–228)

However, although being startled can lead to discomposure and embarrassment, being startled, with all its concomitant behaviors, is not always a negative experience. In the proper social context, it may even be a social asset. For example:

I must admit, like, sometimes the attention you get from it seems OK to me. And it seems like . . . when I was a teenager I probably felt the same way. Um, you know, it brings people's attention to you, if it's a real noticeable start. And I don't mind that; in some situations it's not as good as other situations, but, um, yeah, it brings people's attention to you, and I guess I like that. I can't ever think of having consciously manipulated it, but I'm certainly not above that [laughs]. (Karen Ellis, 1977, interview)

At this point it may be useful to summarize some of the features of hyperstartling:

1. The stimuli that elicit startles in hyperstartlers are like those that elicit startles in ordinary persons, but stimuli of much lesser intensity may also be effective.
2. Most of the responses of hyperstartlers are qualitatively like those of ordinary persons but are more intense.
3. Responses that ordinary persons give rarely may be given frequently by hyperstartlers (e.g., striking out, the assumption of over-

learned defensive postures, naughty talk). However, some responses of hyperstartlers may be quite idiosyncratic.

4. Though ordinary persons may fail to startle or startle less violently if they know when a startle stimulus will occur, this knowledge does not diminish the response of hyperstartlers.

5. Other people are likely to play on a hyperstartler's infirmity.
    a. *How* will depend on local social conditions.
    b. People often startle others to establish or assert status positions. This theme is played out in many contexts, including adolescent male play, courtship, and actual harassment.
    c. A hyperstartler can accept with good grace being repetitively startled by others and integrate hyperstartling into his or her life or may try to resist such teasing, usually without success.

HYPERSTARTLING AS A SIGNIFICANT POSITIVE ASPECT OF A PERSON'S LIFE

The account presented next illustrates how profoundly a high degree of responsiveness to stimuli and an especially strong and dramatic set of responses can color one's social existence. Because it is such a full portrait of what startling violently and readily can be in a person's life, it is instructive to examine it in some detail.[5]

The speaker is Felicia Gould, an attractive, athletic-appearing, professional woman, a behavioral scientist in her early thirties. There is a striking difference between her story and most of the descriptions and anecdotes presented so far. Although she refers to her hyperstartling as "a freaky vulnerability," Ms. Gould repeatedly emphasizes what a positive experience hyperstartling has been for her, how it has been both a social asset and a source of warm, happy feelings.

Ms. Gould begins by describing how she usually responds to startling stimuli. She discusses her response as something that *happens to her* rather than as something *she does*. She explains that, for her, startles are more than the brief, immediate responses most people experience; it takes some time for her to recover fully from being startled.

> I'm simply a person who startles easy. When a noise goes off, I jump, I often scream, I throw my arms, you know, and then after it's over for a while I'm in a state of trauma, just waiting to recover. It's like I'm still afraid. I just have to wait until it passes; I often laugh after that because I realize it's a ridiculous thing to jump and scream. I tend to throw things. I don't know whether other people do that too, but if I have something in my hand I will throw it.

She tells a story about a particularly memorable incident in which, after having been startled, she felt a hand move past her face, which somehow induced her to bite:

I once bit a man when he startled me; I think that's really funny.
I was married at the time and I was working as a waitress. It was
about two in the morning and a customer came in and wanted a
fresh orange. I had to go way back into the kitchen where the wait-
resses usually didn't go in order to get this fresh orange. They took
me back into the coolers . . . and said, "As long as you're getting
one take several." And so I was carrying several oranges in my
hand and I was walking through the kitchen, which had been
deserted up until that time, and one of the men who was scrubbing
the floor, kind of an innocent man, I really feel badly now, I frightened him very badly. There were two aisles, one that crossed the
path that I was walking, and because I was thinking about the person who wanted these oranges I simply did not see him approaching. He stepped into my path and said "Hello!" and it frightened
me so badly that I screamed very loudly, I threw the oranges up
in the air and at this same moment I fell to my knees. As I felt his
hand accidentally move past my face, I bit him on the thumb!
They never let me live it down.

Ms. Gould describes her immediate embarrassment, but also says that
the social consequences were prolonged: "They never let me live it down."
Having been revealed as a hyperstartler, she is identified to others as fair
game for startle-teasing:

"Oh, don't send her in the kitchen, she'll go and get scared and
bite somebody." You know, I was very, very embarrassed, as I said.
I ended up on the floor with my knees and was just traumatized by
this. . . .

Ms. Gould analyzes her experience. She makes a distinction between
startling violently because of being wary and the state she was in in the
anecdote she just told, a weary, introspective state in which she was relatively oblivious to the outside world:

I think the only reason that the fact that the kitchen was isolated
made a difference was that there were few stimuli. I am not an
afraid person; that's what's funny. I don't lock doors and I've no
fear about going out in strange cities at all hours of the night. I
don't mind walking on streets in poor neighborhoods. In fact, I've
been a source of worry to my family, my parents, brothers-in-law,
because I routinely go into situations that they perceive as being
dangerous. So you know I don't think that it was the fact that I was
afraid because it was late at night and I was alone. I think it was
more related to the fact that perhaps I was a little tired and very
much. . . . I'm an introspective person, I kind of get into my own
head, and I was thinking.

Ms. Gould dates the onset of her hyperstartling to her adolescence, within the year after the onset of menstruation. She begins a theme that will characterize the rest of her narrative: Although many of the startle sequences are discomfiting, they are also *pleasurable*. She explains that startle-teasing interactions are experienced by her (quite reasonably) as affectionate rather than hostile.[6] She explains that this vulnerability of hers, and the fact that it is considered socially appropriate to exploit it, has functioned for her as a valuable social lubricant. In high school and in later years Ms. Gould's vulnerability to hyperstartling repeatedly became insti-tutionalized in the small societies in which she lived and worked. She describes her most usual responses and her inability to control them:

> You had asked when I had first noticed this and I'm trying. . . . I really can't remember doing it as a child. The first time that I really remember it first now was when I was in 11th grade, when I was about 16 or 17. I began to menstruate very late so this would be within the year after the onset of menstruation. But in my high school years people became aware that I startled easily and they would do it to tease me. And I actually didn't mind this. I mean I did the whole performance, the screaming, the jumping, and everyone laughed. But I didn't feel it as hostility when they teased me like that. In a sense it was a pleasurable kind of thing; I mean, I was embarrassed and yet you know, but it wasn't an unpleasant thing because I felt warmth from the people around me who had done it, and people would comfort me afterwards. I was an extremely shy person, and all of this was a way of kind of getting positive attention; it's funny I did view it as positive attention from people that I was really too shy to approach in other ways, like the jocks. I was in awe of the jocks, I never could have approached them on my own, but they learned that I would jump and that it was great fun to come up behind me with a paper bag and smash it, and then I'd scream and do the thing.

Ms. Gould's predicament became part of the subculture of the small society in which she lived and, like many other cultural elements, was passed on from cohort to cohort of peers:

> For a time my husband was working on a ranch where they had a school for purebred beef cattle herdsmen. So we would have lots of young men around, I would say ages 17 to 27 from all over the world, who would come in for 6-week sessions to learn to be beef cattle herdsmen. Now I lived on the property, and I had to go into the barn to feed the cats. And of course every class learned that I was a startler. I guess the men who were there full time would pass it on.
> [I]t was a great sport for these boys, when they would hear me

coming with the cat food to hide themselves somewhere and jump out at me and startle me. They did it so often that I came to expect it. I would be walking toward the barn with the cat food and I would try to steel myself against being startled because I would think "somebody's going to jump out of the washroom or hayrack or somewhere and say 'Boo!' and this time I'm not going to give them the satisfaction, I'm not going to jump and scream." And invariably of course they would do it, and I *would* jump and scream. And again if I had something in my hand quite often I would throw it and scream and drop to my knees. One time I hit the person that had scared me by throwing the cat food, but I didn't deliberately throw it at him. I think it just happened.

My husband came in every day at the same time, right at noon for lunch, and one day he came in. I expected him, I knew it was noon, I knew it was lunchtime, but I was thinking about something when he came in. And I had an extreme startle reaction, I really screamed. There was a bed downstairs and I threw myself on that and I screamed and I screamed and I simply could not stop, and I felt deep terror. I remember this, I was really, really. . . . I was frightened, it was like a combination of frightened and startled. Yet it was someone I knew, someone who showed up everyday. . . . He ran back out of the house.

Ms. Gould describes how automatic the reaction seems to her to be, how unrelated to anything rational she can tell herself about the circumstances. She describes the period immediately after the startle as an altered state of consciousness in which she does not have volitional control over her behavior. In that state, despite being able to think of what she wants to say or do, she finds she can't say or do it. She compares her state to being in a prison. In psychiatric jargon, the behavior she describes is "ego-alien," the experience is of something forcing her to do something that she has neither the intention nor the desire to do:

It was like I was two people. One part of me was seeing him, wanting to say, "Don't be an ass, you know I'm like this, don't run out and be afraid, I'm sorry, you didn't do anything, I'm not mad at you, I'm not frightened of you." I wanted to say all of these things, but I was simply unable. It was like . . . until this screaming thing passes, it's like I'm in a prison.

Ms. Gould's children find startling their mother an acceptable way to play with her.

Now my children have picked up on the fact that I'm a startler, and they have fun, you know, waiting at the bottom of the stairs. An easy way to startle me is simply to step out at me, like if I'm walking down a hall, just step out from a room along that hall. You don't have to say "Boo!" You don't have to do anything, you simply have to step out. But it doesn't always work.

Ms. Gould describes a startle sequence in response to a warm, furry tactile stimulus, one that startles her not because such physical properties intrinsically startle, but rather because it is such a radical mismatch from anything she had expected to encounter. Later she tells two other stories in which the stimulus is a mismatch.

One other time I was coming home. I had just been out with friends and we had just had a very silly, giddy evening. I had the housekey on a ledge at the top of a pillar outside my back door, and I reached up for it. When I grabbed it there was a bat sitting on top of it. When I was expecting to hit the cold key, I hit something warm and furry instead, and I responded with a startle response. I screamed and screamed and could not get stopped. I sat down that time, I didn't fall to my knees. There were steps there, and as I was screaming I turned myself around and sat on the steps and just screamed and screamed and screamed, much to the delight of the people that I was with. You know, they find this very funny. And when I'm finished screaming I find it funny too. As soon as I stop screaming I normally start laughing. I find it amusing.

Ms. Gould, who is bright, articulate, self-possessed, and successful, again describes how her hyperstartling is a social asset, an interactional resource that helps her relate to people who might otherwise find her uncomfortably formidable.

I have minor startles when I do that jump thing and major startles where I scream, fall down, and am aware that a period of time is passing in which I'm not able to make myself stop what I'm doing. I want to explain to the people around me to be cool, but I can't until I stop screaming. When I bit the man, I was very aware that time that I wanted to be somehow reassuring him that I wasn't dangerous. I took a lot of ribbing about that. It went through the whole hotel where I worked; everyone knew about it. They teased me like, "Oh, the personnel man has a new place on the form now: They won't hire anyone unless they've had rabies shots," you know this kind of thing. But again I responded pleasurably to that kind of teasing. I did not find that an unpleasant thing; I found that a way to relate to people that I really did not have a whole lot in common with, and it kind of gave us a way to interact that we didn't have otherwise.

At that point I was enrolled in graduate school and so forth,

and when I first started working there I was feeling warm toward
them, but they didn't quite know what to make of me. But once
that incident happened everybody was just teasing with me on a
very human level and that was okay.

It's funny, people that I'm around when it happens then relate
to me in a little different way after it's happened. They're more
human with me. They—it's this teasing thing—they're able to
tease with me, I don't know. But that is interesting. Because they
in a way are put in a position of—it's not really giving comfort,
but in a way it is. It's just like I have this freaky vulnerability that
she's somebody you kind of have to take care of, but she's crazy
and nice and she's funny, you know.

When Ms. Gould subsequently became a teacher, she was frequently
startled by her students. She tells of her class's successful attempts to startle her and expresses pride in their ingenuity. As with other people at different times in her life, her class's playful exploitation of her vulnerability
causes her to feel "bathed in love."

Oh, this reminds me that when I taught, my students knew I startled. I've got dozens of startle stories from my students. Because I
always told them you could misbehave in my class as long as you do
it with creative intelligence, I won't let you get away with stupid
things like spit wads and thumbtacks on the chairs; if you can't
demonstrate intelligence in the jokes you play, don't bother. So they
did some very good jokes. My students always did jokes on me and
again they seized on this ability that I have, or it may be a handicap,
I don't know that it's an ability, to get lost in what I'm doing.

One day when I was working with a student at my desk and
was very involved in what I was doing, they simply turned their
chairs around without my knowing it. It simply amazes me that
they could do that, but I was very engrossed in what I was doing,
so that where before I'd been looking at their faces, now the entire
desks are turned around. And when I looked up from this student
I was working with, looked up from his paper and kind of gazed
with a vacant gaze out across the class and I only see the backs of
heads, and the entire thing's reversed. I had a startle reaction,
screamed, and fell down, the whole thing.

The only time I ever wore glasses was when I was showing film
strips, but I can't talk with glasses on so I put them on as I'm
advancing the thing but when I start talking about what's on I
remove the glasses. Very often I would place them down beside the
projector. Well the boy that sat next to that projector had glasses
very similar to mine, except where I am barely nearsighted he was
extremely nearsighted. And what he would do is substitute his
glasses for mine. He did this every time I showed film strips. I

knew that he did it; I learned to try to steel myself. But I would forget and get engrossed, and when I would reach to put my glasses back on after talking and put them on and they would be his glasses, and now of course the whole world is very distorted for me: startle reaction, the screaming, the "Down." . . . Students did a lot of those things to me. But again I would laugh and they would build rapport with me, and I cannot tell you how close I was with those students. I was not the kind of teacher that the kids drive out by badgering them. I was not a weakling and unable; I always felt in control, but these incidents, it's funny, I never saw it this way but they really broke me down, put me on their level or lower and enabled them to deal with me in a very affectionate, I don't even know what to call it. It's love, I really feel bathed in love. And after every startle reaction I've ever had I feel bathed in love.

Ms. Gould relates her enjoyment and her use of the vulnerability that induces affectionate teasing by others to her perception of herself as essentially a shy person.

I still feel like I'm shy. I was painfully shy, no one could talk to me, I would turn. I'm a blusher, I still blush easily. . . . I just learn to disguise it. It's never left me. I've just learned to cover it up.

Finally, she says something quite remarkable, given the extensive history that she has just related; she says that she has never thought of her condition as something that some people have and others do not, and that she had never "really" discussed it with anyone before!

I don't think that it's anything I've ever really discussed with anybody because I never really thought about it in terms of something some people have and other people don't have. I don't mind being a startle person. I actually do kind of enjoy it. (Felicia Gould, 1983, interview)

Clearly Ms. Gould's hyperstartling has provided her with an important, satisfying, and coherent set of life experiences, and despite her disclaimer, she surely knows that her experience of startle is distinctive and not the norm. Nevertheless, she has no special word to refer to her condition (the awkward term "startle-person" was coined by her for the occasion of the interview) and she had never before "really" (i.e., analytically and at length) discussed it. And this was not because of embarrassment, but rather because in the United States, where she jogs and teaches and helps with the sheep, the condition of hyperstartling has no common name and is not culturally marked. But there are other places in the world where the condition of people like Ms. Gould has a name and where there are customary ways of dealing with and thinking about it.

Although it is not culturally marked, hyperstartling occurs not infrequently in America, and stories about hyperstartlers can be found. The following chapter discusses a rich fictional portrayal of one. That portrayal focuses on the creation of the hyperstartling state and is told from the perspective of one of the perpetrators rather than that of the hyperstartler herself. It is offered to give a hint of the rich narrative potential a truly creative writer can find in this small neurophysiological vagary.

NOTES

1. "Overlearning" is a term that refers to the effect of continued practice after a behavior has been mastered. Riding a bicycle is a frequently cited example. Even after many years without riding, one can mount a bicycle and ride perfectly well because of overlearning, the extensive practice one has put in long after the necessary skill had been acquired.

2. The term "goosed" usually means being poked or pinched on or between the buttocks.

3. A careful study of the distribution of startling patterns in a large, randomly selected population would confirm or be grounds for rejection of this hypothesis. It is a study that should be done.

4. In this experiment we informed subjects that we would count down from ten to one and that the stimulus (the firing of a starter's pistol) would occur at the point that zero would have been reached.

5. This story, like several others in the book, was provided by someone who, after learning of my interest in startle, was kind enough to approach me and volunteer a personal account of witnessed or experienced startles.

6. If the interactions were truly and intractably hostile, this interpretation would be difficult for her to maintain.

REFERENCES

Anonymous. ca. 200 B.C.–A.D. 200/1979. *Mahabharata* (W. Buck, Trans.), pp. 53–54. New York: New American Library.

Ekman, P., Friesen, W.V., & Simons, R.C. (1985). Is the startle reaction an emotion? *Journal of Personality and Social Psychology, 49,* 1416–1426.

Fletcher, W. (1908). *Latah* and crime. *Lancet, 2,* 254–255.

Garrison, V.E. (1986). Letters to R.C.S.

Goffman, E. (1967). *Interaction ritual: Essays on face-to-face behavior.* Garden City, NY: Doubleday.

Jenner, J. A. (1990) Latah as coping. *International Journal of Social Psychiatry, 36,* 194–199.

O'Hanlon, R. (1984). *Into the heart of Borneo.* New York: Vintage Books.

Stevenson, R.L. 1888/1916. *The black arrow.* New York: Scribner's.

Taylor, D.C. (1985). The sick child's predicament. *Australia and New Zealand Journal of Psychiatry, 19,* 130–137.

Thorne, F.C. (1944/45) Startle neurosis. *American Journal of Psychiatry, 101,* 105–109.

3

MAKING PEOPLE JUMPY
Tom Sawyer and Huck Finn Create a Hyperstartler

One day at Harbledown, William Pater, conversant with his brother's antipathy to these creatures [snakes], mischievously twisted a viper around the handle of a door, and Walter, who did not notice the horror until he had clasped it, nearly died of fright. When, in after years he came to write Marius the Epicurean—*and Marius' horror of snakes will be remembered—no incident of his boyhood stood out more sharply. . . .*

Thomas Wright, 1969, *The Life of Walter Pater*, Vol. 2, pp. 52–53

I needed her help in rolling up a dead, six-foot black snake. She refused to touch the thing. The boy down the street and I proceeded without her. We coiled the snake and stuffed it into the mailbox.

Mary Jane Pennington, 1982, *Frontier*, p. 34

People often become hyperstartlers as a result of being startled repetitively and frequently. The fact that this is so is an interactional resource, a bit of neurophysiology that can be exploited socially and culturally in a great number of ways. This chapter analyzes one use of this resource: the story of how and why Aunt Sally Phelps, a character in Mark Twain's *The Adventures of Huckleberry Finn*, was turned into a hyperstartler. Being fictional, the account is a cultural artifact—both in the usual sense of the word "cultural" (it is part of a work of literature), and also in the anthropological sense (shared symbolic, meaning-laden material).

Mark Twain was not only an author but also a professional raconteur who traveled and gave readings from his works with enormous popular success. The story this chapter discusses is typical of his style: a description of plain folk behaving in extravagant fashion, narrated with wry understatement. It is expected that the reader will find both the events depicted and the manner of telling amusing. The story appears to be an exaggerated and fictionalized version of something that Twain himself once witnessed. Whether or not this is so, it contains a clear description of his and his assumed readers' understanding of how hyperstartling might be induced and of the behavior of a person who startles readily and violently.

Huckleberry Finn is generally considered Mark Twain's masterpiece; many believe it to be the greatest novel ever written by an American. It was published in 1884 and is said by Twain to describe events taking place in the early 1800s. The anecdote this chapter discusses can be found near the novel's end. It describes an incident that takes place in the state of Mississippi in a "big double log house" on a "little one-horse cotton plantation" near the Mississippi River. The subject of the anecdote, Aunt Sally Phelps, is the wife of Silas Phelps, the plantation's owner. She is "a white woman . . . about forty-five or fifty years old." The narrator is Huck Finn, an unschooled but clever and perceptive boy of 13. The "Tom" referred to is Tom Sawyer, a boy of about the same age and the hero of a previous successful novel. Unlike Huck, Tom is middle-class and hence both schooled and Sunday-schooled.

Tom and Huck have collected "a couple of dozen" harmless snakes, stored their catch in a bag in their room, and gone off to supper. However, things do not go exactly according to plan:

> [T]here warn't a blessed snake up there when we went back—we didn't half tie the sack, and they worked out somehow, and left. But it didn't matter much, because they were still on the premises somewheres.

The anecdote is the story of what happened next; it is a small self-contained nugget of description that functions as a building block of the larger story. Here it is:

> No, there warn't no real scarcity of snakes about the house for a considerable spell. You'd see them dripping from the rafters and places every now and then; and they generly landed in your plate, or down the back of your neck, and most of the time where you didn't want them. Well, they was handsome and striped, and there warn't no harm in a million of them; but that never made no difference to Aunt Sally; she despised snakes, be the breed what they might, and she couldn't stand them no way you could fix it; and every time one of them flopped down on her, it didn't make no difference what she was doing, she would just lay that work down and light out. I never see such a woman. And you could hear her whoop to Jericho. You couldn't get her take a-holt of one of them with the tongs. And if she turned over and found

one in bed she would scramble out and lift a howl that you would think the house was afire. She disturbed the old man so that he said he could most wish there hadn't ever been no snakes created. Why, after every last snake had been gone clear out of the house for as much as a week Aunt Sally warn't over it yet; she warn't near over it; when she was setting thinking about something you could touch her on the back of her neck with a feather and she would jump right out of her stockings. It was very curious. But Tom said all women was just so. He said they was made that way for some reason or other.

Three weeks after the snakes' escape, the boys embark on a plan to intensify the family's wariness. One night they push a note under the front door, which says: "Beware. Trouble is brewing. Keep a sharp lookout." It is signed, "Unknown Friend." Huck's narrative continues:

Next night we stuck a picture, which Tom drawed in blood, of a skull and crossbones on the front door; and I never see a family in such a sweat. They couldn't a'been worse scared if the place had been full of ghosts laying for them behind everything and under the beds and shivering through the air. If a door banged, Aunt Sally jumped and said "ouch!" if anything fell, she jumped and said "ouch!" if you happened to touch her, when she warn't noticing, she done the same; she couldn't face no way and be satisfied, because she allowed there was something behind her every time—so she was always a-whirling around sudden, and saying "ouch," and before she got two-thirds around she'd whirl back again, and say it again; and she was afraid to go to bed, but she dasn't set up. So the thing was working very well, Tom said he never see a thing work more satisfactory. He said it showed it was done right. (Mark Twain, 1884, p. 258)

This anecdote depends for its effect on a number of explicit assertions and implicit assumptions about startling and about human nature more generally, which can be listed and examined. Here is a brief sentence-by-sentence listing of some of them:

Sentence 1: *No, there warn't no real scarcity of snakes about the house for a considerable spell.*

Aunt Sally, Uncle Silas, Huck, and Tom find themselves in an environment in which potentially startling stimuli (snakes) are frequent and hence likely to be encountered.

Sentence 2: *You'd see them dripping from the rafters and places every now and then; and they generly landed in your plate, or down the back of your neck, and most of the time where you didn't want them.*

Because the snakes are at liberty in the old log house, unexpected visual and tactile encounters with snake stimuli occur every so often. The sightings are often in the form of sinuous "snake" gestalts; snakes may suddenly and unexpectedly appear in front of one, and one may suddenly and unexpectedly be touched by a snake. Even Huck considers these sudden presentations to be for the most part unpleasant.

Sentence 3: *Well, they was handsome and striped, and there warn't no harm in a million of them; but that never made no difference to Aunt Sally; she despised snakes, be the breed what they might, and she couldn't stand them no way you could fix it; and every time one of them flopped down on her, it didn't make no difference what she was doing, she would just lay that work down and light out.*

Though all parties know that there is no real danger, this fact does not reduce either the intensity of Aunt Sally's response or her associated dysphoria. Aunt Sally always responds by dropping whatever she is holding and running. (The phrase "lay that work down" is an ironic understatement, "litotes" in rhetoric, typical of Twain's style. Earlier the plethora of snakes is described as "no real scarcity.")

Sentence 4: *I never see such a woman.*

Huck Finn considers Aunt Sally's response unusual and excessive.

Sentence 5: *And you could hear her whoop to Jericho.*

Aunt Sally's response includes a sudden vocalization with a drawn-out open vowel. It's very loud.

Sentence 6: *You couldn't get her take a-holt of one of them with the tongs.*

For Aunt Sally, the snakes are phobic objects.

Sentence 7: *And if she turned over and found one in bed she would scramble out and lift a howl that you would think the house was afire.*

Aunt Sally's response is especially violent when she unexpectedly finds a snake in her bed. In this situation the encounter is sudden, unexpected, and tactile. Aunt Sally may be presumed to have been lightly clothed, in the dark, and preparing to give up volitional control of attention. In these encounters, Aunt Sally's vocalizations are audible to those in distant rooms and convey alarm as well as distress.

Sentence 8: *She disturbed the old man so that he said he could most wish there hadn't ever been no snakes created.*

The frequency and intensity of these incidents is such as to be a topic of conversation and, for her husband at least, a real nuisance. He attributes the change in her behavior to the presence of the snakes.

Sentence 9: *Why, after every last snake had been gone clear out of the house for as much as a week Aunt Sally warn't over it yet; she warn't near over it; when she was setting thinking about something you could touch her on the back of her neck with a feather and she would jump right out of her stockings.*

The snakes are gone. But something has changed in Aunt Sally: she now startles readily and violently to other stimuli as well. There are certain times during which Aunt Sally is extremely responsive to light tactile stimulation, especially from behind, on bare skin, and on the nape. These times include those during which she is sitting quietly and attending to internal nonenvironmental stimuli. A prominent characteristic of her response during these times is a violent jump. Other (unspecified) persons, presumably including the adolescent male narrator, having observed that she startles readily and dramatically, intentionally stimulate her in order to observe her reaction. Aunt Sally does not exert effective sanctions against being so stimulated. At least during the period immediately after being startled, she is not capable of doing so. This is also observable.

Sentence 10: *It was very curious.*

The narrator (Huck) considers Aunt Sally's excessive response to be unusual and puzzling.

Sentence 11: *But Tom said all women was just so.*

Tom Sawyer explains the difference between Aunt Sally's response and those of Huck, Uncle Silas, and himself as attributable to gender. He asserts that such (dysfunctional) behavior is characteristic of women.

Sentence 12: *He said they was made that way for some reason or other.*

Tom attributes it to something in women's biological constitution, and he locates this in a larger order of coherence, in his world, that of religion.

Three weeks pass.

Sentence 13: *Next night we stuck a picture, which Tom drawed in blood, of a skull and crossbones on the front door; and I never see a family in such a sweat.*

Huck and Tom use another stimulus, this one a symbol and a sign of threat, to make the family wary—that is, to induce them to more acutely and continuously monitor their surroundings for potential dangers.

Sentence 14: *They couldn't a'been worse scared if the place had been full of ghosts laying for them behind everything and under the beds and shivering through the air.*

They are successful in this attempt; the family begins to act as if something dangerous might be encountered everywhere.

Sentence 15: *If a door banged, Aunt Sally jumped and said "ouch!" if anything fell, she jumped and said "ouch!" if you happened to touch her, when she warn't noticing, she done the same; she couldn't face no way and be satisfied, because she allowed there was something behind her every time—so she was always a-whirling around sudden, and saying "ouch," and before she got two-thirds around she'd whirl back again, and say it again; and she was afraid to go to bed, but she dasn't set up.*

Though the entire family has become more wary, Aunt Sally is especially affected. For her a variety of previously innocuous stimuli now elicit intense startles. Her vocalization, described as a "whoop" in sentence 5 and a "howl" in sentence 7, is now a formed English word, "ouch!" She says "ouch!" after sudden loud noises and also after sudden unexpected touches, stimuli, that is, in two modalities. In neither case is "ouch," which means "I have received a pain," a logically appropriate verbalization. Instead, she utters it in a stereotyped fashion in a context in which it is almost but not quite appropriate. Sometimes, acutely flustered, she whirls about repeatedly, even in the absence of a stimulus, saying "ouch!" over and over again.[1] She has also become frightened and extremely wary.

Sentence 16: *So the thing was working very well, Tom said he never see a thing work more satisfactory.*

Huck and Tom attribute the alteration in Aunt Sally's behavior to their activities. They are pleased by their success.

Sentence 17: *He said it showed it was done right.*

For our purposes this is a key assertion. Tom believes that the result that he and Huck have achieved is the natural consequence of activities such as theirs, if properly performed. In this they are correct; one can create a hyperstartler in just this way.

The story begins with a chance observation, Aunt Sally has a strong response to snakes. As she begins to encounter them regularly and frequently, her response, instead of becoming attenuated by familiarity, increases. Possibly because snakes are phobic objects for her, possibly because of temperamental vulnerability, she becomes sensitized rather than habituated to their repeated appearances.

The anecdote reveals much about what Mark Twain believed about both physiological and social aspects of startle and what he expected his readers to believe. These beliefs can be sorted in a number of physiologically and socially meaningful ways. One revealing way to sort them is to group them into assertions about subject, stimulus, response, and setting.

Assertions about the Subject
1. Startles are more readily elicited when a subject is wary or when he or she is drowsy (a "state" difference).
2. People vary in the ease of elicitation of the startle response and the intensity with which it is expressed (a "trait" difference).
3. Ease of elicitation and high intensity of response occur together; people who startle readily also startle violently, and vice versa.

4. Sudden strong startles may be experienced as intensely unpleasant.
5. Once hyperreactivity is induced in a person, it persists.
6. Other people can reliably induce exaggerated startles and consequent flustered behavior in hyperstartling persons.

Assertions about the Stimulus
1. Snake gestalts elicit startles.
2. Sudden unexpected tactile stimuli elicit startles.
3. Phobic stimuli elicit startles.

Assertions about the Response
1. The response to a startling stimulus may include panic, flight, and dropping or throwing held objects.
2. The response may include nonverbal exclamatory vocalizations.
3. The response may include formed English words, relevant but not exactly appropriate to the occasion.

Assertions about the Setting
1. A house with snakes dripping from the rafters is a place in which startling may be especially frequent.
2. A household warned of impending danger by an ominous message is a household in which startling may be especially frequent.

It is easy to see how the practice of creating hyperstartlers and playing with their vulnerability might become institutionalized in different places and at different times. There are a few cultures in which creating hyperstartlers and playing with them is a prominent and expected societal norm. Some of them are discussed in Chapters 8 to 10. But because hyperstartling is a potential reaction in all humans, regardless of the cultures into which they are born, stories of how one might create or exploit the condition appear in many cultures, not just those that name and especially elaborate on the condition of hyperstartling.

Garrison Keillor, a contemporary American humorist who, like Mark Twain, is a keen observer of the vagaries and incongruities of human existence, published another fictional account of how a susceptible person may be made into a hyperstartler. In his account the stimuli used are not snakes but sudden loud noises. In Keillor's story, the subject, "Miss Conway," like Ms. Gould in Chapter 2, teaches school, and again her pupils are included among those who delight in startling her. Unlike Ms. Gould, Miss Conway does not enjoy being startled, and she does not experience being startled as evidence of closeness and warm affection. She appears on the scene already startling easily.

> Miss Conway of fourth grade struck me as suspiciously thin. What was her problem? Nerves, I suppose. She bit her lips and squinted and snaked her skinny hand into her dress to shore up a strap, and she was easily startled by loud noises. Two or three times a day, Paul or Jim or Lance would let go with a book, dropping it flat for maxi-

mum whack, and yell, "Sorry, Miss Conway!" as the poor woman jerked like a fish on the line. It could be done by slamming a door or dropping the window, too, or even scraping a chair, and once a loud slam made her drop a stack of books, which gave us a double jerk. It worked better if we were very quiet before the noise. Often, the class would be so quiet, our little heads bent over our work, that she would look up and congratulate us on our excellent behavior, and when she looked back down at her book, wham! and she did the best jerk we had ever seen. There were five classes of spasms: The Jerk, The Jump, The High Jump, The Pants Jump, and The Loopdeloop, and we knew when she was prime for a big one. It was after we had put her through a hard morning workout, including several good jumps, and a noisy lunch period, and she had lectured us in her thin weepy voice, then we knew she was all wound up for the Loopdeloop. All it required was an extra effort: throwing a dictionary flat at the floor or dropping the globe, which sounded like a car crash.

We thought about possibly driving Miss Conway to a nervous breakdown, an event we were curious about because our mothers spoke of it often. "You're driving me to a nervous breakdown!" they'd yell, but then, to prevent one, they'd grab us and shake us silly. Miss Conway seemed a better candidate. We speculated about what a breakdown might include—some good jumps for sure, maybe a couple hundred, and talking gibberish with spit running down her chin. (Garrison Keillor, 1985, *Lake Wobegone Days*, pp. 173–174)

Miss Conway's little monsters are exquisitely aware not only of her vulnerability but also of how to exploit it maximally. Their picture of her imminent nervous breakdown is interesting too: Startling frequently and violently is part of it, but also "talking gibberish" and a generalized inability to fit behavior within the bounds of conventional social proprieties. How they arrived at this assumption is not told, but it is right on the mark.

NOTE

1. Although saying a not quite appropriate word is sometimes a response to being startled, it is also possible that Mark Twain or his editors substituted "Ouch!" for something stronger, which they considered unprintable. This was, after all, the nineteenth century.

REFERENCES

Keillor, G. (1985). *Lake Wobegone days*. New York: Viking.

Pennington, M. J. (1982, November). *Frontier* (airline magazine).

Twain, M. (Samuel L. Clemens). 1884/1979. *The adventures of Huckleberry Finn*. New York: Signet.

Wright, T. (1969). *The life of Walter Pater* (Vol. 2). New York: Haskell House.

4

VARIATIONS ON A THEME
Being Startled Makes One Ill

The Hmong believe that every organ, or at least every important organ, has a "soul." During infancy it is easy to lose a soul. . . . And in adulthood there are also many occasions where one can lose a soul. One of them is being startled. . . . Then you may lose a soul, and depending on what soul or souls you lose you may become ill, even incurably ill. You can die if important souls leave your body and the shaman can not retrieve them.

Wolfgang Jilek, 1990, personal communication

Faces like those that I loved, faces that haunt and waylay,
Faces so like and unlike, in the dim unforgettable places,
Startling the heart into sickness
        that aches with the sweet of the May

Alfred Noyes, 1908, *The Golden Hynde*
and Other Poems, p. 132

One student included a stuffed mouse with her MSU enrollment application.
    "The mouse was in a little Baggie," chuckled William Turner, director of admissions and scholarships at Michigan State University. . . .
    "It popped out of the envelope and took about ten years off my life," Turner said.

Lansing State Journal, February 13, 1989

Although startle has a benign and humorous aspect, it has a malignant one as well. For example, a persistent belief in a number of subcultures in the West is that if a pregnant woman is startled, the fetus she is carrying will be marked by the startling stimulus. Loudell Snow has reported an instance of this belief:

> You know what, I had a friend one time and she were pregnant. And we were goin' along and was a hog jumped up in front of us, and she slapped her hand to her ear and screamed. Did just like that. And when her baby was born, he had a pushed-up nose like a hog, and his ear was stopped up. (Erma V. [informant], quoted by Snow, 1977, p. 33)

Carol Laderman reported a similar belief from Malaysia. In one of her examples, the startling stimulus was a corpse:

> As she walked up the hill, carrying the baby, dozens of people who had not previously seen the child were appalled at her corpselike appearance. . . . Rohani's mother reminded her of the time, early in her pregnancy, when she was startled by the sight of a young cousin's corpse. (Laderman, 1983, p. 97)

Startling stimuli make strong impressions, and the belief that a startle during pregnancy may print itself on the developing infant is easy to understand. However, it is not only fetuses that are believed to be affected by startling stimuli. In a number of historically unrelated cultures, being startled is strongly associated with illness and debility, and having been startled is a sufficient explanation of why someone has fallen ill. This belief also appears in Western cultures in a somewhat watered-down form, reflected in phrases such as "startled to death" (usually qualified with "nearly"), or "startled out of a year's [or 10 years'] growth."

The association between startle and illness is also easy to empathize with. At least three factors account for it. First, untoward things happen when a person is startled; there is a break in consciousness, one may be different for a time, less appropriately aware, less autonomous. A startled person loses control, is shaken, disturbed, vulnerable. Second, many of the stimuli that elicit startles signal peril, and the essence of startle lies in its relation to threat. The times when being startled is especially likely include times when one is actually in danger of physical harm. Third, persons startle especially strongly when they are debilitated or after they have experienced a significant trauma. For all these reasons, it is not surprising that observations of startle's phenomenology and of the association between jumpiness and debility have often led to the belief that being startled may make one ill.

Sometimes this belief is highly culturally elaborated in ways congruent with other aspects of a local cosmogony. Where there is an equilibrium theory of well-being, startle may be thought to throw things out of balance. Where the attachment of the soul to the body is an issue, it may be believed that the soul is set free by a startle, especially when it is weakly attached, as in infancy, childhood, or debility. A loose soul may wander off, losing its way in some cultural contexts and in others being vulnerable to capture by spirit beings. Healing beliefs are complementary to beliefs about illness. To heal the affliction which a startle may cause, one must restore balance or entice the soul back, free it when necessary from its captors, and fix it more firmly in place.

In some cultures a specific named illness may be thought to follow being startled. What that illness is varies widely from place to place in ways congruent with beliefs about illnesses and health generally and with the disease ecology of the particular site. Often startle is one of a set of disturbances believed to cause illness along with severe fright, the receipt of bad news, or a significant reversal in personal fortune. In a previous publication (Simons & Hughes, 1985) I called this group of folk diagnoses "fright illnesses," using the term employed by Good and Delvecchio-Good in an important paper, which is excerpted below. This chapter discusses six such named and culturally elaborated fright illnesses.

1. *Fright illness*: a report from Iran. An especially penetrating description and analysis of a fright illness is that by Good and Delvecchio-Good. In Iran, fright illness is whatever illness follows a sudden shock, fright, or startle, no matter what the illness is like descriptively. There are, of course, a few consistent descriptive elements, but these are nonspecific, like "tiredness" and "poor sleep," which may be components of almost any affliction. Afflicted persons diagnosed as suffering from fright illness may be ill in any one of a great variety of ways. For example:

> When we first began our research in Maragheh, we discovered that people frequently spoke of illness as caused by "fright." It appeared that sudden fright (shock, trauma) was an important element in Iranian medical culture. We began to speculate whether we had encountered an Iranian culture-bound disorder, and whether any specific psychiatric disorder, such as conversion symptoms, hysteria, and anxiety reactions, or night terrors in children, was associated with fright illness. However, when we saw several cases of fright and analyzed our health survey data, the existence of a particular clinical syndrome associated with the category fright illness was called into question. (Good & Delvecchio-Good, 1982, p. 151)

Good and Delvecchio-Good report that when they interviewed subjects about the symptoms of fright illness, specific symptoms were sometimes described:

> Although many Iranians believe that if a person receives a start or sudden fright it may cause illness, the reported symptoms of the resulting illness vary widely. There is general agreement that the sufferer turns pale or yellow. It is said colloquially that fright may "hurt one's gall bladder" or "cause one's spleen to explode," caus-

ing yellowness of the skin. Other symptoms may include turning pale, fever, excessive nervousness, weak nerves, becoming "jumpy" or easily startled (*tez tez disjinir*—"he is frequently or easily startled"), and shaking or quivering. Sudden shock may also cause heart palpitations and eventuate in chronic "heart distress" (*narahatiye qalb*). Less common results of "fright" may include deformity or twisting of one's mouth or eyes, development of paralysis, or even madness. (1982, p. 151)

However, when they looked at the actual signs and symptoms present in those who had been diagnosed as suffering from fright illness, they found that they were seldom those that people had listed as characteristic of the illness when interrogated about it. Good and Delvecchio-Good concluded:

Fright, it seems, is not distinguished primarily by physical symptoms or particular behaviors, although certain symptoms are commonly associated with the illness in people's minds. Fright illness does not seem to be associated with a single psychiatric syndrome or culture-specific disorder. In addition, in the two cases reported, fright language did not provide a "repertoire of behavior" (Carr, 1978, p. 289), that patterned symptoms and experience into a unique illness syndrome. Rather, *the diagnosis of fright was used primarily by patients and their families retrospectively and interpretively, to make sense of otherwise baffling symptoms and to construct an illness reality appropriate to Iranian culture.* (1982, p. 157; emphasis added)

Good and Delvecchio-Good cite Guimera's 1978 distinction between "descriptive" categories of folk illness, which are diagnosed by their presenting features, and "etiological" categories, which are diagnosed by virtue of their presumed unitary cause. They explain that, in Iran, fright illness is an etiological category, retrospectively diagnosed whenever someone deduces that whatever affliction he or she is suffering from must have been caused by a prior startle or fright.

2. **Susto**: reports from various Latin American cultures. Probably the best documented of the fright illnesses is *susto*, a folk illness widespread in Latin America. As in Iran, the diagnosis is an etiologic one.

A neighbor of theirs explained his own *susto* condition as a result of recently coming upon a dangerous snake ensconced in an *arroyo* (dry gully). He reported being startled, but he could recall no sense of fear until he attempted to kill the creature, only to discover it had disappeared as suddenly as it had revealed itself. His was a short-lived fright, however, and he forgot about it in his preoccupation with other matters on the walk home.

A few weeks later he felt ill enough to consult a physician. The resultant treatment availed him little and, since his discomfort con-

tinued unrelieved—in fact, he thought it worsened after that treatment—he consulted a local *curandera* (healer). During his meeting
with her, she probed for events in the past that would serve to
explain his problem; they agreed that the encounter with the snake
was of importance and that he was suffering *susto* due to that frightening experience. (Rubel, O'Nell, & Collado-Ardón, 1984, p. 34)

A very long time may elapse between the startle or fright which is
alleged to cause the illness and its appearance:

The woman with the uterine tumor explained her incapacitation
by a *susto* that had occurred more than 30 years before and by the
complications of two additional *sustos* that had occurred during
the ensuing years. (Rubel et al., 1984, pp. 44–45)

The diagnosis is a social process. As one observer notes:

I argue that neither organic problems, psychosocial stress, nor psychological variables can possibly account for all cases of *susto*. Further, in this village many illnesses are initially diagnosed as *susto*
and then later as something else (or vice versa) without any change
in symptoms and for reasons that are not diagnostic in the Western sense. That is, any diagnosis of an illness, perhaps especially
susto, is a social process that depends on and affects social, economic, political, and ethnic relations within the village. (Crandon,
1983, p. 154)

Because it is a social process, the diagnosis may be negotiated:

Through the diagnosis of *susto* in children and adults in a context
in which there are multiple other possible diagnoses, individuals
negotiate identity—personal identity, ethnic identity, political
strategies, and economic possibilities. This negotiation process
has more potential in an illness like *susto* which, because of the
general nature of the symptoms, could also be diagnosed as a number of other things. Hence, when *susto* is diagnosed, a statement is
being made about the patient, and the diagnostician as well, at several levels of analysis. (Crandon, 1983, p. 161)

3. *Espanto*: a report from Chiapas, Mexico. *Espanto* appears to be in
most elements identical to *susto*; Tousignant considers the terms to be
equivalent.

Whenever any such belief is widespread over a significant geographic territory there are, of course, some variations in its manifestations. Belief in *espanto* is found throughout a vast geograph-

ical territory. It is known among most Andean countries of Latin America as well as in Guatemala, Mexico and the United States. The most universal trait of the belief is that *espanto* is thought to result from a magical fright through which the victim loses his soul. The soul thereafter remains captive or wanders aimlessly. (Tousignant, 1979, p. 348)

The following case recounts very well the experience:
Melquiaddes was crossing the forest to reach his corn field. The sun had just set and the path was difficult to follow. All of a sudden, he disappeared down a cliff disguised by thick layers of leaves and hit the ground twelve feet below. This was the moment when he felt *espanto* within himself. Some informants translate the event by saying that they feel *l'aire*, as if a draught was crossing through their whole body. (Tousignant, 1979, p. 357)

As with other fright illnesses, the actual symptoms manifested are disparate; the diagnosis is not descriptive but etiological.

[T]he 15 symptoms which reached a frequency of over 80 percent had very little in common: some were truly organic while others referred to behavioral features. They were largely represented by non-specific systemic symptoms such as weakness and loss of appetite or elements suggestive of infections, a result similar to that obtained by Fabrega (1970) with regard to a wide range of folk illness labels. (Tousignant, 1979, pp. 350–351)

Many informants experienced difficulties in answering the questionnaire. Their view of the symptomatology of *espanto* was sometimes so diffuse that their response was often equivocal. Other informants stated very frankly that *espanto* could lead to almost any ailment and that our procedure didn't make much sense to them. (1979, p. 352)

4. ***Lanti***: a report from the Philippines. One aspect of fright illness beliefs in a number of cultural settings is that it is not always the person who experienced the startle who is affected. Sometimes it is someone close to that person, especially his or her child. The fact that the person startled need not be the one who is thereby made ill, but rather someone in close association with that person, was reported by the late Donn Hart from the Philippines.

One rainy morning in a small village (Lalawigan) in eastern Samar I visited a family where the two-year-old daughter was sick.
"What caused her illness?," I inquired.
"Her father," answered the mother.

"How did he make her sick?"

"Two days ago he almost stepped on a big snake in the forest.

"He was alarmed for the snake was poisonous."

"Was his daughter with him at this time?"

"No. This is not necessary with *lanti*."

It was this incident that led me to investigate this illness in the Philippines. (Hart, 1985, p. 371)

Hart reported that the local understanding of how this happens refers to the special bond between parent and child.

Lanti results when one is either directly or indirectly frightened. The patient may be startled or another member of the family is frightened. In the latter instance, since a mystical bond connects these two persons, the emotional shock of this experience is transferred to the child, resulting in sickness. (1985, p. 371)

As with other fright illnesses, the actual symptoms are quite variable, reflecting the range of diseases found in the part of the Philippines where Hart worked:

There are numerous symptoms associated with *lanti*: a high fever that results in boils; loose, greenish excrement; cold extremities; *atas* (white-coated tongue sometimes including the inside of the mouth); *habas* (reddish blotches or skin eruptions where the skin folds on the arms, legs, thighs, and neck); *puno* (a skin disease of the scalp); rapid heart beats; stomach ache; incessant crying; desire to be held by an adult; trembling; shouting during sleep (when awake the patient reports a sensation of falling); and a deepening of the fontanel [a soft spot on an infant's skull, before the bones which comprise the skull grow together] (*bobon*). Those who treat *lanti* claim that of all these symptoms the three most recurrent ones are a high fever, boils, and *habas*. . . . (1985, pp. 375–376)

Belief in fright illness is widespread in the area in which Hart worked.

The identical illness is mentioned, often briefly, in the literature on Samarnon Filipinos residing in eastern Leyte. Arens states that *ugmad* is a sickness caused by fright; the patient is *hinugmaran* or made ill by fear (1971, p. 116; also Makabenta, 1979, p. 187). In a study of etiologies in Guinhangdan, a fishing village of 1,200 people in eastern Leyte, this illness is known as *kalas* (Nurge, 1958, p. 1162). *Kalas* also means sudden emotion, surprise or astonishment (Makabenta, 1979, p. 41). In Cebuan frightening experiences are called *lubatan* (Wolff, 1972, p. 601). It should be noted that illness

rarely occurs in the Bisayas as the putative result of other strong
emotions such as anger, jealousy, or hysteria. (1985, p. 376)

As is true of fright illnesses generally, it is the "weak" who are believed
to be most susceptible.

In Lalawigan *lanti* is considered a natural illness caused by fright
that, with a few exceptions, afflicts only infants or young children,
and almost invariably the youngest child. If there are two children
in the family, the youngest is most apt to be sickened by *lanti*, but
it may strike the elder sibling. When this occurs the explanation
given is that the elder sibling is "weaker than the youngest sibling." (1985, p. 376)

It is the experience of startle or fright that is believed to cause the illness rather than the encounter with any specific stimulus. The stimulus
generating the experience can be anything startling or frightening.

Parents of Lalawigan children who became sick reported such
experiences as being startled by a pig (when defecating outside the
house); seeing two men fighting; hearing barking dogs; seeing a
large fire with black clouds of swirling smoke; playing with a dog
or chicken that frightened them; riding on a bus; almost falling out
of an outrigger boat; being severely scolded or punished; falling
into a ditch; tumbling out of a bamboo walker or a hammock in the
house; and hearing the sudden noise of a passing bulldozer.
Typical incidents that startled a parent or another household
member which resulted in *lanti* in the youngest child (the transferred fright referred to earlier) were: seeing or killing a snake;
mistakening an eel inside a closed basket for a snake; shooting a
gun; fishing with dynamite; being attacked by an angered carabao
(water buffalo); climbing a tall tree; burning a swidden; catching
an unusually large fish; stumbling into a newly dug house post
hole; transferring the body of a neighbor to a coffin or having difficulty in lowering a coffin into the grave; visiting a large cave;
puddling a rice field with two carabaos; being fearful of falling
from a tall building; and slaughtering a large pig or carabao. (1985,
p. 377)

In the area in which Hart worked, the illness thought to be caused by
the startling or frightening experience is believed to have an independent
existence, needing someone on whom to alight:

Immunity to *lanti* occurs once a child is no longer the youngest in
the family. However, an adult who is an only child may suffer *lanti*
for, as one informant explained, "There is no one else to whom it

can be transmitted." For example, a husband had a startling experience that resulted in his wife's becoming ill, since the couple was childless and she was the youngest sibling in her family. (1985, p. 377)

5. *Mogo laya*: a report from New Guinea (the Huli people). In the following example of a fright illness from the southern highlands of New Guinea, a startle intended as a prank turns out to have serious consequences.

> A young man and his betrothed were walking through the forest with some other people of their own age. It was a gay outing, and for fun the young man secretly cut ahead of the others to surprise them further down the track. He jumped out at the girl, who was so terrified that she fainted. She soon recovered, and the incident was treated as a joke. But when he told his mother about it later she advised him not to marry the girl, as she probably had *kuyanda*. If he beat or worried her the *kuyanda* might burst causing her to die. He would then have to compensate her clan. He took her advice, and broke off the engagement. (Frankel, 1985, p. 402)

Frankel explains that *mogo laya*, the Huli word for "startled," is also a diagnosis. The Huli believe in a vital spirit (*bu*), which the body can lose, with dire consequences. It is recognized that some people startle more readily and violently than others, a state attributed to *kuyanda*, "a silent bloodsucker that leechlike swells and contracts." In the case above, the girl's extreme response led to the conclusion that she carried a *kuyanda* and was therefore in danger of dying. Frankel says that children are considered especially vulnerable, and that mothers attempt to shield babies during their first few months of life from anything startling or frightening since a startle or severe fright might lead to illness or even death. If a Huli child should die after being startled, the person responsible for the startling must pay compensation.

6. *Kesambet*: a report from Bali. The Norwegian anthropologist, Uni Wikan, has reported a fright illness from Bali.

> It is the *unexpected* nature of a situation which triggers the psychobiological reaction known as *tekajut* or *mekesiyab*: to be surprised, startled, frightened or shocked. Living in a world where ghosts and supernatural spirits hover about day and night, the characteristic sounds of such creatures come to constitute part of the ordinary round of things and cannot trigger startlement [*sic*] or fright. Fear, which may be a natural reaction considering the ill-intentioned nature of some of these spirits, may also trigger illness but of an altogether different kind. Fear paralyzes the spirit. Fright [i.e., startle] lets it out with a gasp. (Wikan, 1989, p. 29)

In North Bali, if a child cries inexplicably and persistently, the mother is likely to think *"kesambet"* and rush the child off to a traditional healer. *Kesambet* refers to illness from shock, fright, or soul loss, and is not to be taken lightly. It is the illness most commonly adduced as the cause of death in children where the etiology is unknown, and even adults are known to die from it. (Wikan, 1989, p. 25)

In Bali, as is the case in Mexico and the Philippines, the afflicted person may be someone other than the person who was startled:

The traditional healer (*balian* or *dukun*) will focus the treatment on mother or child, depending on whether the child is nursing and whom the fright is believed to have originally struck. In the case of a child believed to be sick because the *mother* was startled, it makes no sense by Balinese conceptions to direct treatment at the child itself. The child receives its vital nourishment through the mother's milk; hence its vitality and balance depend on *her* condition rather than its own. From her blood, in which flows her spiritual essence, she makes the milk that sustains the soul essence of the child. (Wikan, 1989, p. 25)

FRIGHT ILLNESS AND ORGANIC PATHOLOGY

It is not known whether or not in any of the places where belief in fright illness is prevalent there exists a subpopulation of those so diagnosed who have been actually made ill by a severe fright or startle. Given what is known about the posttraumatic stress syndrome, it seems more likely than not. However, this must be a small proportion of those so diagnosed. Survey studies so far have not established the existence of such cases.

The attribution of illness to an antecedent startle is quite reasonable, but it is, as the examples illustrate, often mistaken. It is plausible enough, but often it is wrong. It is hardly credible that the uterine tumors that an informant told Rubel about were really caused by a *susto* fright 30 years earlier or that the 2-year-old whose *lanti* so intrigued Hart fell ill because her father almost stepped on a snake. The children Wikan writes about were sick with something else:

Failing treatment, the child is susceptible to death. In one of the villages where we worked, illness from shock or fright was given as the cause of nearly half of all deaths in children. Child mortality appears to have been around 40%, which meant that over the past ten years a total of some 380 children below the age of two or three were believed to have died from illness from shock or fright in this particular village. (Wikan, 1989, p. 25)

The examples of fright illness cited here are representative but not exhaustive. People in the societies that believe strongly in startle-caused illness may still occasionally play with startle, as in the cited Huli example. However, in these societies the serious and long-lasting negative consequences believed to follow being startled limit this casual social use.

REFERENCES

Espanto

Tousignant, M. (1979). Espanto: A dialogue with the gods. *Culture, Medicine and Psychiatry, 3*, 347–361.

Fright Illness

Good, B.J., & Delvecchio-Good, M.J. (1982). Toward a meaning-centered analysis of popular illness categories: "Fright illness" and "Heart distress" in Iran. In A.J. Marsella & G.M. White (Eds.), *Cultural conceptions of mental health and therapy* (pp. 141–166). Dordrecht: D. Reidel.

Good, B.J., & Kleinman, A.M. (1985). Culture and anxiety: Cross-cultural evidence for the patterning of anxiety disorders. In A.H. Tuma & J. Maser (Eds.), *Anxiety and anxiety disorders* (pp. 297–323). Hillsdale, NJ: Lawrence Erlbaum.

Kesambet

Wikan, U. (1989). Illness from fright or soul loss: A North Balinese culture-bound syndrome? *Culture, Medicine and Psychiatry, 13*, 25–50.

Lanti

Hart, D.V. (1969). Bisayan Filipino and Malayan humoral pathologies: Folk medicine and ethno-history in Southeast Asia. *Southeast Asia Data Paper, 76.* Ithaca, NY: Cornell University Press.

Hart, D.V. (1985). *Lanti,* illness by fright among Bisayan Filipinos. In R.C. Simons & C.C. Hughes (Eds.), *The culture-bound syndromes* (pp. 371–398). Dordrecht: D. Reidel.

Mogo Laya

Frankel, S. (1985). *Mogo laya,* a New Guinea fright illness. In R.C. Simons & C.C. Hughes (Eds.), *The culture-bound syndromes* (pp. 399–404). Dordrecht: D. Reidel.

Susto

Collado-Ardón, R., Rubel, A.J., O'Nell, C.W., & Murray, R.H. (1983). A folk illness (*susto*) as an indicator of real disease. *Lancet, 2*, 1362.

Crandon, L. (1983). Why *susto Ethnology, 22,* 153–167.

Hoff, C. (1968). Reproduction and viability in a Highland Indian population: High altitude adaptation in a Peruvian community. *Occasional Papers in Anthropology, 1.* University Park: Pennsylvania State University Press, pp. 85–129.

Landy, D. (1985). A syndrome and its meaning. *Science, 228,* 850–851.

Langner, T. S. (1965). Psychophysiological symptoms and the status of women in two Mexican communities. In J.M. Murphy & A.H. Leighton (Eds.), *Approaches to cross-cultural psychiatry* (pp. 360–392). Ithaca, NY: Cornell University Press.

Rubel, A., O'Nell, C. W., & Collado-Ardón, R. (1984). *Susto, a folk illness.* Berkeley: University of California Press.

Other Cited References

Guimera, L.M. (1978). Witchcraft illness in the Evuzok nosological system. *Culture, Medicine and Psychiatry, 2,* 373–396.

Laderman, C. (1983). *Wives & midwives: Childbirth and nutrition in rural Malaysia.* Berkeley: University of California Press.

Noyes, A. (1908). *The golden hynde and other poems* (p. 132). New York: Macmillan.

Simons, R.C., & Hughes, C.C., (Eds.). (1985). *The culture-bound syndromes.* Dordrecht: D. Reidel.

Snow, L.F. (1977). Popular medicine in black neighborhoods. In E.H. Spicer (Ed.), *Ethnic medicine in the Southwest* (pp. 19–95). Tucson: University of Arizona Press.

5

THE STARTLE MUSEUM I
Exhibits of Startle Sorted by Their Expository Uses

I'll startle you
Worse than the sacring bell, when the brown wench
Lay kissing in your arms, Lord Cardinal.

William Shakespeare, 1612,
Henry VIII, Act II, scene ii

There was a young lady from hell
Who jumped at the sound of a bell,
Because she was bad—bad—bad,
She jumped at the sound of a bell. . . .

F. Scott Fitzgerald, 1934,
Tender Is the Night, p. 290

But don't worry. . . . It's going to be scary. . . . I have independently counted
thirty shocks or little jumps out of the seat, some much higher than the
others.

William Blatty [film director], *Lansing State Journal*, August 16, 1990

In the passage from *Huckleberry Finn* discussed in Chapter 3, Mark Twain used his understanding of the startle reflex to further an intricate bit of plot development. This chapter and the next examine a collection of similar literary, expository, and artistic uses of the startle reflex, sorted and classified systematically. They present and discuss examples of the ways in which creative persons have described or shown someone or something being startled or have used the word "startle" or any of its variants.

These uses of startle constitute a catalog of the kinds of assertions that cultural, explicitly created references to and depictions of the startle reflex can provide. They reveal something of the ways in which their creators understand the experienced universe generally, the nature of interpersonal relationships, moral values, and the expected consequences of actions.

It is convenient to refer to these examples as "exhibits," both as in "museum" and as in "court of law." The former meaning is the main one, but the second is relevant also. The exhibits are samples of the data on which the argument of this book is based. Like most museum exhibits, these are purposefully arranged specimens, extracted from their native contexts and presented to exemplify a larger collection. Most of the exhibits are quotations from newspapers, magazines, journals, books of fiction and nonfiction, plays, and advertisements. Some are descriptions of cartoons, films, videotapes, slides, paintings, sculpture, ceramics, music, and utilitarian objects such as greeting cards and bookmarks. Virtually all the exhibits are public, "published" cultural materials. They are examples of startle that anyone might encounter in the course of reading and carrying out other activities of ordinary life. Because—with few exceptions—there is no systematic way to seek them out, they were collected as I chanced upon them. For several years I collected every startle I came upon, but as the collection grew to massive proportions, I ultimately limited further collecting to especially interesting, revealing, or amusing ones, or ones that filled gaps in the collection. Because the properties of the reflex are quite specific, it turned out to be easy to identify potential exhibits, although there were a few equivocal candidates.

Most of the exhibits are brief bits of narrative. In each, someone has made use of some aspect of the startle reflex to do some bit of interactional business. Because most of the exhibits are fictional, it would not be proper to conclude from them how startle functions in the real world. They are, however, clear examples of how startles have been *understood* to function in the real world. As the collection demonstrates, these understandings are mostly perceptive and accurate.

When I began collecting startles, I expected to find them in cartoons and in accounts of persons encountering danger, but I never anticipated how many startles I would come upon or the wide variety of contexts in which they would be found. There are startles in American, European, Chinese, and Japanese poetry and fiction, in greeting cards, flower catalogs, bookmarks, nature guides, garden books, and in advertisements for records, films, books, and travel, and this is only a partial list. The contexts in which startles appear include depictions of courtship, falling ill, and curing, and they signify moral statuses from guilty to aesthetically sensitive. The startle reflex, it turns out, is used in a truly impressive number and assortment of ways. It turns up all over. A random *Science* magazine (July 21, 1988) had two, and the 34 pages of a random *New York Times* (July 6, 1988) contained five, none related to the July 4th holiday but instead in descriptions of a tennis game (two references), a recent horror film, children finding a homeless man sleeping in the tunnel of their gym set, and an unexpected turnabout in Korean politics.

Startles are, of course, frequent in cartoons, where they have a standard iconography. No Sunday goes by without several startles appearing in the comics section of most American newspapers. Seven of the 21 cartoons in the Sunday comics section of a recent issue of my local paper depicted or mentioned startles. The book *Garfield Weighs In* (Davis, 1984), a typical collection of newspaper cartoons, contains startles in ten of its four-panel sequences, one repeated on the back cover.

Almost any book-length work of fiction contains some startles; *Victory*, a tale of suspense by Joseph Conrad, for example, contains 37. Because it is a tale of suspense, many of the startles are used to signify a character's being wary, edgy, or in danger. But startles are frequent in nonsuspenseful fiction as well. Volume 1 of D. H. Lawrence's *Short Stories* contains 41 startles, with startles occurring in 14 of the 17 stories (Simons & Salyers, 1980)! In these stories startles are used in a variety of contexts for an extraordinarily diverse assortment of effects. Startles are startlingly frequent, and as a cultural resource, the startle reflex is startlingly useful. But perhaps this should not be startling after all.

Humans interact with their physical and social environments in patterned, recurrent ways that reflect consistencies both in the external material world and in the pattern-imposing organization of the human nervous system. Biologically significant events occur in cultural contexts that pattern them also. Fiction, drama, poetry—in fact, all art—depict and describe experienced regularities such as startle and suggest culturally appropriate attitudes toward them. In all cultures, artistic depictions are intended to resonate in the experiences of their audience, and the degree to which they do is a measure of artistic success.

This chapter and the chapter that follows contain only a small selection from the mass of material that I have collected. The exhibits presented were chosen for brevity and clarity and to illustrate specific points. In choosing exhibits there was a bias toward those in which the phrasing or context makes the assumptions that are implicit in the use especially apparent. Take, for example, an exhibit from Robert Louis Stevenson's *The Black Arrow* (1888, p. 62): "Matcham could not restrain a little cry, which he instantly stifled, and even Dick started with surprise, and dropped the windac from his fingers." "Matcham" is a girl in disguise, and the phrase "even Dick" reveals that Stevenson believed that, because Dick was a boy, he would be less likely to startle to the unexpected arrow than Matcham, a girl of about the same age. This exhibit is therefore an example of the frequent assertion that women startle more readily than men. Statements of the form: "The part that made it startling was . . ." have also been preferentially selected because of their transparency. And of course, other things being equal, exhibits that make their point concisely have been chosen in preference to those that are more prolix.

"ACTUAL" AND "METAPHORIC" STARTLES

Startle figures in the museum collection in two quite distinct ways. First, there are citations of actual or fictional accounts of startle incidents. In these citations, whether or not the actual word "startle" is used, it is asserted that some animate being experienced and displayed a startle reaction. ("When the phone rang, Paul was startled." "When the car backfired, the horse jumped and took off for parts unknown.") But there is also a second usage in which the word "startle" or a related word or phrase is used without suggesting that anyone or anything was actually startled. In the phrase "a startling piece of news," "startling" refers to a property of the news, not to the reaction of any person. Certain information is classified as "news" and subclassified as news of a "startling" type. It is not intended that the reader should infer that anyone actually jumped on hearing it. This second type of usage might be called "metaphoric."

Charles Lamb wrote: "A pun . . . is a pistol let off at the ear" (*Last Essays of Elia*, 1860, p. 433). In what way is this so? What properties of puns and pistol shots did this witty and perceptive observer of the human condition expect his readers to infer? Loudness—that they're both delivered loudly? No, something else. Though the word "startle" is not used, one can safely assume that this is the aspect of the event referred to. How such metaphoric uses of startle come about and how they provide cultural information requires a bit of explanation.

In the second edition of Merriam Webster's unabridged dictionary, "metaphor" is defined as follows:

> Use of a word or phrase literally denoting one kind of object or idea, in place of another, by way of suggesting a likeness or analogy between them (the ship ploughs the sea; a volley of oaths). A metaphor may be regarded as a compressed simile. The comparison implied in the former (a marble brow) being explicit in the latter (a brow white like marble).[1] (p. 1546)

This definition, however, omits an element that is essential to the analysis of the examples used here. It is this: What makes the metaphor intelligible is the shared unnamed superordinate class that contains both the literal term and the term for which it is used metaphorically. The superordinate class is defined by the properties shared. In the examples above, a plough can be a metaphor for a ship because both are "furrow-makers" and marble can be a metaphor for certain brows because both are smooth, cool, and white. Because one can examine startle metaphors for the shared properties that generated them, metaphorical usages also reveal cultural conceptions of startle. Which properties shared by pistol shots and puns did Charles Lamb intend to suggest? Similarly, one can ask, for example, What aspect of the news in the phrase "a startling piece of news" occasioned the use of the term "startling"?

Most of the exhibits are American and contemporary, many from my local newspaper, the *Lansing* (Mich.) *State Journal*. Many others are British or American but older. In some categories I have been able to include a few exhibits from non-Western cultures, most often from Japan.[2] Each reader can do his or her independent verification, which does not require special training or a hunting license. If you watch for startles in cultural materials, you will see them. There is a startle in tonight's newspaper.

SORTING THE EXHIBITS

This chapter and the next discuss the many meanings that the assertion or depiction of a startle can convey and hence demonstrate how the reflex is used as a narrative and artistic resource. Each of the exhibits requires explanation in its own right; in choosing to refer to startle, some creative person has associated a startle with a number of descriptive elements. How can one best explain the creative choice which each exhibit records?

In this chapter, exhibits are sorted by their social or cultural function. It is designed to demonstrate how widely used a resource the reflex is and how many things it can do. It includes, for example, exhibits of startles used for diagnosis, startles used to cure, startles that reveal the moral status of a startled subject, and startles crafted for interest and pleasure. Although in this chapter physiological factors such as stimulus and response are often mentioned, physiological aspects of startle are not used for sorting and are discussed only incidentally. The ways in which the physiology of the reflex provides the raw material for expository use are presented systematically in Chapter 6.

Although each exhibit in each of these two chapters necessarily illustrates more than one feature of the reflex and therefore might have been presented under several headings, each exhibit is presented only once, and the text surrounding it discusses only the aspect of startle usage which the exhibit has been chosen to illustrate. Take, for example, the following exhibit:

> In bed with a cold, I called loudly to my mother to bring me some orange juice. I heard her rustling about. Slam of refrigerator door. Footsteps coming down the hall. I threw myself half off the bed, my head back, my eyes staring wide, tongue extended and hands dragging on the floor. Screech. A shattering of glass. I sat up and laughed. Eventually, after sitting down on my bed to catch her breath and recover, she laughed too. "What a terrible thing to do," she said. (E. L. Doctorow, 1985, *World's Fair*, p. 95)

This exhibit can be found in Chapter 6 under the heading, "Appalling Sights," a subcategory of "Stimuli Which Startle." However, in addition to its illustrating an appalling sight, the exhibit is also an example of a child's use of a startle in play with his mother and it contains examples of a vocal response and of a startled person's dropping a held object. That use of the reflex and those other features are discussed elsewhere in the museum and are illustrated with other exhibits. Thus, by identifying undescribed and undiscussed features of the exhibits, interested readers can use the exhibits supplied to verify or refute the points made in these two chapters and can make their own discoveries even without hunting for additional examples.

The organization of this chapter is given in Table 5.1.

TABLE 5.1   Exhibits of Startle Sorted by Their Expository Uses

I. Startles used for specific social and cultural functions
  A. To diagnose
  B. To cure
  C. To elicit an unplanned revelation
  D. To repel intruders
  E. To murder
  F. In a child's play with his or her mother
  G. In courtship and other sexual play
  H. To change between states of awareness
II. Startles that reveal the moral status of a startled subject
  A. Negative
    1. Of impure mind
    2. Of bad character
    3. Guilty
    4. Afraid
    5. Not enlightened
  B. Positive
    1. Aesthetically sensitive
  C. Not morally responsible
III. Ready and violent startling used to connote:
  A. Low status
  B. Femininity, "girlishness," "spinsterishness"
IV. Failure to startle or rapid recovery from being startled used to connote:
  A. The status of a hero or other great personage
  B. Royalty or nobility
V. Startles used to explain illness or deformity
(Discussed in Chapter 4)
VI. Startles crafted for interest or pleasure
  A. Startles in music
  B. Startles in films and theatrical productions
  C. Startles in advertising
  D. Startle-eliciting and startle-depicting objects
VII. Special terminology: "Boo!" "Oops!" and "Gotcha!"
VIII. Startles used to signify a revelation or massive reconceptualization

THE STARTLE REFLEX AS A SOCIAL
AND CULTURAL RESOURCE

I. STARTLES USED FOR SPECIFIC SOCIAL AND CULTURAL FUNCTIONS

As must be apparent by now, writers may use startles to signify a considerable assortment of meanings. This section of the museum presents exhibits in which a startle (or information about a person's way of startling) is used to accomplish some specific end.

A. To Diagnose

In *Huckleberry Finn*, Jim tells how he was angry because his little daughter didn't seem to obey him:

> My but I wuz mad! I was a gwyne for de chile, but jis' den—it was a do' dat open innerds—jis' den, 'long come de wind an slam it to, behine de chile, keer-blam!—en my lan', de chile never move'!" [Jim then opened the door] "easy an slow, en poke my head in behine de chile, sof an still, en all of a sudden I says pow!, jis' as loud as I could yell. She never budge! ... Oh she was plumb deef en dumb, Huck, plumb deef en dumb—en I'd ben a-treat'n her so! (Mark Twain, 1884, *The Adventures of Huckleberry Finn*, p. 156)

Jim's reasoning, of course, is that while his daughter might be ignoring his commands, unless she were deaf she would show a visible response to the unexpected sound of the slamming door. Just to be sure he makes his own startle test. His daughter's failures to respond not only demonstrate her deafness but also reveal to Jim that he had been unjust in his belief that she had been disobedient. Jim's test is still used:

> By 3 months, baby should startle at loud sounds and be soothed by the sound of mother's voice. (Susan McNamara, "Hearing loss can be corrected in newborns," *Lansing State Journal*, March 22, 1989)

In the next exhibit what is to be diagnosed is not a hearing problem but general nervous system hyperarousal. As part of an evaluation of alcohol and other drug-withdrawal states, an expert on psychiatric interviewing recommends asking:

> Do you find yourself being startled by noises or upset by people moving or talking around you? (Shawn C. Shea, 1988, *Psychiatric Interviewing*, p. 278)

In suspected cases of posttraumatic stress syndrome, ready startling is also asked about.

B. To Cure

Startling stimuli are frequently used in healing ceremonies throughout the world. Startle cures were probably suggested by the observation that startles elicit radical changes in attentional states, thus causing the soul to come, go, or alter, whatever the local concept of soul.

> Navaho clowns during their Mud Dance all of a sudden stop dancing and rush up to a sick person and lift him high above their heads, sometimes tossing him into the air. The Cheyenne "Contraries" also cure by quickly lifting people into the air, sometimes holding the head downward. Another curing method is to run up to a person very fast, in a threatening manner, and then either jump over him or else throw a piece of boiling-hot dog meat at him. . . . By startling people in these ways clowns . . . [cure] them by releasing them from any idle thoughts or worries. (Tedlok, 1975, "The Clown's Way" in *Teachings from the Earth*, p. 111)
>
> In Texas there are two curing procedures for *susto*. In the first, the patient lies with arms outstretched, resembling a cross, the body is swept with the branches of a herb, the curer prays in calm quiet and the patient calls out for his soul to return. Sometime during the calm-enveloped treatment a sudden sputter of liquid, either water or liquor, is emitted from the mouth of the healer, shocking the patient and bathing him about the face. In the second procedure, the patient is also swept with a branch, and then led to a fire where cold liquid is poured into a red-hot copper pot. The hiss given off supposedly frightens the patient terribly, causing him to leap back, shriek, and shudder. (Klein, 1978, p. 26)

Good and Delvecchio-Good have reported a similar use of startle in Iran:

> A hot wire or piece of burning thread will be touched to the patient, causing him to start and causing the fright to be "frightened" out of the body. (Good & Delvecchio-Good, 1982, p. 153)

In the next exhibit, the movement which is part of the unreflective defensive startle response is itself the cure:

> The great Razi healed an emir of Raiy . . . struck by a chronic paralysis of his legs, by a combined therapy: after a long hot bath and a drink which was "to ripen the humors" he suddenly threat-

ened the prince with a knife as if he intended to kill him, whereupon the prince sprang to his feet. Razi fled on a horse kept in
readiness, and after reaching a safe place wrote a letter to the emir
in which he explained his "psychological therapy" (*iladj-e nafsani*).
(Browne, *Arabian Medicine*, 1921, p. 82, cited in Leslie, 1976, *Asian
Medical Systems*, p. 51)

Startle is also believed to cure in Western medicine. This may occur as
part of a planned therapy or spontaneously. In *Battle for the Mind*, William
Sargant (1957, p. 75) tells of a case of hysterical blindness cured by a
thunderclap. And the following exhibit describes the use of startle in the
treatment of obsessive thoughts:

In this procedure ["thought-stopping"] the patient is relaxed and
is asked to think of the obsessive thought. The therapist shouts
"stop" and makes a sudden noise at the same time. (Marks, 1981,
p. 591)

In the same paper, Marks notes that related techniques include self-
administered electric shock and snapping a rubber band on the wrist.

In Western folk medicine, being startled is, of course, the classic
folk remedy for hiccups—see, for example, "Treatment of Hiccup" (in
Jefferson, 1981, p. 64). In the following anecdote, an ingenious stimulus is
used effectively:

Patients in the waiting room were startled by a loud scream from
the doctor's office. A few minutes later, a woman, obviously in her
late 60s and visibly shaken, came out, paid her bill, and left. The
doctor emerged and signalled for the next patient to come in. As
they walked, the patient asked, "What happened?"

"Oh," the doctor replied, "I told her she was pregnant." The
patient looked astonished. "But doctor, you couldn't have been
serious!"

"Of course not," he answered. "But it sure cured her hiccups."
(Ann Landers, *Lansing State Journal*, March 13, 1983)

C. To Elicit an Unplanned Revelation

Startling someone may elicit a disclosure that the victim may not have
planned to reveal. Nathaniel Hawthorne describes this stratagem twice in
the same novel. It works for his protagonist on the second try:[3]

After sitting awhile, in contemplation of this person's familiar con-
tour, I was irresistibly moved to step over the intervening benches,
lay my hand on his shoulder, put my mouth close to his ear, and
address him in a sepulchral, melodramatic whisper:

"Hollingsworth! Where have you left Zenobia?"

His nerves, however, were proof against my attack. (Nathaniel Hawthorne, 1852, *The Blithedale Romance*, p. 197)

A quick association of ideas made me shudder, from head to foot; and, again, like an evil spirit, bringing up reminiscences of a man's sins, I whispered a question in Hollingsworth's ear.

"What have you done with Priscilla?"

He gave a convulsive start, as if I had thrust a knife into him, ... (1852, p. 200)

D. To Repel Intruders

Commercial devices that emit a sudden loud noise are sold on the theory that this stimulus will make a felon flee.

You're walking to your front door, late at night, alone. Suddenly you hear footsteps behind you. You press a button in your pocket and instantly a bright light goes on in the house and a piercing siren blares. The startled intruder flees. You're inside—and safe. (Advertisement for "Hot Button Electronic Pocket Bodyguard," 1983, *Sharper Image* catalog)

One such device is called "The Startler."

Simply hang *Startler* on inside door knob.... Scares intruders away. (Advertisement for "Startler Portable Electronic Burglar Alarm," n.d., text on package)

E. To Murder

Referring to the potential effect of a startle on heart rate and on alerting, arousing physiologic mechanisms generally, the comedienne Joan Rivers once humorously advocated using a startle as a lethal weapon:

Marry rich! Buy him a pacemaker, then stand behind him and say "Boo!" (Interview in *Newsweek*, October 10, 1983)

F. In a Child's Play with His or Her Mother

In many cultures, children intentionally startle their mothers in their play with them. I suppose the instantaneous status reversal is part of the payoff (Fig. 5.1). Fathers are played with like this less often, perhaps because they may less easily accept the reversal.

Figure 5.1 In many cultures, in many contexts, children's play with their mothers includes startling them. The instantaneous status reversal is probably part of the payoff. Calvin and Hobbes © Watterson. Reprinted with permission of Universal Press Syndicate. All rights reserved.

Archer and Jacob jumped up from behind the mound where they had been crouching with the intention of springing upon their mother unexpectedly, and they all began to walk slowly home. (Virginia Woolf, 1922, *Jacob's Room*, pp. 19–20)

I often saw children startling their mothers in Malaysia and in the Philippines, and a friend raised in Ireland who told me that both he and his mother say "Jesus, Mary, and Joseph!" when startled also told me that when young he used to drop a brass shoehorn to startle her. This sort of play is frequent in the United States as well. Here's a commercial application from an Advertisement for a plastic "dinosaur egg":

"Leave it in Mom's terrarium to startle the wits out of her!" (*Jerryco catalog*, 1990).

Mom is also the one who is chosen as the subject to be startled in an exhibit presented in Chapter 6 under "Appalling Sights."

G. In Courtship and Other Sexual Play

Startles are used in teasing interactions between men and women in many cultural contexts. In most of the exhibits that I have, it is he who startles her. It is interesting to speculate on why startle is used in this context and why the direction is so sexually asymmetrical. Startling someone and the comfortable acceptance of being startled can imply intimacy and to a certain extent physical access. Stimuli can be quite varied as long as there is a meta-message that the startle is playfully intended. In the next exhibit, Kurt Vonnegut refers to this teasing as "ancient." Perhaps it is.

Vera had not sensed my approach. She was peering into [a microscope]. . . . I stole closer to her, and then I said, "Boo!"

She jerked her head away from the eyepiece.

"Hello," I said.

"You scared me to death," she said.

"Sorry," I said, and I laughed.

These ancient games go on and on. It's nice they do. (Kurt Vonnegut, 1976, *Slapstick*, p. 204)

Here is a scene from a Japanese film:

An attractive woman in her twenties is out for a day's holiday with a plain, middle-aged man, "Tora." With arm outstretched, he dangles a piece of rope like a snake at her. She startles strongly, which both find amusing. (*Tora and The Song Of Love*, 1982)

With the teasing startle, Tora violates their previously negotiated, more politely formal, relationship. By accepting the teasing, the woman accepts the increased intimacy. Tora is now defined as a man who might play with her and with whom she might play.

And here is the caption to a photograph of a Leningrad (now Saint Petersburg) street scene:

This World War II memorial, one of the most prominent in Leningrad, offers a sharp contrast to the soldiers of today's Red Army Band, who took a break from practice to toy with a band member's rubber snake. (Patrick Kelly, 1984, "Mission to Moscow," *Campus Voice*, pp. 10–11)

The accompanying picture shows the young officer holding the snake in a manner that permits him to startle passersby by thrusting it at them. I'll bet his targets are often attractive young women.

Pictures of startled pretty girls are common—for example, an advertisement for Fujichrome 400 film in which an attractive model in a bathing suit facing left is hit in the back with a stream of water from a hose held by someone off right. A scene reproduced with variations in girly calendars and the like shows a bikini-clad sunbather dozing prone with a playful male about to sprinkle cold water, readily available from pool, lake, ocean, or hose on her back. In a variant, she is lying with her top straps untied.

H. To Change Between States of Awareness

As many of the above exhibits illustrate, a startle is often used ritually or therapeutically as the boundary or "limen" between states of awareness. Here is another such use, startle as it was employed in early nineteenth century mesmerism:

The second stage, *catalepsy*, was brought about by the experimenter suddenly opening the patient's eyes. The patients now proceeded to manifest waxy flexibility of the limbs which could be molded into any position. This state could also be induced by the application of a sudden intense stimulus such as a bright light in a darkened room or the clanging of a Chinese gong. Indeed once at a patients' ball at the Salpêtriére, a gong was inadvertently struck, and many of the female hysterical patients immediately became cataleptically frozen into the position they were in at the sound of the gong. (Sheehan & Perry, 1976, "The Demise of Magnetic Doctrines," *Methodologies of Hypnosis*, p. 35)

II. STARTLES THAT REVEAL THE MORAL STATUS OF A STARTLED SUBJECT

A. Negative

1. Of Impure Mind

Though the usual charitable view is that lapses caused by startle are morally neutral, a less charitable interpretation is equally available to an antagonist.

> "You can answer me, can't you?," he said.
> For reply, she suddenly jabbed a knife across his thick, pale hand. He started up with a vulgar curse.
> "Shows what you are," said Minette in contempt." (D. H. Lawrence, 1920, *Women in Love*, p. 63)

This moral ambiguity was reflected in comments once made to me about *latah* (see Chapter 8).

2. Of Bad Character

The association of startle with character defect is sometimes explicit, as in the exhibit just above and the first exhibit below, and sometimes implicit, as in the next two.

> There was a young lady from hell
> Who jumped at the sound of a bell,
> Because she was bad—bad—bad,
> She jumped at the sound of a bell. . . .
> (F. Scott Fitzgerald, 1934, *Tender Is the Night*, p. 290)

Charles Darwin, in *The Voyage of the Beagle*, described the natives of Tierra del Fuego in a strikingly uncomplimentary way:

> Their very attitudes were abject, and the expression of their countenances distrustful, surprised, and startled. (1840, p. 177)

Here is a contemporary version from a newsmagazine of the same negative connotation that "startled" can have:

> Cazale found his widest success as Fredo, the slow, shy, forever startled, finally traitorous older brother in Francis Coppola's Godfather films. (*Time*, March 27, 1978)

The negative connotations of startling apparently go back a long way. In his scathing description of the emperor Caligula, the historian Suetonius reported:

> For he that set so light by the gods and despised them as he did, yet at the least thunder and lightning used to wink close with both eyes, to enwrap also and cover his whole head. (ca. 100 A.D., *The Lives of the Twelve Caesars* [original in Latin], p. 254)

3. Guilty

Perhaps the association of startling with bad character results, in part, from observing how guilt may predispose one to startle. Shakespeare, for example, often used startle to reveal an uneasy conscience. Because startles are visible, they allow otherwise hidden states of mind to be seen by others.[4] In the following exhibit, two nobles in Macbeth's court comment on his state of mind:

> ANGUS: Now does he feel
> His secret murders sticking on his hands ...
> ... now does he feel his title
> Hang loosely about him, like a giant's robe
> Upon a dwarfish thief.
>
> MENTEITH: Who then shall blame his pester'd senses to recoil and
>   start...?
> (1606, *Macbeth*, Act V, scene ii)

Macbeth himself also considers his ready startling to be the result of his unquiet conscience.[5] Just after Duncan's murder, Lady Macbeth takes the daggers and goes to plant them on the grooms, leaving Macbeth alone. There is a loud knocking at the gate.

> MACBETH: Whence is that knocking? How is it with me, when every
>   noise appalls me?
> (1606, *Macbeth*, Act II, scene iii)

Shakespeare, an especially keen observer, often refers to the neurophysiology of emotional states. The association of startle with guilt is also used in *Hamlet, All's Well That Ends Well,* and *Henry VIII:*

And then it started like a guilty thing
Upon a fearful summons.
(1602, *Hamlet*, Act I, scene i)

You boggle shrewdly, every feather starts you.[6]
(1599, *All's Well That Ends Well*, Act V, scene iii)

Lord Surrey threatens Cardinal Wolsey:

I'll startle you
Worse than the sacring bell, when the brown
    wench
Lay kissing in your arms, Lord Cardinal.
    (1612, *Henry VIII*, Act II, scene ii)

Also see the Shakespeare entries in Chapter 6 under "Significant, Sometimes Idiosyncratically Significant Words." Not only Shakespeare uses this device:

I don't know why I started when the door opened behind me; I suppose because I felt as though I were snooping even if I'd been invited to snoop. (Judith Rossner, 1984, *To the Precipice*, p. 25)

BRADY: Why would you think that man was a drug dealer?

REX: He was startled when he came into the room and found us there. ("Rex Morgan, M.D." [comic strip], *Lansing State Journal*, September 18, 1985)

The neurologically effective mechanism in these "guilty" startles is probably "wariness." The subject is not necessarily aware of being hyperalert but is hyperalert all the same, because being detected would have unfortunate consequences.

4. Afraid

Startling may be taken as a sign that one is afraid. Other persons may infer fear from observing someone startle, and after starting, one may have to admit being afraid to oneself.

A little while later, however, a bullet shot past my ear with a vicious crack and banged into the parados behind. Alas! I ducked. All my life I had sworn that I would not duck the first time a bullet passed over me; but the movement appears to be instinctive, and almost everybody does it at least once. (George Orwell, 1938, *Homage to Catalonia*, p. 22)

With "Alas!" Orwell makes it clear that he would have preferred not to so respond. Thornton Burgess's Peter Rabbit feels the same way:

> Boom! Peter Rabbit jumped as if he had been shot. It was all so sudden and unexpected that Peter jumped before he had time to think. Then he looked foolish. He felt foolish. He had been scared when there was nothing to be afraid of. [It was only Boomer, the nighthawk. Later Peter explains:] If I had seen him about he wouldn't have made me jump. It was the unexpectedness of it. (Burgess, 1924, *The Burgess Bird Book for Children*, p. 16)

Here is a similar exhibit from Japan. The point of the poem is the contemptuous evaluation of a hyperstartler:

> A big rain drop falls,
>   And he sounds
> As if he had been killed!
> (Author not given, n. d. [original in Japanese], in R. H. Blyth, 1960, *Japanese Life and Character in Senryu*, p. 135)

5. Not Enlightened

A major goal in the quest for "enlightenment" is to become free from the tyranny of stimuli, to no longer be rocked in one's soul by things of the world but to be able instead to accept whatever occurs dispassionately. In the exhibits below, startles reveal an "unenlightened" state to another person.

> A young [Zen] master went to the hills to visit an old master at his hideout in the hills. As they were sitting on the old master's favorite seat, a lion roared in the distance. The younger master jumped, and the older one said, "I see it is still with you." (Wayland Young, 1964, *Eros Denied*, p. 254)

> The zen priest
>   Leaps into the air
> At the poisonous millipede.
> (Kenkabo, ca. 1800 [original in Japanese], in R. H. Blyth, 1960, *Japanese Life and Character in Senryu*, p. 444)

An alternative explanation of the haiku is that even enlightenment does not free one from the demands of this basic reflex.

The desired state is that of the Great Buddha at Kamakura, who does not flinch even in a hailstorm:

> The Great Buddha! Not at all
>   does he blink an eyelid—

as the hailstones fall.
(Shiki, ca. 1890 [original in Japanese], in H. Henderson, *An Introduction to Haiku*, 1958, p. 179)

Henderson also gives a transliterated version: "Great Buddha's blinking, even not doing, hailstones." Shiki's observation is especially interesting in the light of a finding by Landis and Hunt that of all the externally visible aspects of the startle reflex, the eyeblink was the only one that otherwise habituated subjects (police marksmen) could not suppress.

B. Positive

In all the exhibits so far given under the heading "startles that reveal the moral status of a startled subject," the evaluations are negative. Although uncommon, positive evaluations are also possible.

1. Aesthetically Sensitive

Being strongly affected by the song of the cuckoo (*hototogisu*), is used in the following example to attest to aesthetic refinement. To Western ears, the poem seems a bit forced and effete:

I did not drop my chopsticks
  At the thunder and lightning
But when the *hototogisu* sang. . . .
(Mucho, ca. 1780 [original in Japanese], in R.H. Blyth, 1964, *A History of Haiku, Vol. 2*, p. 1)

C. Not Morally Responsible

In most if not all cultures, behavior by a just-startled person is not subject to the moral evaluation by which it would be judged under usual circumstances. Everyone who has been severely startled recognizes that the behaviors which follow a startle may have been unplanned. Earlier chapters contain many examples, and the chapters that follow contain many others. Here is one further exhibit:

A popular and nationally known Philippine radio announcer in the Marcos era would follow intimations of graft or the like with a simulated startle, excusing himself by saying something like "See what you made me say!" or "Don't startle me so much, I say things I don't mean!" (Reported by J. N. Gutmann, field notes, October 5, 1977)

III. READY AND VIOLENT STARTLING USED TO CONNOTE:

A. Low Status

Largely because of the social vulnerability that is a defining characteristic of low and equivocal status, low and equivocal statuses are regularly associated with hyperstartling.

> A mouse from the family altar,
>   And the second wife
> Leaps into the air.
> (Author not given, n. d. [original in Japanese], in R.H. Blyth, 1960, *Japanese Life and Character in Senryu*, p. 385)

In addition to feeling wary in the presence of the family altar (where the deceased first wife's name tablet may be presumed to hang), the second wife is also on guard because of her equivocal status. The haiku is amusing because of the leakage—the mouse reveals an aspect of reality that is otherwise not visible. Here is another example from Shakespeare:

> MALVOLIO: Seven of my people, with an obedient start
> Make out for him. I frown the while;
> And perchance wind up my watch. . . .
> (William Shakespeare, 1601, *Twelfth Night*, Act II, scene v)

In Malvolio's fantasy his servants monitor him so closely in order to be able to respond promptly to his wishes that when he speaks they startle "obediently." In the following exhibit, Tom Wolfe uses the same literary device to convey a character's high status relative to the status of the people about him.

> "Well. . .which did your husband do?"
>   "What your father said, of course. When he spoke—people jumped!" (Tom Wolfe, 1987, *The Bonfire of the Vanities*, p. 336)

Stepin Fetchit was a shiftless, low-status character in early radio and film, a portrayal later much criticized as a negative black stereotype. When his creator died, Stepin Fetchit's easily elicited startles were mentioned in his radio obituary (*All Things Considered* [radio program], November 20, 1985)

B. Femininity, "Girlishness," "Spinsterishness"

Whether there is indeed any difference between the sexes in susceptibility to startle is not known. Writers, however, regularly assert that women startle more easily than men. At least in part this has to do with the more general need in most cultures for men to retain self-control as a mark of superior status.

> There was a great fizzing and banging of guns, and starting of
> ladies—and then a mine was sprung to the gratification of every-
> body—and when the mine had gone off, the military and the com-
> pany followed its example, and went off too. (Charles Dickens,
> 1837, *Posthumous Papers of the Pickwick Club*, p. 56)

Startling readily is not only considered more appropriate for women
but is often said to be especially likely in young women or older women
who are "girly" (whose mode of self-presentation is behaviorally much like
that considered typical of adolescence), or "spinsterish" (often described as
including defensiveness against being touched).[7]

> Rosalind opened the door to him. She started slightly, as a young
> girl will. . . (D. H. Lawrence, 1920, *Women in Love*, p. 247)

> Baby was a tall, fine-looking woman, deeply engaged in being just
> over thirty. . . . Baby had certain spinster's characteristics—she
> was alien from touch, she started if she was touched suddenly, and
> such lingering touches as kisses and embraces slipped directly
> through the flesh into the forefront of her consciousness. (F. Scott
> Fitzgerald, 1934, *Tender Is the Night*, p. 191)

> [T]he spinsterish herons, who keep their hair up with fish bones. . . ,
> would fall down in a faint if a boy could stalk them and shout before
> he was seen. (T. H. White, 1977, *The Book of Merlyn*, p. 151)

IV. FAILURE TO STARTLE OR RAPID RECOVERY FROM BEING STARTLED USED TO CONNOTE:

A. The Status of a Hero or Other Great Personage

Under some circumstances a startle is so expected that the failure to startle becomes a noteworthy event. This is possible, of course, only because of
the consensus on the circumstances in which a startle should occur. Just as
to be easily startled often signifies a problem, it is generally considered a
virtue not to be easily startled. Easy startling is not only inconvenient, it
is also interactionally expensive and hence it is usually disvalued. The converse, failure to startle when one might have been expected to, is associated
with strength, with heroic and otherwise special personages, with nobility, and, above all, with royalty.

Great or admirable persons ("heroes") are considered to startle less
readily than the rest of us. This is in spite of (or perhaps in part because of)
their frequent encounters with dangers and despite their frequent need to
be wary. Several of the museum exhibits show cartoon characters—for
example, Lois Lane, Superman's friend—conspicuously failing to startle
in a situation where one might have reasonably expected a startle and a

flustered response. The following two exhibits from novels by Joseph Conrad nicely show how failure to startle can be used to signify the special status of a "great man."

> "He startled me," repeated Heyst. . . . "It must have been something—to startle *you*," she said. (Joseph Conrad, 1915, *Victory*, p. 353)

> It was a special form of the great man's extravagance, sanctioned by a moral intention big enough to flatter his vanity. Even in this aberration of his genius he served the progress of the world. Charles Gould felt sure of being understood with precision and judged with the indulgence of their common passion. Nothing now could surprise or startle this great man. (Joseph Conrad, 1904, *Nostromo*, pp. 421–422)

Rapid recovery from a startle, which is also a mark of strength and power, is asserted explicitly in the next exhibit:

> Being a woman of high courage, she soon got over the first startling effect of what I had to communicate. (Wilkie Collins, 1860, *The Moonstone*, p. 118)

B. Royalty or Nobility

Statements about the composure of royalty and nobility—including failure to startle in potentially startling circumstances, startling little, and recovering rapidly when startled, and of course lapses from these ideals—are regularly reported as news in the Western press. When I sorted the collection of startles from newspapers, I was surprised at how frequently the composure of members of the British royal family, or a lapse in expected composure, was reported in the press.

> Caption to birthday photo of Princess Diana: "Twenty-two today, and a picture of serenity." (*Lansing State Journal*, July 2, 1983)

As in, of course, "Her Serene Highness." The caption implies Diana's suitability for elevation to royal status. When such a person startles, it is news. More often, what is reported is the failure of a royal personage to startle when an ordinary mortal would be expected to. That after a startle royal composure is rapidly and effectively regained is also frequently reported. Here is an account of the reaction of the queen:

> The British royal family carried on its public appearances as usual today despite the scare Saturday when six blank shots were fired at Queen Elizabeth II as she rode on horseback through London on a military parade. . . . The queen . . . looked startled, and her

horse shied at the noise of the firing ten feet away. . . . The Queen was unharmed, calmed her horse, and carried on with the parade as police grabbed the youth who fired the blanks. (*Lansing State Journal*, June 15, 1981)

A fuller report the day earlier included the following:

Two riders in the procession—believed to be her husband, Prince Philip, and the heir to the throne, Prince Charles—spurred their mounts to shield the Queen, seen by thousands in the crowd and millions more watching on television. But Elizabeth, dressed in scarlet military tunic and black riding skirt, controlled the horse, and within a minute she was again smiling and waving.

Here is a princess's reaction:

Edward Adcock, a carpenter, said he meant no harm to the 27-year-old princess [Diana] when he jumped over railings as she spoke to a crowd outside a workshop for the mentally handicapped. Television pictures show the princess was startled. She stepped backward as three detectives hurled themselves between her and Adcock, but quickly regained her composure. (*Lansing State Journal*, April 14, 1989)

And here is an account of the reaction of an heir apparent:

On Jan. 26, in Sydney, Australia, a student fired blanks from a starter's pistol at him [Prince Charles] during an outdoor ceremony. The prince barely flinched and was later praised for his calm. In an interview published today . . . the prince joked about his cool demeanor when threatened in Sydney: "A thousand years of breeding have gone into this, you know." (*Seattle Times*, February 7, 1994)

Prince Charles evidently believes that there is something special about royal neurophysiology, a sort of princess-and-the-pea phenomenon in reverse. Unlike Charles, Princess Diana, whose startle was shown on television, was not to royalty born.

In *Interaction Ritual*, Erving Goffman noted that

Composure in all its different dimensions has traditionally been associated with the aristocratic ethic. . . . The significant point here is that we find composure a concern and a value in many different cultures and across many different strata. (1967, p. 227)

One might reasonably speculate that royal composure or rather the cultural expectation of royal composure arises from three factors:

1. Relative insulation of such persons from intentionally provided startling stimuli. One doesn't say "Boo!" to the king, poke him in the ribs, or drop a rubber spider down inside his robe.
2. As a demonstration of legitimacy and power; the lack of a need to feel wary. A wary king is an insecure king.
3. The distribution of social attention. The distribution of social attention in small groups of both human and nonhuman primates has been studied by Michael Chance (Chance & Larson, 1976). Chance suggested that who watches whom is a major component of the social structure of small primate groups. Attention, of course, is generally directed up a dominance hierarchy, to those most likely to influence events, especially by administering negative sanctions. But social attention is more than wariness. If attention merely reflected wariness, more dominant animals in nonhuman primate groups would be given a wide berth. In fact, they are highly attractive social foci. At any rate, in a gathering in which royalty are present, all others are constrained to maintain awareness of the location and deportment of the royal personages. However, a royal personage, in theory at least, may gaze and move about as he or she pleases.

That royalty and nobility are not exposed to potentially startling stimuli is a point sometimes made in fiction. In the next exhibit the personage who fails to startle is a count, not quite royal, only noble. Here is how he is described:

He dined in an evening waistcoat and a "smoking" (he called it so) with a black tie. All of this of very good cut, not new—just as these things should be. He was, morning or evening, very correct in his dress. I have no doubt that his whole existence had been correct, well ordered and conventional, undisturbed by startling events. (Joseph Conrad, 1908, in "Il Conde" [a short story from] *A Set of Six*, p. 332)

The American presidency has some features in common with the status of royalty. For one thing, the president's startles, both real and metaphoric, are also news. The headline above the next exhibit was "Revelations Startle Reagan"; the term "mesmerized" is in this context a metaphoric reference to the capture of attention after a startle, which is discussed in Chapter 7.

"I will confirm to you that he is startled and surprised from some of the testimony in the ["Iran-contra"] hearings, and his reaction is about what you would expect. . . . The White House must not be mesmerized by these hearings and must continue to discharge the obligations of government," Baker said. (*Seattle Post Intelligencer*, January 28, 1987)

V. STARTLES USED TO EXPLAIN ILLNESS OR DEFORMITY

In many societies, startle is commonly used as an explanation for disease, and almost any illness or deformity may be explained by attributing it to some prior startle. Because this is such a large topic, it was discussed separately in Chapter 4.

VI. STARTLES CRAFTED FOR INTEREST OR PLEASURE

In most of the museum's exhibits, being startled is an unpleasant experience, but it can also be a pleasant one, even one that is sought out. Sometimes it is nice to be startled; we know that we will be startled in the haunted houses that are featured at amusement parks, fairs, and in the celebration of Halloween. It is a big part of why we pay admission to tour them. The museum has many examples, both actual and metaphoric, of people seeking to be startled or enjoying startles.

A. Startles in Music

There is a beautiful illustration of how music plays on us in Ingmar Bergman's film of Mozart's *The Magic Flute*. During the overture, as the camera pans over the audience, we see on the rapt faces changing expressions that parallel the evolving pattern of the music.

Not infrequently, music is used to elicit a startle. The best known musical startle is, of course, the startle that is the surprise in Haydn's Symphony no. 94, "The Symphony with the Surprise." In Rossini's overture to *William Tell* a sudden trumpet call interrupts a slow, dreamy, soothing passage. A diminuendo is followed by a crash in von Weber's overture to *Oberon*. Many similar musical startles could be cited. Romantic composers frequently wrote the second movements of symphonies in a slow, quiet, and introspective style, but began the third movement with notes that are loud, abrupt, and percussive to elicit a radical change in listeners' mood. Tchaikovsky, for example, used a startle in this way just after the slow movement of his Symphony Pathetique. Cymbals may be used to exaggerate the effect of drums and increase the sharpness of the front edge of the stimulus. This technique is especially useful in opera, in which audience members can be startled by a musical passage at the same time that some character in the opera is startled by an event onstage.

> The scene is of a temple, "the atmosphere [depicted is one] of the weird, exotic mystery of the banks of the Nile bathed in soft moonlight." (*Victrola Book of the Opera*, 1929, p. 32).

The music is serene, soft, and gentle. Aida waits there for her lover. Suddenly, unexpectedly, and portentously she catches sight of her father. She cries out: "Ciel! Mi padre!" The accompanying music is sudden and loud, and the audience is startled right along with the heroine.

B. Startles in Films and Theatrical Productions

People attend theatrical productions in large part to experience induced
emotional states, and theatrical productions are often classified in terms of
the states they promise to induce—for example, comedies, "tear-jerkers,"
suspense films, and horror films. Many people include being startled in the
list of experiences they seek from a certain genre of films. These startles are
like the pleasurable arousal sought from roller-coaster rides. There is an
intense anticipatory state, then a sudden violent release, experienced as
exciting and pleasurable. Advertising and reviews frequently note that a
film offers startles:

> The results suffer a little bit from predictability. . . . But the film
> offers more than enough plot and character development to hold
> your attention and throws some jolts that will make you spill your
> popcorn. (Jack Garner, review of film *Misery*, in *Lansing State Jour-
> nal*, November 29, 1990)

> But don't worry. . . it's going to be scary. . . . I have independently
> counted 30 shocks, or little jumps out of the seat, some much
> higher than others. (William Blatty [director of *The Exorcist III*],
> *Lansing State Journal*, August 16, 1990)

> One can learn how to evoke startles at film school.

> "*The Thing* was the first movie that made me jump out of my seat—
> literally!" said the 33-year-old filmmaker, John Carpenter. . . . Car-
> penter recalls that he wasn't traumatized by his youthful exposure to
> *The Thing*. Instead, his reaction was: "Boy, that's neat! How can I do
> that?" He found out at film school and applied his learning to a non-
> union quickie, *Halloween*. . . . "The audience knows it is going to be
> scared, but it doesn't know when it is going to be scared; the trick is
> to scare them when they least expect it." (*Lansing State Journal*, June
> 27, 1982)

In the following excerpt from a radio interview, interviewer Gahan
Wilson has just asked Steven King, author of several best-selling books
that were turned into successful horror movies (including *Carrie* and *The
Shining*), "Why do you do it?" King gives a psychological answer, but he
also describes his ability to elicit audience startles as a technical skill, necessary for his type of filmcraft:

> It's probably a sadistic thing to a certain degree. I like to scare peo-
> ple because it's fun to watch them jump. I like to see people jump,
> and that is a lot of it right there. But I feel the effect inside, and it
> isn't really a terrified effect, where I'm jumping or my hair is

standing on end; it's just a feeling of being in the right place and things are going right. So that, for instance, if somebody slammed a door in the house at that time, I would jump, where otherwise I wouldn't. The feeling is just one of sort of pleasure at having it just right, you know, at that time.[8] (*All Things Considered* [radio program], October 31, 1981 [Halloween Broadcast])

I recently came across a reference to a popular category of film called in the trade "Womjeops" for "Women in Jeopardy." Womjeops are films whose main interest centers on the portrayal of some woman, usually young and nubile, in a series of dangerous situations that constitute the body of the film. Like horror movies, such films are filled with startles.

In the following exhibit, Columbian writer Gabriel García Márquez describes peasants at a country fair paying to be startled (or metaphorically startled) by a feat that must have seemed radically uncanny to this unsophisticated audience.

There was no lack of people standing open-mouthed watching kettles fall and pots roll and who paid fifty cents to be startled as a gypsy woman put in her false teeth and took them out again. (Gabriel García Márquez, 1967, *One Hundred Years Of Solitude* [original in Spanish], p. 351)

C. Startles in Advertising

Advertising also makes it clear that being startled, at least metaphorically, may be a desired experience. The advertising display for the Pacific Northwest ballet company's production of Tchaikovsky's *Nutcracker* ballet contained only a single quote, spread across the advertisment in large type above the logo:

We jumped a foot when we saw the Giant Mouse. (*Seattle Times*, November 12, 1994)

The following exhibits also urge readers to attend or purchase something and be startled.

THE FUNNIEST, CRAZIEST, DIRTIEST, MOST PERVERSELY BEAUTIFUL SCIENCE-FICTION MOVIE EVER MADE!.... GENUINELY STARTLING!... (Advertisement for *Liquid Sky*, in *State News* (Lansing, Mich.) April 4, 1986)

They've seen the world. And they've never left town. They're Pirates. Rickie Lee Jones tells their tales on a startling second album. (*Psychology Today*, August 1981)

Figure 5.2 Cans and boxes of spring-loaded snakes are sold for use as startle-eliciting devices. Various devices made expressly to startle are used in many cultures. THE BORN LOSER reprinted by permission of Newspaper Enterprise Association, Inc.

D. Startle-eliciting and Startle-depicting Objects

A number of objects are made specifically to startle. These include models of snakes and spiders meant to be hidden and then to be discovered by the unwary; burglar alarms; innocuous-appearing items that explode; spring-loaded snakes in cans and other containers (Fig. 5.2); mugs with ceramic frogs fixed deep inside; and, of course, jack-in-the-boxes. I have a soapstone box from Nigeria out of which pops a carved snake, aimed at the hand of the person opening it. I recently received an advertisement for a high-tech way of accomplishing a similar result, a computer program called "Boo!" that

> emits a frightening noise and puts a monster face on the screen in response to any keystroke. (*Software Labs* catalog, Summer 1993)

The next exhibit is for decals of what appear to be bullet holes. It's from a catalog for hunters. The bold print and italics are in the original.

Startling Bullet Holes **stick on anywhere!**
    Put a couple on a friend's windshield and watch their mouth drop open. . . . When people first see them, **their minds grind to a halt**. Self-stick, peel off, clear plastic, bullet holes. Pack of 40. **Startle your friends!** (*The Sportsman's Guide* catalog, 1993)

Figure 5.3 Garfield, a sociopathic cat, delights in startling others, and is frequently shown doing so. Here, he makes himself into a stimulus which is unexpected, in sudden motion, and threatening. A booby-trapped mailbox is also used to startle in the second of the quotations that heads Chapter 3 (p. 38). Garfield © 1984 PAWS, Inc. Reprinted with permission of Universal Press Syndicate. All rights reserved.

Moral evaluations of those who habitually startle others for fun tend to be negative, but amused and somewhat tolerant. Bugs Bunny, a sociopathic rabbit, and Garfield, a sociopathic cat, delight in startling others (Fig. 5.3). So do villains in Superman and Batman cartoons and nuisances in the cartoon "They'll Do It Every Time" (Fig. 5.4). The popular American advice columnist Ann Landers is frequently asked for advice on how to think about and deal with such people:

> Dear Ann Landers: I am married to a 52-year-old man who believes he has a fabulous sense of humor. Everyone else (me included) thinks he's nuts. This holiday weekend was the worst. He slid a plastic snake down the bosom of an 80-year-old woman at a cocktail party. She fainted and could not be revived. An ambulance had to be called.... (*Lansing State Journal*, March 31, 1980)

Ms. Landers generally advocates some sort of social ostracism.

Depictions of startle can be found on greeting cards, bookmarks, statuary, china, and works of popular art designed to be hung on walls. Frederick Remington sculpted two versions of a horse startled by a rattlesnake. A *Saturday Evening Post* cover by Norman Rockwell showing an elderly gentleman feigning an intense startle to a small sheet-covered child carrying a jack-o'-lantern head has been reproduced as a postcard, as a bit of kitsch sculpture, and as a commemorative plate (Fig. 5.5).

VII. SPECIAL TERMINOLOGY: "BOO!" "OOPS!" AND "GOTCHA!"

The Malay language has a special term, *cucuk* (pronounced "chuchuk"), for the sudden sharp poke in the ribs that is the prototypic Malaysian intentional-startle stimulus. English also has special terms associated with startle, all usually followed by exclamation points. In both British and American culture, the prototypical intentional-startle stimulus is, of course,

Figure 5.4 This cartoon from the late 1970s shows disapproval of a person who inappropriately startles others. There is an element of sexual harrassment as well. Copyright (c) 1979. Reprinted with special permission of King Features Syndicate.

"Boo!"—a word with no other meaning or use. It's usually pronounced loudly and explosively, and thus it is often printed in bold variant type. (It might, however, even be effective when whispered if the sound of that whispered voice were sufficiently unexpected.) As the word "Boo!" has a sharp front edge (the sound begins abruptly), and as it can be pronounced loudly, it is a good choice for a neurophysiologically effective stimulus. "Pow!" would probably work equally well, but "Ahm!" probably would not. Because it is the culturally appropriate way to startle someone with the voice, it signifies unequivocally that the person eliciting the startle is doing so deliberately. Its use suggests a playful rather than a threatening context.

"Oops!" is the prototypical verbal response in American and British English. "Oops!" is frequent, but other vocalizations occur also. Here are 38 consecutively collected examples from cartoons:

Figure 5.5 The *Saturday Evening Post* cover that was the model for this bit of popular sculpture has also been reproduced as a postcard and a holiday plate.

"AAK!", "AAGHHH!!", "AHHHUUUGGGHHH!!", "What—??", "WHAAA!", "GAHHH!", "GAAA!", "GAAAAAA!", "GAAAAA AAAA!", "GASP!", "YAA!!", "YAGHH!!", "EEK!", "EEEK!", "EEEEK!", "EEEEEEEK", "EEE-E-E!", "YEEOW!", "YIKE!", "Yikes!, "Yiiii", "YII-I!", "YIPE!", "YIIIPE!", "YIPES!", "MY NANNY!", "OW!", "YOW!", "YOWP!" "YEOW", "YOWK-!", "YOWFF! [sound made by a startled dog]", "OH NO!", "HOLY TOLEDO!", "HUNH—?", "ULP!", "GAZORNIN PLOTZ!" [vocalization of startled extraterrestrial], "?" [by Snoopy, a dog who does not speak]), "@#%#!!" [not reproduced exactly; it signifies naughty rather than silly talk].

Note the regular appearance of any one of an assortment of extended vowels, often followed by a glottal stop or lip closure, as in "EEK!" and "YIPES!"

Because it signifies having been startled, "Oops!" can be used to identify a mismatch that necessitates a massive reconceptualization, as discussed later in this chapter. In the song "High Hopes," for example, confident, determined creatures accomplish, contrary to expectation, feats that had appeared extravagant. A determined ant carries off a potted rubber tree, a ram pushes down a hydroelectric dam. The choruses run, "Oops! There goes another rubber tree plant!", "Oops! There goes a million kilowatt dam!," etc.

"Gotcha!" is always written with an exclamation mark and means "Now I've startled you!"; "Now I've captured you!"; "Now I've bested you!"; "Now you are stumped!" or "Now I've got your meaning!" The meta-message is that this is playful. A clothing company for youth that features playfully imprinted sports clothing has adopted "Gotcha!" as a trademark. Though "Gotcha" is etymologically derived from "Got you," it is not merely a colloquial variant, and the terms are not interchangeable. Try substituting "gotcha" for "got you" in "I've got you under my skin." In the following anecdote, "Gotcha!" is used to announce that someone has been startled and also to denote the less than competent performance that divided attention may produce when one anticipates being startled.

> An amateur golfer challenged his club pro to a match. "But," said the amateur, "you've got to give me a handicap of two 'gotchas.'" Although the pro had no idea what a "gotcha" was, he was confident and agreed to the terms. Just as the pro was about to tee off, the amateur crept up, grabbed him around the waist and shouted, "Gotcha!" They finished the game without incident, but the pro played terribly and was beaten. Asked why he had lost, he mumbled, "Have you ever played 18 holes of golf waiting for a second 'gotcha'?" (*Reader's Digest*, September 1977, p. 665)

VIII. STARTLES USED TO SIGNIFY A REVELATION OR MASSIVE RECONCEPTUALIZATION

A thought identified as "startling" is both an unexpected thought and also a thought that, because of its failure to fit into a previous conceptual scheme, requires a wholesale restructuring of that scheme. Oliver Wendell Holmes once described the process poetically:

> It is enough to stun and scare anybody, to have a hot thought come crashing into his brain, and ploughing up those parallel ruts where the wagon trains of common ideas were jogging along in their regular sequences of association. (1858, *The Autocrat of the Breakfast-Table*, p. 88)

The same process was described analytically rather than poetically by William James in *The Varieties of Religious Experience*:

> A mind is a system of ideas, each with the excitement it arouses, and with tendencies impulsive and inhibitive, which mutually check or reinforce one another. . . . A new perception, a sudden emotional shock, or an occasion which lays bare the organic alteration, will make the whole fabric fall together; and then the centre of gravity sinks into an attitude more stable, for the new ideas that reach the centre in the rearrangement seem now to be locked there, and the new structure remains permanent.[9] (William James, 1903, p. 194)

Novel information or an insight is often referred to as "startling," and the reconceptualization after "startling" information is sometimes compared to a physically disorienting experience.

> In fact, at a recent meeting at Cold Spring Harbor, two highly respected neuroscientists presented startling findings, based on new techniques, that threaten to turn present views of the phenomenon on their head. (*Science, 248*, 1990, p. 1603)

The use of the terms "startled" and "startling" to identify a datum requiring a reevaluation of some previous belief is illustrated in the following two exhibits:

> But everyone in American politics was startled by the mere fact that the Robertson forces could find and put up and qualify 4,500 people to have a try at getting into a convention primary in Michigan. The Kemp forces qualified only 3,400.
> The event was startling partly because the Rev. Mr. Robertson is a relative unknown in politics . . . and partly because he ranks with the Rev. Jerry Falwell as a top radio and television preacher of religious fundamentalism. (*Christian Science Monitor*, June 5, 1986)

> The second and more dramatic event that changed the nature of psychology at this time was Pavlov's discovery of *stimulus substitution:* that pairing an arbitrary stimulus with a stimulus that naturally elicits some response will empower the arbitrary stimulus to elicit the same response. This was a startling discovery because it suggested that "reflexes" could be learned. (D. Dellarosa, 1988, "A History of Thinking," in Sternberg and Smith, *The Psychology of Human Thought*, p. 5)

Note the words "The event was startling partly because," and "This was . . . startling . . . because." The use of some variant of this set phrase informs readers who might otherwise be ignorant of its significance that a bit of information is contrary to expectation.

In the following exhibit this pointer function of "startling" is used twice. As in the two exhibits just above, that which is identified as startling is something thereby identified as radically different from what one had previously believed.

> In what one official acknowledged was "a startling change," the Defense Department said Thursday it has slashed the cost of the first phase of a Star Wars defensive shield from $115 billion to $69 billion. . . . "This is a startling change," acknowledged Robert Costello, undersecretary of defense for acquisition. (*Lansing State Journal*, October 7, 1988)

Phrases that signal this usage include "startling aspect," "contrast," "conclusion," "experience," "exposé," "fact," "improvement," "naivete," "news," "revelation," "sight," "turnabout," and so forth.

There is a difference between the connotation of the "startling" and "surprising" in these set phrases. "Startling news" is more unexpected then merely "surprising news." A "startling revelation" is more unexpected than a merely "surprising" one.[10] "Startling" connotes a greater disparity between expected and observed and, more important, the expectation of a greater effect on the perceiver. Though "startling" may also imply "disconcerting," in most of the exhibits in which this usage is employed, it is the need to reassess a previously assessed situation that appears to have determined the choice of "startling" over "surprising." There are degrees of effect: The word "startling" is often modified by a quantifying adjective: "somewhat startling," "rather startling," "more startling," "most startling," "less startling" and so forth:

> In perhaps the most startling revelation, Attorney General Ed Meese told a stunned press corps Nov. 25 that his investigators had, over the weekend, unearthed an unauthorized White House scheme to funnel $30 million in profits from the Iran arms deal to Nicaraguan rebels. (*Lansing State Journal*, December 7, 1986)

"Startling" may also be used when the new datum engenders a massive reconceptualization by only a specific individual, as in the next two exhibits. In the exhibit below, "that was a startler" can be taken to mean "that caused my world to significantly alter, and that shook me up and disabled me for a time."

> I tell you, that *was* a startler to begin with, the revelation that Sally was a wedded wife. . . . (A. E. Coppard, 1931, *The Collected Tales of A.E. Coppard*, p. 267)

In the exhibit below, what is asserted is a woman's incipient discovery that the speaker is in love with her. Any one of countless slips might make the truth apparent and cause a massive reconceptualization of their history, current situation, and future.

> We had parted one night as usual. No word had fallen from my lips, at that time or at any time before it, that could betray me or startle her into sudden knowledge of the truth. (Wilkie Collins, 1860, *The Woman in White*, p. 52)

Because of the use of "startling" to signal reappraisal, terms such as "unstartling" and "hardly startling" can be used to characterize trite or banal events, events that present no news, no surprise, or events that are ordinary and of frequent occurrence.

> When we tested ceiling fans in 1982, we came to the unstartling conclusion that big fans moved more air than smaller ones. (*Consumer Reports*, July 1989)

> An American would need a low threshold of amazement to be startled by the news that the U.S. had swapped information with Tai Li or trained his forces. (*Lansing State Journal*, December 20, 1978)

> The new Surgeon General's report is based on no specific new research and contained no startling new conclusions. (*Lansing State Journal*, January 11, 1979)

In Chapter 6, further examples of this usage are discussed under the heading "Stimuli Which Startle." In that chapter, exhibits similar to those presented above are sorted by the biologically significant components of startling that they display. To stretch the museum metaphor a bit, one might think of Chapter 6 as the next gallery.

NOTES

1. Among contemporary students of language, the term "metaphor" currently has a denotation much broader than that given in the dictionary definition. See, for example, the collection of essays, *On Metaphor*, edited by Sheldon Sacks (1970).

2. The choice of Japan is occasioned by nothing more significant than the reading I happened to be doing while collecting the exhibits.

3. For further examples, see "Secret or Hidden Thought" in the section on "Unintended Speech," under "Responses When Startled" in Chapter 6.

4. "Leakage" is Paul Ekman's useful term for the general case of this process.

5. Interestingly, by the last act, Macbeth habituates and no longer startles. See the exhibit under "Familiarity with a Stimulus" in Chapter 6.

6. "Boggle" = take fright; "shrewdly" = cursedly.

7. See also the haiku by Santaro, under "Creepy-Crawlies," a category of stimuli discussed in Chapter 6.

8. As Tom Sawyer said in the passage from *Huckleberry Finn* discussed in Chapter 3, "It showed it was done right."

9. A striking illustration of this process, unfortunately too long to quote here, can be found in Dashiell Hammett's classic mystery novel, *The Maltese Falcon*. In the novel a Mr. Flitcraft, after being accidently startled, leaves his job and family and assumes an entirely new life (Hammett, 1930, pp. 77–79).

10. Take, for example, the following advertisement:

> General Electric has some surprising news for anyone who thought we made only the finest *electric* ranges. Now we're proudly introducing a full line of gas ranges as well. (Ad in *Bon Appetite* [magazine], August 1986)

General Electric does not suggest that its news will result in a massive reconceptualization; substituting "startling" for "surprising would be excessive.

REFERENCES

Blyth, R.H. (1960). *Japanese life and character in Senryu*. Tokyo: Hokuseido Press.

Burgess, T.W. (1924). *The Burgess bird book for children*. Boston: Little, Brown.

Chance, M.R.A., & Larson, R.R. (1976). *The social structure of attention*. New York: John Wiley.

Collins, W. 1860/1964. *The woman in white*. New York: Heritage Press.

Conrad, J. 1904/1917. *Nostromo*. Garden City, NY: Doubleday, Page and Co.

Conrad, J. 1908/1915. *A set of six*. Garden City, NY: Doubleday, Page and Co.

Conrad, J. 1915/1918. *Victory*. Garden City, NY: Doubleday, Page and Co.

Coppard, A.E. (1948). *The collected tales of A.E. Coppard*. New York: Knopf.

Darwin, C. 1840/1955. *The voyage of the Beagle*. New York: Dutton.

Davis, J. (1984). *Garfield weighs in*. New York: Ballantine.

Dellarosa, D. (1988). "A history of thinking. In R.T. Sternberg & E.E. Smith (Eds.), *The psychology of human thought*. New York: Cambridge University Press.

Dickens, C. 1837/1948. *Posthumous papers of the Pickwick Club: New Oxford Illustrated Dickens*. Oxford: Oxford University Press.

Doctorow, E.L. (1985). *World's fair*. New York: Random House.

Fitzgerald, F. Scott (1934). *Tender is the night*. New York: Scribner.

García Márquez, G. 1967/1970. *One hundred years of solitude* (G. Rabassa, Trans.). New York: Harper & Row.

Goffman, E. (1967). Interaction ritual: Essays in face-to-face behavior. Chicago: Aldine.

Good, B., & Delvecchio-Good, M.J. (1982). Toward a meaning-centered analysis of popular illness categories: "Fright illness" and "Heart distress" in Iran. In A.J. Marsella & G. White (Eds.), *Cultural conceptions of mental health and therapy*. Dordrecht: D. Reidel.

Hammett, D. 1930/1987. *The Maltese falcon*. San Francisco: North Point Press.

Hawthorne, N. 1852/1958. *The Blithedale romance*. New York: Norton.

Holmes, O.W. 1858/1955. *The autocrat of the breakfast table*. New York: Heritage Press.

James, W. 1903/1936. *The varieties of religious experience*. New York: The Modern Library.

Jefferson, J.W. (1981) *Neuropsychiatric features of medical disorders*. New York: Plenum.

Kelly, P. (1984). Mission to Moscow. *Campus Voice*, pp. 10–11.

Kenkabo. (ca. 1800). In R.H. Blyth (Ed.). (1960). *Japanese life and character in Senryu*. Tokyo: Hokuseido Press.

Klein, J. (1978). *Susto*: The anthropological study of the diseases of adaptation. *Social Science and Medicine, 12,* 23–28.

Lamb, C. (1860). *Last essays of Elia*. Boston: William Veazie.

Lawrence, D.H. 1920/1954. *Women in love*. London: Heinemann.

Lawrence, D.H. (1955). *The complete short stories* (Vol. 1). London: Heinemann.

Leslie, C. (1976). *Asian medical systems: A comparative study*. Berkeley: University of California Press.

Marks, I. (1981). Obsessive-compulsive disorders. *American Journal of Psychiatry, 138;*591.

Mucho. (ca. 1780) In R.H. Blyth (Ed.). (1964). *A history of haiku* (Vol. 2). Tokyo: Hokuseido Press.

Orwell, G. 1938/1952. *Homage to Catalonia*. New York: Harcourt, Brace.

Rossner, J. (1984). *To the precipice*. New York: Warner Books.

Sacks, S. (1970). *On metaphor*. Chicago: University of Chicago Press.

Sargant, W.W. (1957). *Battle for the mind: A physiology of conversion and brain washing*. London: Heinemann.

Shea, S. C. (1988). *Psychiatric interviewing*. Philadelphia: Saunders.

Sheehan, P.W., & Perry, C.W. (1976). *The demise of magnetic doctrines: Methodologies of hypnosis*. Hillsdale, NJ: Lawrence Erlbaum.

Shiki. (ca. 1890). in H.G. Henderson (Ed.). (1958). *An introduction to haiku: An anthology of poems and poets from Basho to Shiki*. Garden City, NY: Doubleday.

Simons, R.C., & Salyers, M. (1980). *Startle in American and English fiction*. Unpublished manuscript.

Stevenson, R.L. 1888/1916. *The black arrow*. New York: Gilberton.

Suetonius. (ca. A.D. 100). *The lives of the twelve Caesars* (1965 ed.). New York: Heritage Press.

Tedlock, B. (1975). The clown's way. In *Teachings from the earth: Indian religion and philosophy*. New York: Liveright.

Twain, M. 1884/1951. *The adventures of Huckleberry Finn*. New York: Harper & Row.

Victrola book of the opera. (1929). Camden, NJ: Victor Talking Machine Company.

Vonnegut, K. (1976). *Slapstick: Or lonesome no more*. London: J. Cape.

Webster's New International Dictionary. (1960). Springfield, MA: G.&C. Merriam.

White, T.H. (1977). *The book of Merlyn: The unpublished conclusion to The once and future king*. Austin: University of Texas Press.

Wolfe, T. (1987). *The bonfire of the vanities*. New York: Farrar, Strauss, Giroux.

Woolf, V. 1922/1959. *Jacob's room*. New York: Harcourt, Brace.

Young, W. (1964). *Eros denied: Sex in Western society*. New York: Grove Press.

6

THE STARTLE MUSEUM II
Exhibits of Startle Sorted by Properties of Startle Events

> "If oo want to startle people," said Bruno, "oo should put live frogs on their backs."
>
> Lewis Carroll, 1893, *Sylvie & Bruno Concluded*, p. 668

In my lap is a book titled *Startling Experiences*, published in the early 1900s. Its cover is an intense red, and the words "Startling" and "Experiences" are in flamboyant gold letters, outlined in black. The book's title page reveals that its subject is rather more narrow than the title implies; it's really "Startling Experiences in Three Wars." The title page also tells the potential reader that "all the thrilling stories of the three wars" consist of "exciting stories of bravery," "wonderful descriptions of battles," and "startling personal experiences." A mounted copy of *Startling Stories*, a science-fiction magazine popular from the late 1930s to the mid-1950s, hangs on my office wall. Although the connotation of "startling" in the magazine's title is mostly metaphoric, the covers of some issues show someone actually being startled. On the cover of this one it's an attractive young woman. A flask of strange electric energies has burst in her grasp, and she stands startled and transfixed by an intense brilliance (Fig. 6.1).

Startling Experiences and *Startling Stories* as titles, "startling personal experiences" as a title-page descriptor, the typography of the book's title, and the illustration on the magazine's cover, all result from informed creative decisions. All were chosen in order to convey certain culture-typical meanings and values, and all were designed to induce positive buyer interest and hence purchase. The title's typography is especially interesting. It

Figure 6.1 *Startling Stories* was a popular science-fiction magazine from the late 1930s to the mid-1950s. The woman on the cover of this issue is shown, as illustrators often show startle, with eyes and mouth open. High-speed films show that in the initial reaction to being startled, eyes are squeezed shut, and the mouth is closed in a characteristic grimace.

is intended to induce a certain feeling in the viewer, and it asserts something about the contents of the book. But are the feeling and the assertion matters of culture only?

It is true that to understand creative artistic choices fully one must understand relevant cultural meanings. However, this truth is a tautology (the operative word is "fully"), and it is not the whole story. To understand these choices "fully," one must also consider the underlying biology, not in some vague general sense but rather in its minute and particular features. I believe the error arises in large part from a false dichotomy—the belief that explanations of human behavior are cultural or biological but not both, that cultural explanations are somehow in opposition to biological ones. This way of thinking is nicely illustrated in the following quote from the anthropologist Ruth Benedict:

> We must accept all the implications of our human inheritance, one of the most important of which is the small scope of biologically transmitted behavior, and the enormous role of the cultural process of the transmission of tradition. (1934, *Patterns of Culture*, p. 15)

The fallacy lies in believing that, because the contribution of culture is demonstrably "large," that of biology must in consequence be "small." But this, of course, is a nonsequitur. It does not follow logically and it has never been demonstrated. In point of fact, the contributions of both culture and biology are "large."

Attention to the biological factors that shape human lives does not inhibit attention to the cultural factors that shape those same lives—in fact, its effect may be quite the opposite. Considering the relevant biology can provide powerful insights into the nature of cultural choices. This chapter is intended to demonstrate that cultural understanding is demonstrably enhanced when biological shaping is taken into account.

For many, the role of biology in contemporary cultural anthropology is worse than suspect intellectually. In some circles, it is considered naive, reductionistic, reactionary, politically incorrect, and quite possibly fascist. Guild issues account in part for the persistence of this radical culturalist position, but there is at least one other set of considerations underlying cultural anthropologists' wariness about conceding a role for biology in explanations of culturally shaped events. There are good reasons for their wariness.

Cultural anthropology's wariness regarding biological explanations of behavior stems in part from early uses of evolutionary determinism to justify racism, sexism, and various other sorts of oppression, usually the status quo. Morgan (1877), Tylor (1871), and most of the rest of the Western world believed that cultures evolved along a specific path, creating a hierarchy of evolutionary stages that were exemplified by more and less progressively evolved "races." The force behind the radical culturalists' wariness about attributing shaping force to specific evolved biology is in large part the aftermath of World War II, when racist doctrines of appalling evil were justified on the grounds of alleged evolved biological differences between groups. The general reaction in anthropology has been to take the position that is the polar opposite, as stated classically, shortly after the war by Leslie White:

> (1) As a matter of fact, it cannot be shown that *any* [emphasis in original] variation of human behavior is due to variation of biological nature.
> (2) In other words, in the whole range and scope of human

behavior, differences in custom or tradition can nowhere be cor-
related in a structural or functional sense with differences of physical structure. (1949, *The Science of Culture*, p. 134)

There is, however, a lapse in logic here. In spite of the phrase "In other
words," the second proposition is not a restatement of the first. Although
the second proposition is probably true, the first is demonstrably false.
Whether or not *groups* differ biologically in ways relevant to their behavior, *individuals* differ biologically in ways which account for many differences in their behavior. Some ways in which this fact shapes cultural productions are demonstrated in this chapter.

Of equal importance are the many ways in which the biology that
humans share also shapes cultural productions, and this is what most of
the exhibits in this chapter show. Human experience tends to follow certain species-typical ruts. This is, after all, what all the poets tell us, and the
holy books. It is the source of the notion that children should be tenderly
cared for, that all men are brothers (mutatis mutandis, women), and that
love is real.

One way in which culture-typical references to startle, such as the
exhibits, can be sorted is by the properties of startle that are used or
referred to: the stimulus used, the setting in which the startle is said to
occur, the subject who startles, and the nature of the response. This
approach allows the elements of startle occurrences to be systematically
compared across quite disparate contexts as, for example, comparison of
startles occurring in American short stories with film records of *latah*
behavior in Southeast Asia. Each of the major categories of stimulus, setting, subject, and response can be further subdivided in more than one
way. Stimuli may be compared by modality ("channel"), categorized as
being deliberately or inadvertently presented, and so forth. Phenomeno-
logic, behaviorally descriptive, and neurophysiologic aspects of responses
can also be compared. This chapter presents examples of startles sorted in
this way.

To present the most exhibits in the least space, different exhibits are
presented in Chapters 5 and 6. However, there is only one corpus of data;
the two parts of the museum are simply the result of applying two sorting
systems. The exhibits in Chapter 5 can readily be sorted into the categories
of Chapter 6 and vice versa.

The plan of this chapter (see Table 6.1) closely follows the sequence
outlined in Table 1.2 in Chapter 1, "Properties of Startle Events," with
minor changes. A few of the categories of Table 1.2 are discussed in such
detail elsewhere in the book that it seemed unnecessary to repeat the points
made in those places here, and in a few categories it seemed clearer to separate metaphoric from actual exhibits of startle explicitly.

Table 6.1 Exhibits of Startle Sorted by Properties of Startle Events Used or Referred To

I. Stimuli that startle
    A. Dangerous or appalling sights
        1. Snakes and creepy-crawlies
            a. Actual snakes and snakelike objects
            b. Metaphoric snakes (snakes as paradigmatic of startling stimuli)
            c. Creepy-crawlies (toads, lizards, scorpions, centipedes, wasps, spiders, etc.)
        2. Other dangers
        3. Appalling sights
    B. Loud noises, bright lights, and other intense stimulations
        1. Actual
        2. Metaphoric
    C. The unexpected
        1. Sudden motion
            a. Motions in general
            b. Startles of other persons
        2. Unexpected occurrences
            a. Unexpected events
            b. Prohibited words (naughty talk)
            c. Significant, sometimes idiosyncratically significant, words
        3. Radical novelty (extreme unfamiliarity, mismatch of scale, etc.)
        4. Metaphoric unexpectedness
    D. Great beauty or value
        1. Great female beauty
        2. Great prizes or treasures
        3. Other and metaphoric beauty, prizes, or treasures
    E. Cessation of a stimulus

II. Responses when startled
    A. Jumping, blinking, or vocalizing
    B. Striking out
    C. Dropping or flinging something that had been held
    D. Being stopped in thought or action
    E. Releasing an action that had been held in check
    F. Unintended speech
        1. Prohibited words (naughty talk)
        2. Improper reference to a deity
        3. Idiosyncratically stereotyped thought or utterance
        4. Secret or hidden thought
        5. Disorganized talk
    G. Matching
    H. Obedience

III. States in which persons startle especially readily and violently
    A. When ill or debilitated
    B. When wary
    C. When in a state of high anticipation
    D. When drowsy, dozing, or dropping off to sleep

(continued)

Table 6.1 (*continued*)

    E. When asleep

    F. When lost in thought

IV. Settings in which startles are likely to occur

    A. Spooky and dangerous places

    B. Quiet places

 V. Sensitization and habituation

    A. Being frequently startled may lead to hyperstartling

    B. Severe or prolonged trauma may lead to hyperstartling

    C. Familiarity with a stimulus may reduce the likelihood of startling to its presentation and may reduce the violence of the response when it occurs

VI. Miscellaneous other expository uses of startle's biology

    A. Stimuli in any modality may elicit startles

    B. Animals startle to equivalent stimuli in equivalent ways

EXHIBITS OF STARTLE SORTED BY PROPERTIES OF STARTLE EVENTS USED OR REFERRED TO

I. STIMULI THAT STARTLE

A. Dangerous or Appalling Sights

1. Snakes and Creepy-Crawlies

As in Chapter 3 in which Tom Sawyer and Huck Finn use snakes to create a hyperstartler, snakes are a frequently described startling stimulus. The museum has many startles to both actual and metaphoric snakes, from many times and many places.

a. Actual Snakes and Snakelike Objects

> I dropped my eyes, then, to the foot of the wall—and I leaped into the air. There before me, facing the little prince, was one of those yellow snakes that take just thirty seconds to bring your life to an end. (Antoine de Saint Exupery, 1943, *The Little Prince* [original in French], p. 81)

> My life is embittered by the abundance of these reptiles—rattlesnakes and moccasin snakes, both deadly, carpet snakes and "green racers," reputed dangerous, water snakes, tree snakes, and mouse snakes, harmless but abominable. Seven rattlesnakes have been killed just outside the cabin since I came. A snake, three feet long was found coiled under the pillow of the sick woman. I see snakes in all withered twigs, and am ready to flee at "the sound of a shaken leaf." (Isabella Bird, 1879, *A Lady's Life in the Rocky Mountains*, p. 48)

In four sentences Isabella Bird uses the word "snake" nine times, perhaps to convey her experience by inducing a ghost of it in the reader. She has come to perceive withered twigs as snakes. The phrase she quotes "at the sound of a shaken leaf" may be a reference to a passage from *The Odes* of Horace, quoted in "Creepy-Crawlies" below.

The stimulus in the next example is not really a snake but an eel, which has the same perceptual gestalt.

> But my mother, Fenwoman though she was and far from squeamish, could not abide them. She would scream if she saw a not quite dead eel begin to slither on the kitchen table. . . . (Graham Swift, 1983, *Waterland*, p. 130)

b. Metaphoric Snakes (snakes as paradigmatic of startling stimuli). Startle to snake stimuli is so ubiquitous that it is frequently used metaphorically as paradigmatic of all startling. In asserting that someone has been startled, the author includes some variant of the phrase "as if he had seen a snake."

> When I said "a mother,"
>   Methought you saw a serpent. What's in
> "mother",
>   That you start at it?
> (William Shakespeare, 1599, *All's Well That Ends Well*, Act I, scene iii)

> For the tax collector—and he was a man of courage: he had fought at Bautzen and Lützen, and taken part in the French campaign, and had even been proposed for the Legion of Honor— suddenly recoiled as though he had seen a snake. (Gustave Flaubert, 1857, *Madame Bovary* [original in French], p. 348)

In the short novel *Victory*, Joseph Conrad uses this device twice within the space of 10 pages.

> The unexpected outburst affected Mr. Jones strangely. He had a horrified recoil, chair and all, as if Schomberg had thrust a wriggling viper in his face. (Joseph Conrad, 1915, *Victory*, p. 128)

> Wandering about his premises in profound solitude, Schomberg recoiled at the door of the billiard-room, as if he had seen a snake in his path. (1915, p. 138)

c. Creepy-Crawlies (toads, lizards, scorpions, centipedes, wasps, spiders, etc.). "Creepy-crawlies" is a conglomerate category consisting of toads, lizards, scorpions, centipedes, wasps, spiders (Fig. 6.2), and all other

Figure 6.2 Startled by a spider, Miss Muffett drops her bowl of porridge. Of all the illustrations in this edition of *Mother Goose*, a startle was chosen for the cover. Illustration by E. Bachmann reprinted by permission of The Putnam & Grosset Group, from *Mother Goose Rhymes and Nursery Tales* edited by Watty Piper, copyright 1922 by Platt & Munk Co.

small potentially venomous creatures that may appear or be noticed suddenly.[1] As in encounters with snakes, immediate evasive action is probably hard-wired into our species. Although the vast majority of small, suddenly appearing animals pose no danger, some are dangerous indeed, especially in the tropics, and some people have serious and sometimes fatal allergic reactions to their stings and bites. The whole point of the startle reflex is to permit an evasive response to be made even before there is sufficient time to make an accurate assessment. The rule is "Jump first, consider later." In radio terms, the tuner is sensitive but not selective.

Chloe, you will not venture near,
Just like a lost young mountain deer

Seeking her frantic dam; for whom each
Gust in the trees is a needless fear.
Whether the spring-announcing breeze
Shudders the light leaves or she sees
The brambles twitched by a green lizard,
Panic sets racing her heart and knees.
(Horace, ca. 70 B.C., *The Odes of Horace* [original in Latin], p. 24)

In the Latin, "*Nam . . . seu virides rubum/ dimovere lacertae,/ et corde et genibus tremit,*" the words "panic sets racing" do not appear, just the leaves moved by the lizard making Chloe's heart and knees shake.

"If oo want to startle people," said Bruno, "oo should put live frogs on their backs." (Lewis Carroll, 1893, *Sylvie and Bruno Concluded*, p. 668)

A toad appears,
     And the girls' school
Is on its feet.
(Santaro, ca. 1930 [original in Japanese], in Blyth, 1960, *Japanese Life and Character in Senryu*, p. 285)

The following text was used in an advertisement for a rack used to store firewood.

It eliminates infestation by termites and other ruinous insect pests. It minimizes "critter surprise," discouraging nesting behavior by snakes, rats, mice and other undesirable animals.

"Critter surprise" is, of course, a witty way of saying "being unpleasantly startled by the sudden unexpected appearance of a mouse, snake, or other small animal."
    Creepy-crawlies may also be used metaphorically, but for this purpose, in English at least, "as if one saw a snake" is much more frequent:

She started away as if from an unclean thing. (D. H. Lawrence, 1915, *The Rainbow*, p. 333.)

2. Other Dangers

With the exception of snakes, the museum has surprisingly few examples of startle to suddenly presented objects that are actually dangerous. Perhaps this is because startling to a suddenly presented danger is less useful to authors since it is relatively unrevealing.[2] Save for general human vulnerability, startle to a suddenly encountered danger does not reveal significant information about character, motivation, or internal state, making such startles less useful as a narrative resource than many other properties of the reflex. In film, where the danger can be actually shown, startles to dangerous objects are frequent. The next exhibit is one of the few I have been able to find in print. There is an epidemic in the city. The narrator's friend is watching by the bedside of a dying girl.

> Suddenly a terrific yell rent the sky, and my friend rushed from his room, fairly plunging into mine as he slammed the door after him.
> I asked him in terror and surprise, "Are you mad? . . . Why are you shouting so?"
> He gasped, "There is a tiger in the house." (Dhan Gopal Mukerji, 1923, *Jungle Beasts and Men*, p. 32)

Startle to other dangers is sometimes used metaphorically:

> You had not turned your back on me then. You had not started away from me as if I had got the plague. (Wilkie Collins, 1868, *The Moonstone* p. 376)

> . . . Why shrinks the soul
> Back on herself, and startles at
>   destruction?
> (Joseph Addison, 1713, "Cato," p. 299)

3. Appalling Sights

The term "appall" is here used in the sense "to shock or overcome with sudden terror or horror" (*Webster's*, 1960). In the next exhibit, a boy turns himself into an appalling sight in order to startle his mother.

> In bed with a cold, I called loudly to my mother to bring me some orange juice. I heard her rustling about. Slam of refrigerator door. Footsteps coming down the hall. I threw myself half off the bed, my head back, my eyes staring wide, tongue extended and hands dragging on the floor. Screech. A shattering of glass. I sat up and laughed. Eventually, after sitting down on my bed to catch her breath and recover, she laughed too. "What a terrible thing to do," she said. (E. L. Doctorow, 1985, *World's Fair*, p. 95)

B. Loud Noises, Bright Lights, and Other Intense Stimulations

Because they are so easily controlled and quantified, intense stimuli are often used to elicit startles in experimental research. Both actual and metaphoric startling to intense stimuli are used in a wide variety of literary and expository contexts.

1. Actual

"Startling" can be used to mean "sudden and intense":

> The logging truck horn fills the air with a startling blast. (Carolyn Chute, 1985, *The Beans of Egypt, Maine*, p. 107)

In the following example, a reporter cites startles to signify how intense some earthquakes have been.

> Most of [the earthquakes] have been too small to be registered by anything but instruments, but many have been strong enough to startle residents 20 to 30 miles away. . . . ("Mt. Shasta's Eastern Slope Jiggling," *Lansing State Journal*, September 4, 1978)

Here is a startle to a sudden, intense bright light:

> He eventually lent him the money to set up his photography studio, and from the time he took his first picture of a child startled by the magnesium flash, Jeremiah de Saint-Amour paid back every last penny with religious regularity. (Gabriel García Márquez, 1985, *Love in the Time of Cholera* [original in Spanish], pp. 10-11)

The following single-panel cartoon uses a startle to signify how intense a sonic boom was.

> A woman with her hair standing on end asks, "WOW! Did you hear that sonic boom?" The man she is asking has startled so violently that he has kicked off the cast which had encased his leg. We deduce that yes indeed he has heard it. (*King-Sized Cracked* [magazine], 1975 [annual])

In the next example, a cartoon in four panels, a sudden loud stimulus is used for revenge. The victim is "The Born Loser," a man who is frequently depicted in a one-down situation and who often is shown startling violently.[3] Before giving the startling stimulus, the perpetrator sets up the startle by manipulating the victim's attention.

> After the Born Loser refuses a panhandler the panhandler asks him: "Did'ja hear about the cheapskate who was hard of hearing?" The last four words are in smaller and smaller print, signifying dropping the voice to near inaudibility. When the Born Loser replies, "What?" The panhandler shouts, "HARD OF HEARING!" represented in the cartoon by huge black capital letters. The Born Loser flips upside-down three feet off the sidewalk. (*Lansing State Journal*, January 7, 1982)

2. Metaphoric

The idea of startle to an intense stimulus is often used metaphorically. In the first example the stimulus is a new fact, the idea of an immense new force:

> Boyer's main point echoes the comment . . . that the bomb caused "an explosion in men's minds as shattering as the obliteration of Hiroshima". . . . In all levels, in all ways, Americans had to confront a startling new force. (A. M. Winkler, 1986, "By the Bomb's Early Light," in *Science, 232,* p. 407)

In the next example it is a sharp, bright picture on one's computer monitor. The reporter does not mean that anyone will actually be startled by the new terminal displays, only that the displays are unexpectedly intense.

> But the eye-popping, high density, multihued views you get with these extended display modes can startle even the most jaded disk jockey. (A. Poor, *PC Magazine 8*; July, 1989)

C. The Unexpected

The fact that unexpected objects, unexpected properties of objects, and unexpected events all may startle is used both literally and metaphorically for a wide variety of expository purposes.

1. Sudden Motion

Many kinds of sudden unexpected motions can elicit startles. Among adolescent American boys sudden feints to the head, body, or upper arm are frequently used in play in which the object is to avoid revealing weakness by startling. He who startles least to a sudden feint at his head or body retains most status. This is a game played among males; when adolescent boys startle adolescent girls in teasing courtship, they choose other stimuli.

a. Motions in General.   One may or may not be able to habituate to a startling stimulus, even if it is repeatedly encountered:

> When it [a praying mantis] strikes, it jerks so suddenly and with such a fearful clatter of raised wings, that even a hardened entomologist like J. Henry Fabre confessed to being startled witless every time. (Annie Dillard, 1974, *Pilgrim at Tinker Creek*, p. 56)

The subject in the next exhibit has seen what appears to be a head in the branches of a ginkgo tree. With the words "ill-omened," "ghost," "ghosts," "uncanny," "another world," "weird," "beautiful," "dangerous," "coming nearer," "demonic," and "haunted," which appear in the 25 lines that precede the sentence exhibited below, the author foreshadows the startle.

> Then a sudden movement nearer to her made her startle and step back. (Iris Murdoch, 1983, *The Philosopher's Pupil*, p. 423)

Here are two exhibits from Japan in which poets describe startling to sudden unexpected motion:

> The skylark, starting up,
>   Stumbles
> The cowherd.
> (Kenkabo, ca. 1930 [original in Japanese], in Blyth, 1960, *Japanese Life and Character in Senryu*, p. 275)

> A pheasant flew up
>   And startled us,
> Over the withered moor.
> (Issa, ca. 1800 [original in Japanese], in Blyth, 1949, *Haiku, Vol. 1*, p. 294)

Discussing the first exhibit, Blyth explains: "This is not a very grammatical translation but it may convey the idea of the Japanese [version] that the skylark pushes the cowherd over." Skylarks feed and nest in bare places in open fields, not sites where one expects sudden excitement. Many ground-dwelling birds—for example, grouse and woodcock—explode from the ground with a loud whir and a big show. This appears to be an evolved defensive maneuver; the just-startled predator or human hunter must gather his wits before he can act effectively, providing time for at least a head start if not a complete escape. A hunter who startles markedly and misses his shot reveals relative inexperience or worse.

b. Startles of Other Persons.   An interesting subcategory of "Sudden Motion" is the startle of another person. Because the movement of the startled person is itself sudden and abrupt it can startle someone else, especially if it is violent. Here is a startle to the sudden motion of another as used by D. H. Lawrence:

> Then there was the sound of the door softly opening. Gerald started. He was chagrined. It was his starting that really startled Gudrun. (D. H. Lawrence, 1920, *Women in Love*, p. 318)

2. Unexpected Occurrences

a. Unexpected Events.   In each of the next five exhibits, an author has used a startle to signify the unexpectedness of an event.

She had so little expected to see him that she started back in alarm. (Marcel Proust, 1913, *Swann's Way* [original in French], p. 332)

Another day, at tea time, as he sat alone at table, there came a knock at the front door. It startled him like a portent. No one ever knocked at the front door. (D. H. Lawrence, 1915, *The Rainbow*, p. 34)

"Tessie," Katharine said, startling her slightly because she hadn't heard her name in so long. (Judith Rossner, 1975, *Looking for Mr. Goodbar*, p. 78)

She lifted his hand to her lips and let it go. He was startled. "Lena!" he cried out under his breath. (Joseph Conrad, 1915, *Victory*, p. 420)

Dear Ann Landers: Regarding the letter from the distraught husband whose wife enjoyed answering the door stark naked to watch the startled reaction of visitors, salesmen, paper boys, etc. . . . (*Lansing State Journal*, April 8, 1979)

In another Ann Landers column (*Lansing State Journal*, August 2, 1987), Ann's criticism of a woman who drove naked is: "That woman is a hazard to public safety. Such a sight could easily startle a driver, causing him or her to plow into another vehicle or straight into a ditch." That it is dangerous to startle a driver is an assertion repeated frequently in a variety of expository contexts.

The museum has a number of cartoons in which the joke is that a violent startle is elicited when someone, often a spouse, turns up where the startled subject knew that he or she could not appear. Surely most readers have been so jolted at least once. There is an initial gap in experience and in social performance as the mind attempts to assimilate the new data.

b. Prohibited Words (naughty talk). Hearing a normally prohibited word, especially suddenly and unexpectedly, can also produce a startle response. This is probably only a special case of an unexpected stimulus, but it is possible that it is determined in part by the special neurologic encoding of naughty talk as well. In the following exhibits it is not the physical properties of the stimuli that evoke startles but rather their meanings.

[A] most horrible change came over his tallowy face, and he ordered me in with an oath that made me jump. (Robert Louis Stevenson, 1884, *Treasure Island*, p. 13)

He shot out an infamous word which made Davidson start. (Joseph Conrad, 1915, *Victory*, p. 52)

In the next exhibit, a young woman is the speaker:

"Now the question is why the fuck I said it." He flinched. (Judith Rossner, 1975, *Looking For Mr. Goodbar*, p. 194)

c. Significant, Sometimes Idiosyncratically Significant, Words. In the next exhibit, a reporter describes actual startles; in the second, they are metaphoric:

County Commissioner Jess Sobel at a board of commissioners meeting:
"The sheriff's department is very good," he added, "but I think the sheriff himself is dishonest, corrupt, and unethical."
The blunt statement brought a few gasps from other board members. (*Lansing State Journal*, October 24, 1984)

Masaru Yoshitomi, the senior official of Japan's Economic Planning Agency, startled his listeners with the directness of his message that American policy was riddled with contradictions and that Japanese and other foreign investors would surely retreat if Washington did not put its financial house in order. (Robert D. Hershey, Jr., "Political Sparring Erupts at Economists Meeting," *New York Times*, September 28, 1988)

In the exhibits above the statements are startling because of their "bluntness"—that is, both speakers say something that normally would not be said in such a direct and uncompromising way in the public settings in which the statements were made. It is easy to imagine being in the audience and being similarly startled. However, in most of the museum's exhibits in which someone is startled by the significance of something said, words that would normally be innocuous have a disturbing significance only to a particular recipient, and the startle they cause is expositorily useful leakage.

The next exhibit is from *Macbeth*. Out on the lonely moor in strange weather, Macbeth startles when the three witches hail him as Thane of Glamis and Cawdor and as he "that shall be king after." Their greeting has hit too closely on hopes he had thought secret. Banquo notices and asks:

Good sir, why do you start and seem to fear
Things that sound so fair?
(William Shakespeare, 1606, *Macbeth*, Act I, scene iii)

This use of startle leakage is a dramatic expository device that has been used by many writers in a wide variety of circumstances:

"So far, miss (as you have remarked), this is the story of your regretted father. Now comes the difference. If your father had not died when he did—Don't be frightened! How you start!" She did, indeed, start. And she caught his wrist with both her hands. (Charles Dickens, 1859, *A Tale of Two Cities*, p. 67)

You mention no names in the letter; but Miss Farlie knows that the person you write of is Sir Percival Glyde——

The instant I pronounced that name she started from her feet and a scream burst from her that rang through the churchyard and made my heart leap in me at the terror of it. (Wilkie Collins, 1868, *The Moonstone*, p. 85)

Woody was startled when Pop used the word, "trust." It was as if from all corners of the world a Sousa band blew a blast to warn the entire world: "Crook! This is a crook!" (Saul Bellow, 1984, *Him With His Foot In His Mouth and Other Stories*, pp. 246–247)

3. Radical Novelty (Extreme Unfamiliarity, Mismatch of Scale, etc.)

Otherwise innocuous objects may elicit startles if they are improbable enough.

In a room downstairs they had been startled to open a cupboard door and be confronted by a staring bevy of little gods, made out of clay and *papier maché* and painted in gaudy colors. (Iris Murdoch, 1983, *The Philosopher's Pupil*, p. 235)

Clinton County Sheriff's deputies on Sunday captured a 230-pound pig that had been startling motorists on U.S. 27 near St. Johns, said Deputy Eric Schroeder. (*Lansing State Journal*, July 9, 1990)

The improbability may be only situational, with the startle occurring because some new stimulus is radically inconsistent with a person's current perceptual set. Here are startles elicited by two mismatches of scale.

I have been almost knocked off my kitchen chair on several occasions when, as I was following [through a microscope] the tiny career of a monostyla rotifer, an enormous red roundworm whipped into the scene, blocking everything, and writhing in huge, flapping convulsions that seemed to sweep my face and fill the kitchen. (Annie Dillard, 1974, *Pilgrim at Tinker Creek*, p. 123)

Size and distance and the sudden swelling of meanings confuse me, bowl me over. . . . If I'm thinking minnows, a carp will fill my brain till I scream. I look at the water's surface: skaters bubbles, and leaves sliding down. Suddenly my own face, reflected, startles me witless. . . . [Later, hawk-watching:] I followed a sharp-shinned hawk against a featureless sky, rotating my head unawares as it flew, and when I lowered the glass a glimpse of my own looming shoulder sent me staggering. (Annie Dillard, 1974, *Pilgrim at Tinker Creek*, p. 25)

The author apparently startles violently and easily; *Pilgrim at Tinker Creek* is full of such startles.

Sidney Harris, the regular cartoonist of *American Scientist*, published a cartoon based on observations parallel to Dillard's:

> "Ashley," wearing a lab coat, is shown massively startled. The person walking by who had been the unintentional stimulus is told, "Don't mind Ashley. After looking through a microscope all day, anything large startles him." (1984, *American Scientist*, *70*; p. 175)

4. Metaphoric Unexpectedness

As noted in Chapter 5 in the section of the museum titled "Startles Used to Signify a Revelation or Massive Reconceptualization," the word "startling" or some variant of it can be used to mean "very unexpected." This is a frequent metaphoric usage and occurs in a wide variety of contexts:

> In laboratory tests at San Francisco General Hospital, GLQ223 [an experimental antiviral drug] revealed a startling property: When injected into a test tube of cells infected with the AIDS virus, GLQ223 not only eliminated all trace of the virus within five days but also protected other cells from infection. (*Business Week*, April 24, 1989)

> It was a startling result. The researcher placed palladium electrodes in water and ran a current across them, and the cell produced heat and helium. (*Science*, *248*; April 28, 1989)

> Dear Dr. Reinisch, My wife and I recently had a startling phone call from our daughter. Her husband has told her of his desire to have a sex change and assume the role of a woman. (*Lansing State Journal*, April 4, 1990)

In the next exhibit, the author emphasizes the "startling" incongruity of the stimulus by using the words "solemn," "august," and "shrouds of antiquity":

> As the solemn Opening Day exercises of October 8, 1913, drew to a close in the new building's august Hall of Casts, a football team in Dandelion Yellow burst through the doors, snaking its way through the shrouds of antiquity and the startled assemblage of frock coats and afternoon dresses. (*Rochester Review*, summer, 1987)

After a speech at a trade meeting, a Libyan translator unexpectedly presented 20 teenage dancers in traditional dress who swirled down the aisle of the Miami Beach Convention Center and onto the stage. Amid flute and drum music . . . [The performance] included a solo that came very close to being a belly dance. . . . Playing flutes and drums and twirling with enthusiasm, a group of Libyan dancers startled a somewhat embarrassed group of American farmers Tuesday. (*Lansing State Journal*, January 17, 1979)

Neither the *Rochester Review* feature writer nor the *Lansing State Journal* reporter is reporting observed general startles. Instead, they are using startle metaphorically to convey the degree of mismatch. The farmers-meet-dancers example may also have a sexual component, as in the exhibits in the section of the museum that follows.

Referring to a startle to signify the unexpected is perhaps the most frequent metaphoric use of startle in contemporary American writing. Although the exhibits were not collected in a systematic enough manner to make this assertion unequivocally, the museum contains many more exhibits with this feature than with any other.

D. Great Beauty or Value

In marked contrast to the above unpleasant stimuli, great, beautiful, and good objects may also startle. High degrees of beauty and status are often said to elicit startle both actually and metaphorically.

1. Great Female Beauty

In the following exhibits some man is said to be startled by the beauty of some woman, as Dante reports that he was startled by his first sight of Beatrice (*Vita Nuova*, 1292). I suspect that writers have also described women being startled by the beauty of men, but I have no such examples.

[T]hen he gazed upon the girls and he was startled and he marvelled with exceeding marvel at their beauty and loveliness. (Sir Richard Burton, 1885, "The Porter and the Three Ladies," *The Arabian Nights*, pp. 60–61.)

A puff of wind—oh, those blessed breaths of wind, coming from nowhere in the stifling hot-weather days!—had caught her cotton frock and blown it against her, showing the outline of her body, slender and strong like a tree. Her sudden appearance beside the older, sun-scorched woman was a revelation to Verrall. He started so that the Arab mare felt it and would have reared on her hind legs, and he had to tighten the rein. (George Orwell, 1934, *Burmese Days*, p. 187)

"Startling" can thus be used to signify extreme beauty or sexual desirability. In the following exhibit a reporter uses the term "startlingly" in this way to signify just how sexually attractive an actress is:

An 18-year-old Montreal teen with no experience except for some high school plays, Ms. Gilbert is startlingly beautiful. (*Lansing State Journal*, January 29, 1981)

The following exhibit is from "Sonnets to a Red-haired Lady." The speaker is Bluebeard.

Comet, shake out your locks and let them
    flare
Across the startled heaven of my soul!
Pluck out the hairpins, Sue and let her roll!
Don't be so stingy with your blooming hair.
(Don Marquis, 1922, *The Best of Don Marquis*, p. 666)

The next is from India:

The queen of the Hindus stepped out, and when they saw the marvel of her face they were startled by the beauty and majesty of it. (Dhan Gopal Mukerji, 1923, *Jungle Beasts and Men*, p. 119)

In the following exhibit, a startle reveals an otherwise hidden appreciation of feminine beauty, another example of Ekman's "leakage" and one highly consequential for the person whose inner state is thus revealed. Edwin Arnold describes the parade of beautiful women held to select a wife for young Prince Siddartha, who will ultimately become the Buddha. A parade of young women will be held, and courtiers will "mark it when one or two/Change the fixed sadness of his tender cheek." The last beauty to be shown is Yasodhara:

. . . and they that stood
Nearest Siddartha saw the princely boy
Start, as the radiant girl approached. A form
Of heavenly mold. . . .
(Edwin Arnold, 1882, *The Light of Asia*: p. 28)

The startle makes visible Siddhartha's interior response and hence is useful information, just the sort of thing the courtiers were watching for, and a marriage is arranged. It is probably because such leakage is so useful to writers as an expository resource that the museum has so many examples.

2. Great Prizes or Treasures

Benvenuto Cellini, writing between 1558 and 1562, records that King Francis I of France startled when first shown that famous and extravagant salt cellar:

When I exhibited this piece to his Majesty, he uttered a loud outcry of astonishment, and could not satiate his eyes with gazing at it. (Benvenuto Cellini, ca. 1560, *Autobiography* [original in Italian], p. 294)

The next example is contemporary:

In Dubai the queen [Elizabeth II] gasped. It happened when Sheikh Rashid presented her with a two-foot square box containing a necklace of sapphires and surrounded by 300 diamonds, with matching earrings and a ring. (*Lansing State Journal*, March 6, 1979)

That's rather charming, isn't it; she's only human after all. This is not merely a report of a royal gift. The structure of the paragraph illustrates the proposition that the composure of royalty is news.

3. Other and Metaphoric Beauty, Prizes, or Treasures

The exhibits above all describe actual startles. Metaphoric uses are also common:

Lady Duff Gordon boasted that she had "loosed upon a startled London,. . . dropped skirts which opened to reveal slender legs."
    (Caption in costume exhibit, *Victoria and Albert Museum*, quote from 1932)

In the next exhibit the metaphor is more extreme:

Ursula . . . would brush his teeth with charcoal powder so that he would have the radiant smile of a Pope, and she would cut and polish his nails so that the pilgrims who came to Rome from all over the world would be startled at the beauty of the Pope's hands. . . . (Gabriel García Márquez, 1967, *One Hundred Years of Solitude* [original in Spanish], p. 375)

At least in metaphor the beauty need not be human and sexual:

The great advantages of hybrid peonies, aside from their startling beauty, are that. . . . (Katharine S. White, 1979, *Onward and Upward in The Garden*, p. 122)

This startlingly beautiful *Hydnum* [the bear's head fungus, a mass of snow-white icicles several feet in breadth and length], . . . its pure whiteness seen in contrast with the dark colors of some fallen, moss-covered monarch of the forest, will cause even the most callous to stop in wonder and admiration. (Krieger, 1936, *The Mushroom Handbook*, quoted in Marteka, *Mushrooms Wild And Edible*, p. 100)

Both Krieger and Marteka report that Elias Magnus Fries, the founder of modern mycological taxonomy, decided when still a boy to devote his life to the study of fungi after coming across one of these.

E. Cessation of a Stimulus

The absence of an expected or accustomed object can startle—for example, "My God, he/she/it's not there!"

> Sometimes for minutes together invisible cicadas would keep up a shrill, metallic pinging like the twanging of a steel guitar, and then, by stopping, make a silence that startled one. (George Orwell, 1934, *Burmese Days*, p. 150)

> They shot through an underpass. The rain stopped completely for one blank, startling second. Sarah gave a little gasp of relief, but even before it was uttered the hammering on the roof resumed. (Anne Tyler, 1985, *The Accidental Tourist*, p. 2)

In the next exhibit, William Wordsworth uses much startle physiology. There's the lulling monotony of the "hoof after hoof," the initial words, "Oh mercy!" and the experience of an unexpected thought as a surprising intrusion. The sudden unexpected disappearance of the moon somehow precipitates the specific morbid thought.

> My horse moved on: hoof after hoof
> He raised and never stopped:
> When down behind the Cottage roof
> At once the bright moon dropped.
> What fond and wayward thoughts will slide
> Into a lover's head!
> "Oh mercy!" to myself I cried,
> "If Lucy should be dead!"
> (William Wordsworth, 1800, "Strange Fits of Passion I Have
> Known," in *Selections from Wordsworth*, pp. 49–50)

II. RESPONSES WHEN STARTLED

A. Jumping, Blinking, or Vocalizing

Because these responses are so very frequent, are mentioned in so many of the exhibits, and are discussed throughout the book, further examples need not be presented here.

Figure 6.3 The "Born Loser" is an American cartoon character whose startles are a frequent feature of Sunday newspaper comics. This is the last of a four-panel sequence. Distracted, the "Born Loser" sips a cup of scalding coffee, which causes him to startle, vocalize, drop his newspaper, and fling the cup full of coffee. Readers are expected to find this funny. THE BORN LOSER reprinted by permission of Newspaper Enterprise Association, Inc.

B. Striking Out

In the next exhibit, T. H. White uses unreflective striking out to explain the breaking of a truce and the start of devastating hostilities. To heighten the irony, he makes the snake which is the stimulus harmless.

> A grass-snake moved in the meadow near their feet, close to an officer of Mordred's staff. This officer stepped back instinctively and swung his hand across his body, his armlet with the whip showing for a second's flash. The bright sword flamed into being, to destroy the so-called viper. The waiting armies, taking it for treachery, raised their shout of rage. (T. H. White, 1977, *The Book of Merlyn*, pp. 183–184)

C. Dropping or Flinging Something that Had Been Held

In cartoons a flung or dropped object somewhere in the panel is a useful piece of startle iconography; it is one of the symbols signifying that someone has been startled.[4] The released object is not aimed but rather is propelled targetless into the air. In the last panel of one such cartoon in four panels, the panel with the denouement, "The Born Loser" responds to the

unexpected hotness of the coffee in a cup he's just put to his mouth by startling violently and flinging away the cup (Fig. 6.3). We are expected to find
humor in his doing so (*Lansing State Journal*, January 28, 1979).

In the next exhibit a newspaper reporter describes an actual occurrence
with serious consequences:

> Rep. Edward J. Derwinski, R-Ill., was wounded in the right hand
> and abdomen Sunday when the shotgun of his son Michael acci-
> dentally discharged while he was loading it on a skeet range, police
> said. After the first blast, Derwinski's wife, Patricia, dropped her
> shotgun, causing it to hit the congressman in his left hand and left
> side. (*Lansing State Journal*, April 26, 1982)

Two further examples of dropping objects after being startled follow:

> We followed him into the room. A little old lady, in a corner, very
> nicely dressed, and very deeply absorbed over a smart piece of
> embroidery, dropped her work in her lap, and uttered a faint little
> scream at the sight of my gipsy complexion and my piebald hair.
> (Wilkie Collins, 1868, *The Moonstone*, p. 467)

> On Basho's "Frog"
> Under the cloudy cliff, near the temple door,
> Between dusky spring plants on the pond,
> A frog jumps in the water, plop!
> Startled, the poet drops his brush.
> (Sengai, ca. 1800, In *On Love and Barley: Haiku of Basho Translated
> and edited by Lucien Stryk*, p. 21. Copyright University of Hawaii
> Press. Used with permission.)

D. Being Stopped in Thought or Action

Being startled may stop one dead in one's tracks, sometimes briefly, sometimes for a considerable period of time. The myth of Medusa makes use of
this fact, its logic being that catching sight of a snake is to being startled
and stopped in thought and action as catching sight of the appalling vision
of a human head covered with writhing, striking, venomous snakes is to
being turned to stone.

The museum has many examples. The phenomenon is discussed further in Chapter 7 under the heading "Attention Capture."

> It happened one day about noon, going towards my boat, I was
> exceedingly surpriz'd with the print of a man's naked foot on the
> shore, which was very plain to be seen in the sand. I stood like one
> thunderstruck, or as if I had seen an apparition. (Daniel Defoe,
> 1719, *Robinson Crusoe*, p. 125)

"What do you want?" I called. He must have been startled. It took him a moment to answer. (John Steinbeck, 1962, *Travels with Charley*, pp. 56–57)

Further reflections along these lines were cut short by a heavy, short-handled ax which hurtled through the air and buried itself with an astounding thud in the wall about three inches from his left ear and for a moment blotted out all thought. (Douglas Adams, 1990, *The Long Dark Tea-Time of the Soul*, p. 272)

E. Releasing an Action that Had Been Held in Check

A person prepared to perform an action but holding it in check will often release that hold and perform the action when startled. Being prepared to do something is apparently neurophysiologically different from both doing it and not doing it. In the next exhibit, Robert Louis Stevenson uses the release of an action held in check in an especially interesting way. Jim Hawkins is up a mast holding two pistols cocked at pirate Israel Hands, who has been climbing up after him with a knife. Hands offers to surrender, and Jim is feeling cocky and a bit smug.

> I was drinking in his words and smiling away when. . .I felt a blow and then a sharp pang. [Hands has thrown the knife, pinning Jim's shoulder to the mast.] In the horrid pain and surprise of the moment—I scarcely can say it was by my own volition, and I am sure it was without conscious aim—both my pistols went off and both escaped out of my hands. (Robert Louis Stevenson, 1884, *Treasure Island*, p. 204)

Startled, Jim squeezed the triggers. Because actions performed while in a startled state are usually considered involuntary and hence not subject to moral evaluation, this literary stratagem saves Jim, a boy in his early teens, from responsibility for the killing.

In the one-act Kabuki drama *Yasaku no Kamabara*, a vendetta play first performed in 1791, I counted six startles. One of these releases a sequestered action:

> Holding a scythe blade against his abdomen as if it were a sword, a farmer has been trying to summon up the courage to commit *seppuku* (ritual suicide in the manner of a samurai). Suddenly there is a loud pounding at the door. Startled, the farmer stabs, completing the action he had been unable to perform voluntarily. (Nakawa Shimesuke [1791], as performed at the Kabuki-za Theater, Tokyo, April 18, 1978)

The next exhibit is an actual instance of the same phenomenon. It was encountered while we were filming crowds being startled by muskets and cannons at a popular tourist attraction, the restored Fort Michelmackinac, in Michigan. A guide who was demonstrating a British .75-caliber smooth-bore flintlock musket included the following in his patter:

> Now if you'd like a still photograph of the musket going off I have one suggestion. Instead of anticipating my firing commands or accidentally getting a picture of one of the misfires, if you'll simply aim your camera at the musket, place your finger on the shutter button, and then relax, I'll almost guarantee that if and when this musket does go off you'll take one instantaneous photograph out of sheer fright.

The museum has several other accounts of actual occurrences. This one is from a news feature describing a policeman who, while wearing a new bullet-proof vest that he had received as a Christmas gift, was shot in the abdomen from three feet away by someone with a .45-caliber pistol.

> "I apparently blacked out for a moment from the concussion and, by instinct, I pulled my revolver and fired all six chambers at him, missing all six times," Schaefer said. (*New Straits Times*, Kuala Lumpur, Malyasia, December 27, 1977)

In the following, this same process is apparently assumed:

> Janitor Raymond Pettit, 28, took at least two bullets when he startled the gunman near the back door. ("Two Die in Restaurant Robbery," *Lansing State Journal*, December 14, 1987)

This fact about startle may have partly determined the Southland Corporation's (7-Eleven stores) policy of training clerks to protect robbers from potentially startling circumstances. If the robbers are startled, who knows what they might do?

> They are told to cooperate with the robber, to do exactly as the robber says, to alert the robber to what might be any startling occurrences. (*Lansing State Journal*, July 10, 1987)

F. Unintended Speech

When startled, people sometimes say unintended things: naughty talk (including improper references to a deity), idiosyncratically stereotyped utterances, and disorganized or "silly" talk. Matching something they have just heard with their own speech is discussed in the next section of the museum.

1. Prohibited Words (Naughty Talk)

The museum has both literary and actual exhibits of prohibited words following a startle. Erving Goffman has explained the nature of the lapse: "Situational requirements are of a moral character: the individual is obliged to maintain them; he is expected to desire to do so; and if he fails, some kind of public cognizance is taken of his failure" (1963, p. 240) One such requirement is to refrain from using naughty language in many social situations, even though everyone knows that everyone else knows such language and that he or she may use it at other times.

> The Professor jumped at the explosion. . . . At the same time he let off one of those big words which lie at the bottom of the best man's vocabulary, but perhaps never turn up in his life, just as every man's hair may stand on end, but in most men it never does. (Oliver Wendell Holmes, 1858, *The Autocrat of the Breakfast Table*, p. 185)

> Sticky Situation of the Month: You use a swear word at the wrong time in the wrong place. Situation: You're having lunch with a business colleague and accidentally spill your wine. Without thinking you blurt out "Oh, s——!" [In the accompanying illustration, a cartoon, the startled young woman says, "Oh *@#*@!=*!"] It's the last thing you mean to say to a fellow professional, but it's too late now. What can you do to save face? (*Glamour* [magazine], May, 1982; see Figure 2.1, p. 23)

> In a newspaper account of a heroic rescue from a fire by Mayor Flynn: "When the mayor of Boston burst into his living room, 68 year old Manuel Rose was so startled he said, "What the hell are you doing here?" (*Lansing State Journal*, July 29, 1987)

Although his startle excuses Mr. Rose from what would have otherwise been an ungracious greeting, such lapses are reportable news. Here is a parallel account of such a lapse in the presence of royalty, excused because actions following startles are generally understood to be involuntary. A chambermaid has come upon an intruder in the queen's bedroom:

> Two minutes later a chambermaid arrived, took one look at the scene and exclaimed [to the queen]: "Bloody hell, ma'am, what's he doing in there?" ("Intruder at the Palace," *Newsweek*, July 26, 1982)

In the next exhibit, the startled person blurts out both a deity reference (Holy) and a naughty word.

> In Palatka, Florida, WIYD disc jockey Bob Henry startled his midday listeners with a "Holy ——! It's a snake." Listeners then heard fast moving feet and the control room door slamming. . . . [A four-foot long snake is subsequently captured.] . . . Henry . . .

said he thinks he suffered "a mini-heart attack." (*Seattle Post Intel-ligencer*, October 1, 1981)

The offending word was omitted from the newspaper account. Mr. Henry did not lose his job over this incident; everyone understood that the startle-elicited impropriety was involuntary.

2. Improper Reference to a Deity

In a number of cultures, a frequent component of the startle response includes unthinkingly exclaiming the name or title of a deity.[5] The museum, however, has surprisingly few examples; it seems to be a behavior that writers tend to avoid describing. The following example is the verbal part of a startle response used to exemplify dropping or flinging objects in Chapter 2, p. 24.

"Jesus Christ!" said James. (Redmond O'Hanlon, 1984, *Into the Heart of Borneo*, p. 140)

The exclaimed god name or title is often modified slightly, which mitigates the offense against propriety. Thus "Jesus!" may be modified to "[J]Cheese and crackers! and, as in the translated example below, "Lord!" to "Lordy!"[6] When this is done, the modification is on a syllable other than the first; the first syllable appears to be harder to control.

Suddenly she reached out her hand and touched him. "Lordy!" she said, sincerely startled, and that was all she could say. (Gabriel García Márquez, 1967, *One Hundred Years of Solitude* [original in Spanish], p. 26)

In the next example, the improper reference to a deity is the eighteenth century (and earlier) curse, "God's wounds!," often dampened down to "Zounds!" Here a hot chestnut has just rolled down into "a hiatus" in Phutatorius's breeches:

"Zounds!— — — — — — — — — — — — — — — — — —
— —   — — — — — — — — — — — — — — — —   — — — — —
— — — — — — — —   — — — — — — — —   — — — — — —
— — — — — — — — — — — — —   –Z——ds!   cried Phutatorius. . . ."

The dashes are in the original; Laurence Sterne, the author, uses them to signify naughty talk. Sterne explains:

[T]he soul of Phutatorius, together with all his ideas, his thoughts, his attention, his imagination, judgement, resolution, delibera-tion, ratiocination, memory, fancy, with ten battalions of animal spirits, all tumultuously crowded down, through different defiles and circuits, to the place in danger, leaving all his upper regions, as you may imagine, as empty as air. (1759, *Tristram Shandy*, p. 318)

3. Idiosyncratically Stereotyped Thought or Utterance

A person's spoken (or thought) response to certain startling stimuli may be idiosyncratically stereotypic, like other stereotyped startle responses. In the next exhibit Oliver Wendell Holmes describes how for him a particular stimulus generates a stereotypic mental response even in a grossly inappropriate context:

Now, the sloop-of-war the *Wasp* . . . had disappeared from the face of the ocean, and was supposed to be lost. . . . Let me make a clean breast of it now . . . [and even though the sloop disappeared when I was a boy and I am now full grown] . . . when the roar of the cannon has struck suddenly on my ear, I have started with a thrill of vague expectation and tremulous delight, and the long-unspoken words have articulated themselves in the mind's dull whisper, The Wasp has come! (Oliver Wendell Holmes, 1858, *The Autocrat of the Breakfast Table*, p. 185)

The next exhibit also asserts that a startle may instantly take you back to an earlier time of life:

You hit the bump and see George Washington's face on the schoolroom wall and hear the Nicene Creed, "I believe in one God the Father Almighty, Maker of heaven and earth, and of all things visible and invisible," and smell tunafish casserole. (Garrison Keillor, 1987, *Leaving Home*, p. 24)

One might speculate how a certain frequently repeated behavior typical of dentists generates the response in the next exhibit:

My dentist tells me that sometimes when he runs into another person while trying to get through a door he finds himself saying, "Open, please!" instead of "Excuse me!" (Rudolf Arnheim, 1990, quoted in *American Scientist*, 78, p. 266)

4. Secret or Hidden Thought

After a startle, a person may blurt out a secret, especially if the secret is laden with emotion.

Elizabeth made desperate efforts to find out; she sprang all sorts of Jack-in-the-box questions on Lucia in the hope that she would startle her into revealing the unknown destination. (E. F. Benson, 1935, *The Worshipful Lucia*, p. 294)

But then there was a *bang* in the fireplace. Steam had to escape from a trap in a sappy log.

Yes, and Mother, because she was a symphony of chemical reactions like all other living things, gave a terrified shriek. Her chemicals insisted that she shriek in response to the *bang*.

After the chemicals got her to do that, though, they wanted a lot more from her. They thought it was high time she said what she really felt about Eliza and me, which she did. Her hands closed convulsively. Her spine buckled and her face shriveled to turn her into an old, old witch.

"I hate, them, I hate them, I hate them," she said. (Kurt Vonnegut, 1976, *Slapstick*, p. 66)

Not only Mother's statement but also her bodily expression leak the secret thought.

5. Disorganized Talk

Sometimes the speech after a startle is disorganized, with incongruent words or phrases and sometimes grammatical infractions. In the following exhibits, a sports writer and a cartoonist use this fact humorously:

When human approaches to within 3 feet, grouse erupts with a great thundering of wings. Flight path carries it within 6 inches of human's nose. Human gasps. Noise, violent swirling of dry leaves, and confusion ensue. Human turns a sickly off-white. Grouse disappears behind trunk of large tree in .89 seconds. Human begins babbling incoherently about mortgage rates and college tuition credits. ("Ruffled Grouse Ruffles Human," *Lansing State Journal*, October 21, 1984)

A cartoon in four panels: A balding, male "born-loser" type is dozing at his office desk. Standing behind him, his vigorous, well-dressed boss imitates a woman's voice (there are musical notes sprinkled over and under the text): saying "Honey, aren't you up yet, you'll be late for work." In the next two panels, the dozer replies sleepily, as if at home, in bed, and to his wife. In the last panel, having caught sight of the boss, he springs to the top of a filing cabinet (movement lines and a little puff of cloud at the seat just vacated), and sweating he shouts: "Ho! Judas Priest on a pony, sir!" ("Graves, Inc.," in *Seattle Times*, October 8, 1981)

G. Matching

Matching the actions or speech of others after being startled is one of the defining characteristics of *latah* and the other startle-matching syndromes, many examples of which are given in Chapters 8 to 10. Although it is much less common in other contexts, the museum has a few examples. In the first, from England, the startled speaker who echoes the words he has just heard is "Eccles," a somewhat retarded, stock comic character in the old B.B.C. Goon shows:

NEDDIE SEAGOON: Now long lad, tell me where can I hire a ship to take me to Africa?

ECCLES: Ah, where can you hire a ship to take you to Africa? Uh-hum, yah. Well let me see. I know some fellers. I know these fellers, yep. Umm, let me see. Jim Crunja, nope not him, nope. He comes like a wood. . . . I know another fellah. Ah. Oh. Oh. Oh. Um. Yea. There's a fellah in Bedford. Oh no, not him. This shouldn't be difficult, you know, this shouldn't be difficult. I once caught quite a few fellahs. . . . Now let me think now. (pause) What was the question again?

NEDDIE SEAGOON [a sudden startling shout]:   You idiot, Eccles!

ECCLES[immediately]:   You idiot, Eccles!
("The White Box of Great Bardfield," *The Goon Show* [radio program], May 2, 1977)

In the Woody Allen movie *Sleeper*, Woody (the hero) and Diane (the heroine) have just made a discovery of earth-shaking dimensions. They are in disguise and in imminent danger of detection and capture by sinister opponents. Their extreme nervous arousal is dramatically exaggerated in their jerky movements and in their rapid, breathless, urgent speech:

WOODY: I dropped the radio!

DIANE: You dropped the radio?

WOODY: It fell out of my pocket when I was hanging out the window.

DIANE: It fell out of your pocket when you were hanging out the. . . .

WOODY: Will you stop repeating everything I say?

DIANE: Will you stop repeating everything I say?

WOODY: Get a grip on yourself! (1973)

Such verbal matching probably occurs frequently but unremarkably in everyday life. Once Gunter Pfaff and Betsy Shipley, the filmmaker and sound recordist with whom I worked were sitting on the front steps of our home in Malaysia. Betsy said, "She went into the house, you get her this time." Gunter, speaking simultaneously, began a sentence with "That was more of a normal . . . ," at which point there was a loud squawk from a chicken. Startled, he finished the sentence with the word "house."

Although the context makes it clear that he had meant to say "night," being startled induced him somehow to extract the word "house" from the sentence that he had just heard and insert it in his own. As Gunter and Betsy were speaking at the same time, his use of the word immediately followed hers.

In the next exhibit, which is from Japan, action rather than speech is matched. It is from the same Kabuki play, *Yasaku no Kamabara*, which was cited earlier.

> Two brothers are talking, one a samurai, the other a farmer. The samurai is holding a knife, the farmer, a writing brush. When the samurai makes a sudden, unexpected gesture with the knife as if to stab himself, the farmer brother, startled, stabs at himself with the brush. (Nakawa Shimesuke [1791], as performed at the Kabuki-za Theater, Tokyo, April 18, 1978)

H. Obedience

As Chapters 7 to 10 will show, hyperstartling persons will sometimes obey commands they might otherwise ignore. However, because a just-startled person can obey an order only if he or she is given one, obedience can only be a response to being startled if another person issues a command. Issuing commands to hyperstartlers is common in the cultural settings discussed in Chapters 8 through 10, and as Chapter 7 demonstrates, it also occurs, though uncommonly, in the West. As yet, the museum has no exhibits showing Western literary or other artistic use of this phenomenon. For actual Western exhibits, see Chapter 7.

III. STATES IN WHICH PERSONS STARTLE ESPECIALLY READILY AND VIOLENTLY

Though everyone startles, as shown in previous chapters, there are certain states in which people startle especially readily and violently. This fact is a rich resource for narrative elaboration.

A. When Ill or Debilitated

> Now, dear Sir, what if ... tho' terror of it, natural to so young a traveller, my little gentleman had got to his journey's end miserably spent;—his muscular strength and virility worn down to a thread; his own animal spirits ruffled beyond description,—and that in this sad, disorder'd state of nerves, he had laid down a prey to sudden starts. . . . (Laurence Sterne, 1759, *Tristram Shandy*, p. 6)

Sterne's work, which was immensely popular in its day, is "naughty"; he says things that are universally known but not usually spoken about. Here the "little gentleman, so young a traveller" is a distressed spermatozoon. Sterne apparently believed (and apparently believed that his readers believed), that debility made one "a prey to sudden starts."

As part of an "experiment" in Wilkie Collins's *The Moonstone*, debility is intentionally produced by sleep deprivation and by stopping heavy smoking:

> He is this afternoon in a state of nervous sensitiveness which stops just short of nervous irritation. He changes color readily; his hand is not quite steady; and he starts at chance noises and at unexpected appearances of persons and things. (Wilkie Collins, 1868, p. 462)

In *A Tale of Two Cities*, the heroine, Lucy Manet, begins to startle excessively because of the strain of the situation in which she finds herself:

> "What is that!" she cried, all at once.
> "My dear!" said her father, stopping in his story, and laying his hand on hers, "command yourself. What a disordered state you are in! The least thing—nothing—startles you. *You*, your father's daughter?" (Charles Dickens, 1859, p. 479)

In the following exhibit from Japan, R. H. Blyth explains that the context makes it clear that Shiki's violent startle to the minimal stimulus of a flower's falling took place during a debilitating illness. Shiki uses the startle to illustrate the extent of his debility.

> A sound at midnight,
>   How I jumped!
> An evening-glory had fallen.
> (Shiki, ca. 1890, in Blyth, 1964, *A History of Haiku, Vol. 2*, p. 90)

Jane Austen also used startling violently to minimal stimuli to signify the lingering effect of a severe illness. Asked if he believes the young woman in question to have recovered, a friend answers:

> He answered rather hesitatingly, "Yes, I believe I do—very much recovered; but she is altered; there is no running or jumping about, no laughing or dancing; it is quite different. If one happens only to shut the door a little hard, she starts and wriggles like a young dabchick in the water. . . ." (Jane Austen, 1818, *Persuasion*, p. 218)

B. When Wary

A startle or readiness to startle can be used by an author to signify wariness, as in the next two exhibits:

She looked round; and as if her eyes had just been opened, she perceived the shades of the forest surrounding her, not so much with gloom, but with a sullen, dumb, menacing hostility. Her heart sank in the engulfing stillness; at that moment she felt the nearness of death breathing on her and on the man with her. If there had been a sudden stir of leaves, the crack of a dry branch, the faintest rustle, she would have screamed aloud. (Joseph Conrad, 1915, *Victory*, p. 396)

Caroline Heftshank, who had just arrived from London, was absolutely petrified with fear of street crime in New York, which she read about every day in London, and she jumped at every shadow, which was funny at first. (Tom Wolfe, 1987, *The Bonfire of the Vanities*, p. 159)

The following exhibit is not fictional but rather is from a news report after a major clampdown on demonstrations by the Chinese government:

China's capital now is barely functioning. People have stopped going to work and students have stopped going to school. Banks are open but most shops are closed and garbage is piling up in the streets. People buying melons and tomatoes from the neighborhood vendor are uncharacteristically quiet, even sullen. They jump at every unexpected sound, and when they do, no one laughs. (*All Things Considered* [radio program], June 7, 1989)

C. When in a State of High Anticipation

When people are in states of high anticipation, they are also especially prone to startle. In the following exhibit, Nathaniel Hawthorne uses a startle to signify just how high anticipation has been. Hepzibah is a gentlewoman whose meager circumstances reduce her to opening a "cent shop." She is waiting for the bell that will signal her first customer and the change of status that encounter will bring.

But at this moment the shop bell, right over her head, tinkled as if it were bewitched. The old gentle-woman's heart seemed to be attached to the same steel spring, for it went through a series of sharp jerks, in unison with the sound.... Hepzibah ... stood at a gaze, with her hands clasped, looking very much as if she had summoned up an evil spirit. (Nathaniel Hawthorne, 1851, *The House of the Seven Gables*, pp. 67–68)

In the next exhibit, with repetition and italics, the author signifies, of course, that the heroine's repeated assertion is not true, she *had* been focusing on the phone: If only he would call! Waiting for the portentous call and startling when the phone rings is a set scene in post–Alexander Graham Bell fiction.

She started every time the phone rang, then got angry at herself; reminding herself that she hadn't expected him to call; it would be *ridiculous* to expect him to call. (Judith Rossner, 1975, *Looking For Mr. Goodbar*, p. 38)

In the next exhibit, Henri Fauconnier uses the relationship between startle and anticipation metaphorically:

. . . like people who screw up their faces when a bottle of champagne is being opened; what upsets them is not the detonation itself, but their uncertainty as to the exact moment when it will take place. (Henri Fauconnier, 1931, *The Soul of Malaya* [original in French], p. 229)

D. When Drowsy, Dozing, or Dropping Off to Sleep

As one dozes or begins to drop off to sleep, the trigger that alerts and focuses attention is set to "sensitive" for an initial period before one falls fully asleep. As when one is warily alert, this is a state of the central nervous system in which the mechanisms controlling attention operate in an altered manner.

Sleep for a long time fled my eyelids; and just as I was beginning to feel quiet stealing over my limbs, and settling densely in my mind, a noise at my head startled me broad awake again, and, I will frankly confess it, brought my heart into my mouth. (Robert Louis Stevenson, 1879, *Travels with a Donkey in the Cevennes*, p. 261)

Because people often enter a scene through a door, and because they can do this suddenly and unexpectedly, in situations in which the subject is drowsy, wary, guilty, anticipating, and so on, a writer can place a sounding device on a door and thereby create a potential startle for one of his or her characters, as in the exhibit from Nathaniel Hawthorne under "When in a state of high anticipation." Pounding on the door works too— for example, the pounding that begins the well-known porter scene in Macbeth. (See under "Guilty" in "Moral Evaluations" in Chapter 5.)

Jane . . . had "dropped-off" as she frequently did on a Sunday afternoon, and her head was drooping over against the back of the chair; her mouth was slightly open too. She had just been reading and somehow this had set her nodding. She was conscious of Flora coming into the room and she seemed to remember that she had said something about having cleaned the bath. . . . After that all was blessed oblivion until the cruel shrilling of the front doorbell startled her into uttering a cry and sitting bolt upright in her chair. (Barbara Pym, 1981, *Jane and Prudence*, p. 60)

E. When Asleep

Most people can recall at least some instances of awakening from sleep with a strong startle. Describing someone's doing so is used by writers in a number of ways. Sometimes the startle is a unique event, occasioned by something special about the stimulus or setting. Sometimes it reflects on the state of mind of the person awakened. Sleeping fitfully and awakening easily with starts has long been associated with disability, wariness, or guilt. Early in the second century A.D., Aretaeus of Cappadocia, who recognized and recorded the association between melancholia and mania, listed starting up from sleep as a symptom of melancholia:

> Those affected with melancholia are not everyone of them affected according to one particular form; they are either suspicious of poisoning or flee to the desert from misanthropy, or turn superstitious, or contract a hatred of life. If at any time a relaxation takes place, in most cases hilarity supervenes. . . . [T]he patients are dull or stern, dejected or unreasonably torpid, without any manifest cause . . . they also become peevish, dispirited, sleepless, and start up from a disturbed sleep. (Aretaeus of Cappadocia, in Goodwin & Guze, 1984, *Psychiatric Diagnosis*, p. 4)

The next two exhibits are from ancient Japan. In the first, Lady Murasaki, an eleventh-century Japanese writer, describes starting up from sleep in a "spooky" setting. In the second, it is a particular feeling tone that is commented on.

> It was growing late. Outside from a gloomy, sodden sky the rain swept across the woods, and the wind howled. A sudden gust shook everything in the house, and Kozeri awoke with a start. (Lady Murasaki, ca. 1020, *The Tale of Genji* [original in Japanese], p. 881)

> [These] meetings in dreams
> How sad they are!
> When, waking up startled
> One gropes about,
> And there is no contact to the hand.
> (Yakamochi, ca. A.D. 760 [original in Japanese], in *Japanese Poetry, The Uta*, p. 34)

The *Robinson Crusoe* and *Treasure Island* exhibits that follow are associated with bad dreams, as in the posttraumatic stress syndrome, discussed later in this chapter.

> The perturbation in my mind, during this fifteen or sixteen months was very great; I slept unquiet, dreamed always frightful

dreams, and often started out of my sleep in the night. (Daniel Defoe, 1719, *Robinson Crusoe*, p. 182)

Oxen and wain-ropes would not bring me back again to that accursed island; and the worst dreams that ever I have are when I hear the surf booming about its coasts, or start upright in bed, with the sharp voice of Captain Flint still ringing in my ears: "Pieces of eight! Pieces of eight!" (Robert Louis Stevenson, 1884, [concluding words of] *Treasure Island*, p. 273)

In a contemporary exhibit, a person writing to Ann Landers uses a hyperbolic description of his response to signify the unexpectedness, inappropriateness, and unpleasantness of being aroused by a ringing telephone in the early morning:

Dear Ann Landers: This morning at 5:45, California time, my phone rang. I peeled myself off the ceiling and answered it. . . . (*Detroit Free Press*, November 2, 1980)

F. When Lost in Thought

Because one may be readily startled when lost in thought, an author may cite a startle to signify just how lost in thought a character is:

It was altogether a confusion of Images & Doubts—a perplexity, an agitation which she could not see the end of—and she was in Gay St. & still so much engrossed, that she started on being addressed by Admiral Croft, as if he were a person unlikely to be met there. It was within a few steps of his own door. (Jane Austen, 1818, *Persuasion*, p. 258)

Lucia's eyes wore a concentrated though far-away expression as if she were absorbed in some train of transcendent reasoning. She gave a little start as Diva spoke, and recalled herself to the High Street. (E. F. Benson, 1935, *The Worshipful Lucia*, p. 46)

In the next exhibit, Miss Brown, a villainous governess, is daydreaming about the fortune that would be hers "if an accident were to happen to Maria."

The vicar startled her from the reverie. (T. H. White, 1946, *Mistress Masham's Repose*, p. 190)

IV. SETTINGS IN WHICH STARTLES ARE LIKELY TO OCCUR

A. Spooky and Dangerous Places

Persons will sometimes startle to otherwise innocuous stimuli if they are presented in settings that are "spooky" or otherwise appear dangerous. The effect is mediated by the neurophysiological state of the subject; in such settings people are especially wary and hyperalert. The museum has a cartoon in which the Born Loser startles right off the top of the panel in such a setting (*Lansing State Journal*, August 29, 1982). Here are a few other exhibits in which a startle occurs in a spooky or dangerous place. In the first, Ursula, a young woman, is alone in a woods:

> The night had fallen, it was dark. . . . She started, noticing something on her right hand, between the tree-trunks. It was like a great presence, watching her, dodging her. She started violently. It was only the moon, risen through the thin trees. (D. H. Lawrence, 1920, *Women in Love*, p. 237)

In the second, the site where the startle occurs is specifically associated with strange and fearsome happenings:

> Uncle Mel Shelton was afraid of no man, beast or devil. But he was afraid when he passed the well where men mysteriously drowned. It was here that something invisible with the flutter of wings came down and lifted Uncle Mel's coal bank cap from his head and put out the flame. Uncle Mel said he jumped four feet high and squealed when it happened. ("Poet's Hollow His Paradise," *Lansing State Journal*, November 8, 1979)

Jizo Bosatsu is a beneficent deity, a protector, especially of children and travelers. The next exhibit, a haiku, makes the point that in a properly spooky setting even a statue of Jizo, the protector, may elicit a startle.

> In the gloom under the trees,
> Jizo
> Gives one a start.
> (Shiki, ca. 1890a [original in Japanese], in Blyth, 1952, *Haiku, Vol. 3*, p. 268)

Blyth notes that Jizo's statue is often set up at crossroads and other lonely places. A Japanese reader would be expected to infer the isolation of the locale. In Japanese, the word order is "Gloom under the trees, startle, Jizo! [It's only Jizo!]" closely paralleling the experience being described.

In the following example the spooky setting is only being read about.

> Dagwood, getting into bed with a book says, "Tonight I get to read my scary chapter. He's tensely intent on reading when Blondie says, "I hear something downstairs." Dagwood sits bolt upright, flinging the book, and in the last panel, from under the bed, says, "It was definitely the wrong time to say that." Blondie, incidentally, apologizes. ("Blondie," cartoon in four panels, *Lansing State Journal*, July 28, 1987)

B. Quiet Places

People startle especially readily and strongly to sounds when they are in places that are exceptionally quiet, even when the silence is unrelated to any sense of menace. A number of factors contribute to this. In quiet places such as churches and theaters people may especially monitor their own behaviors, and sometimes quiet places are associated with drowsiness or with deep introspection or concentrated study. In a setting that is notably quiet, startling stimuli may be especially unexpected. The absence of auditory stimuli just before the stimulus which startles may also sometimes be physiologically significant, as noted in Chapter 1.

> The morning advanced. The heated air grew quite easily hotter. . .; even the insects were too languorous to pipe, the basking lizards hid themselves and panted. It was so still you could have heard the least buzz a mile off. Not a naked fish would willingly move his tail. The ponies advanced because they must. The children ceased even to muse.
>
> They all very nearly jumped out of their skins; for close at hand a crane had trumpeted once desperately. Then the broken silence closed down as flawless as before. (Richard Hughes, 1929, *A High Wind in Jamaica*, p. 16)

V. SENSITIZATION AND HABITUATION

A. Being Frequently Startled May Lead to Hyperstartling

Because examples of sensitization resulting from repeated startling are presented and discussed extensively throughout the book, special exhibits need not be presented here. (For examples of this phenomenon, see especially Chapters 3 and 8.)

B. Severe or Prolonged Trauma May Lead to Hyperstartling

One way a person becomes a hyperstartler is to be repetitively startled. Another is to be placed in an intensely dangerous situation, especially for a prolonged period or repeatedly. After such exposure many people develop some version of what has come to be called the "posttraumatic stress syndrome," which includes hyperstartling among its symptoms. The proximate mechanism for the hyperstartling of both persons who have been repetitively startled and those with posttraumatic stress syndrome may be hypervigilance. Tkachik was a foreman at Chrysler's Eldon Avenue plant in Detroit, where James Johnson killed three men on June 15, 1970.

> Tkachik cried when the telephone rang, screamed at the sound of the doorbell, refused his two daughters' visitors, was terrified of

the back-yard, and went to pieces if a door slammed, his wife reported. ("Husband scared to death," *Lansing State Journal*, February 18, 1980)

While fighting in the jungles of Vietnam's Quang Ngai Province in 1966, Ted Calhoun's infantry unit lost so many men that its flag bore the emblem of a skull and crossbones.

During one search-and-destroy mission, Calhoun's thigh was shredded by an exploding grenade. The wound cost him 20 percent of the muscle movement in his leg.

But shell-shock, the 32-year-old Grand Ledge man said, never caught up with him—at least not during the war.

Today, 14 years after combat, the ex-Marine can't bring himself to blow up balloons for his children. The fear that they'll pop jangles his nerves. ("Viet Vets Relive Horrors," *Lansing State Journal*, August 3, 1980)

Traumatized children continue to startle readily long after their exposure to danger. The first exhibit that follows reports hyperstartling by the classmates of a child who was abducted; the second, hyperstartling by children who were on a school bus that was hijacked.

Melissa's classmates were distraught at school Monday. "Every little noise they'd jump," Johnson said. "They were scared to go outdoors. . . . Some were crying and wondering if they would ever see her again." ("Illinois Village Wary after Girl's Abduction," *Lansing State Journal*, June 5, 1985)

Some children say they are afraid of playing outside. Others jump at sudden noises, while others have experienced nightmares, irritability and aggressiveness. (*Lansing State Journal*, December 7, 1987)

Some persons exploit the propensity to startle of those who have been traumatized for their own amusement, as in the exhibit below:

John Beverly of Waterloo, Wisconsin, has been awarded $86,000 in a workers' compensation suit against the Miller Brewing Company. Here's what John Beverly says happened. Learning that he suffered from posttraumatic stress syndrome, a disorder shared by many veterans of the Viet Nam War, his co-workers began to create situations to which Beverly would react. For two years, the suit alleges, Miller employees dropped tables, broke beer bottles, popped milk cartons, and set off fireworks and watched their coworker hit the deck. After a couple of years John Beverly quit. He sued and won. (*All Things Considered* [radio program], June 21, 1989)

C. Familiarity with a Stimulus May Reduce the Likelihood of Startling to Its Presentation and May Reduce the Violence of the Response when It Occurs

Sometimes a person may fail to startle to a stimulus that would startle most people because he or she has encountered it often and is thus unusually accustomed to it. This observation suggests the question: Why does repeated exposure to a stimulus sometimes lead to habituation and sometimes to sensitivity? Why do some people, under some circumstances, become accustomed to a stimulus and cease to startle when it appears, whereas others respond by startling more and more readily and violently? Aunt Sally never did get used to those snakes, and the entomologist, Fabre, continued to startle to the strike of a praying mantis even though he had seen it many times. However, under some circumstances, some people do habituate. Here are some exhibits illustrating habituation as the result of familiarity.

After his crime Macbeth has been startling especially easily, something that both he and those about him have noticed. But by the last act of the play, in the collapse of his bloody rule, he observes that stimuli that once would have elicited startles no longer affect him. It is a sign of his moral decay.[7] At the very end of the act, just before the final battle, the court women cry out, signaling the death of Lady Macbeth. Unaffected, Macbeth observes:

> The time has been, my senses would have
>   cool'd
> To hear a night-shriek. . . .
> [but now] I have supped full with horrors;
> Direness, familiar to my slaughterous
>   thoughts,
> Cannot once start me.
> (William Shakespeare, 1606, *Macbeth*, Act V, scene v)

In the following exhibit, contrary to expectation, a lawyer startles. The phrase, "Lawyer as he was" means that it might have been expected that he should not have, because as a lawyer he should have heard much before of violence, betrayal, and horror. The fact that he now startles is used to signify just how very unexpected the news is.

> Lawyer as he was to the very marrow of his bones, I startled him
> out of his professional composure. (Wilkie Collins, *The Moonstone*,
> 1860, p. 375)

VI. MISCELLANEOUS OTHER EXPOSITORY USES OF STARTLE'S BIOLOGY

The concluding section of the museum contains exhibits in which writers make use of two further aspects of the physiology of the reflex.

A. Stimuli in any Modality May Elicit Startles

Stimuli in most of the exhibits in the museum are tactile, auditory, or visual. But since stimuli in any sensory modality may startle, the museum has a few examples of startling to a unexpected taste and an unexpected temperature.

In the next three exhibits a writer refers to a taste that startles, either actually or metaphorically.

> General Loewenhiem, somewhat suspicious of his wine, took a sip of it, startled, raised the glass first to his nose and then to his eyes, and sat it down bewildered. "This is very strange!" he thought. "Amontillado!" (Isak Dinesen, 1953, "Babette's Feast," *Anecdotes of Destiny*, p. 35)

> Lace this [sauteed finely chopped mushrooms] into mashed rutabaga for a startling good flavor combination. (James Beard, "Turnip at root of good taste," *Detroit News*, September 19, 1979)

> Chunn . . . also was startled by the light taste of the dark beer. (*Lansing State Journal*, July 27, 1988)

An unexpected encounter with cold is the stimulus that startles in the next exhibit in which untraveled tropical villagers encounter a manufactured block of ice. The author uses the startle to signify unsophistication.

> Jose Arcadia Buendia paid them and put his hand on the ice and held it there as his heart filled with fear and jubilation at the contact with mystery. . . . Aurelio . . . took a step forward and put his hand on it, withdrawing it immediately. "It's boiling," he exclaimed, startled. (Gabriel García Márquez, 1967, *One Hundred Years of Solitude* [original in Spanish], p. 18)

In the next exhibit, startling at the touch of unexpected cold is used metaphorically:

> "Twenty times," adds Chesterton, "we have taken Dickens' hand and it has been sometimes hot with revelry and sometimes weak with weariness; but this time we start a little, for it is inhumanly cold; and then we realize that we have touched his gauntlet of steel." (Dingle Foot, 1955, in the Introduction to *Hard Times*, *New Oxford Illustrated Dickens*, p. i)

B. Animals Startle to Equivalent Stimuli in Equivalent Ways

Because startle is generally understood to be a physiological phenomenon, many writers describe animals' startling to much the same sorts of stimuli as humans.

White said his life may have been saved by the lion's roar, because the startled tiger jumped and went the other way. ("Police Kill Escaped Tiger," *Lansing State Journal*, December 26, 1978)

"When Zed [a dog] saw the front gate he began to run on towards it, but was startled by George's turning and his threatening gesture. (Iris Murdoch, 1983, *The Philosopher's Pupil*, p. 249)

In a newspaper pet advice column, "Dr. Miller Advises," a veterinarian offers advice about an upcoming holiday:

Time's running out to prepare your pooch for a typical bang-up Fourth of July. Some canines will ignore loud, sudden noises unless they're close enough to physically batter sensitive eardrums. Most others can cope . . . without losing their canine cool.

But then there's that substantial group that becomes completely unstrung with the first firecracker. Those Nervous Nellies. . . . (*Seattle Post Intelligencer*, July 23, 1987)

Note the contemptuous negative evaluation, "Nervous Nellies." A feature on "What to do with your dog on July Fourth" is run in many newspapers each year when the holiday comes round. An exhibit from the *Lansing State Journal* of July 4, 1991, noted that

While humans enjoy the bright colors exploding across the skies this holiday week, many dogs will be doing their best to keep from going crazy.

It suggested boarding vulnerable dogs at a "well insulated kennel," or consulting a veterinarian "who can prescribe a mild tranquilizer." Dogs that cannot be trained to habituate to the sound of a gun's firing are called "gunshy" and cannot be used as hunting partners.

Even more than is the case with dogs, easy startling is problematic in horses. Easily startled horses are often referred to as "skittish." In the next exhibit, which is from Japan, the poet Shiki cites a startle as evidence that a horse, like a human, experiences a withered moor as a place to be wary. The withered moor ("kareno" in Japanese), a sad and spooky place, is a set subject in haiku poetry:

A bird flies up,
   The pack horse shies,
The withered moor.
(Shiki, ca. 1890b [original in Japanese], in Blyth, 1954, *Haiku, Vol. 4*, p. 278)

R.H. Blyth, the translator and editor, comments on the sudden motion: "The driver is startled in his turn." See the parallel human version by Issa under "Sudden Moves."

In the next exhibit, Dickens's character (Sam Weller) is shown to believe that horses, like humans, startle to the unexpected, the horse he is renting to Pickwick, of course, being an exception. Pickwick is hiring a horse:

> "He doesn't shy, does he?" inquired Mr. Pickwick.
>
> "Shy, Sir?—He wouldn't shy if he was to meet a vagin-load of monkeys, with their tails burnt off."
>
> The last recommendation was indisputable. (Charles Dickens, 1837, *Posthumous Papers of the Pickwick Club*, p. 60)

The belief that unexpected events startle animals is stated explicitly by Wister in *The Virginian*:

> I am convinced that any community which shares some of our instincts will share some of the resulting feelings, and that birds and beasts have conventions, the breach of which startles them. If there be anything in evolution, this would seem inevitable. (Owen Wister, 1902, *The Virginian*, p. 77)

SUMMARY AND CONCLUDING COMMENTS

Because the properties of startle penetrate so deeply into the fabric of our culture (perhaps all cultures), the startle reflex is a major resource for writers and other creative artists. By referring to a startle, one can convey an enormous range of meanings, among them the loudness of a sound, the brightness of a light, the beauty of a man, woman, flower or mountain, guilt, wariness, danger, nobility, unexpectedness, and aesthetic sensibility. Startle is such a rich and varied resource precisely because all of its minute and specific aspects are available for expository use. The museum has been arranged to show that these minute and specific aspects are indeed used.

Culturally determined meanings and values shape every exhibit. Nevertheless, the museum collection demonstrates that evolved biology is also a shaping factor. So many of the exhibits make physiological sense that it is hard to come up with a tenable alternative hypothesis. The properties of startle are embedded in a complex net of meaning that includes culture-typical notions of gender, of status, of propriety, of love, and of hate. Sometimes objects or events are referred to as startling because of their properties, sometimes because of their effects. Sometimes the meaning is ambiguous, and often both properties and effects are referred to. I was surprised to discover that references to startle often had multiple determinants, two or more aspects of the reflex being relevant to what is being asserted. Sometimes the inference to be drawn from an exhibit is available only because a startle-precipitated violation of some culture-typical convention makes that convention visible.

Most of the exhibits are American or English and contemporary; only a small number are from non-Western contexts or remote times. What the selection currently available demonstrates is ubiquity, not universality; certainly not all aspects of the reflex are used in the same way in all places or at all times. But the limited data available do show a surprising cross-cultural consensus about what the startle reflex is like, and many of the meanings that a reference to startle can convey appear to be widespread. It would be useful to make systematic, extensive single-culture collections and then sort and compare them, but this work has yet to be done. The list of categories used here might be taken as an initial search list. It is extensive but not exhaustive; work in other cultural settings would undoubtedly suggest others.

The exhibits are representative of a much larger corpus, which cannot be presented. This is inevitable. As in all museums, there is only a limited amount of display space, and the boxes in the basement contain some lovely exhibits.

NOTES

1. In *Proverbs and Common Sayings from the Chinese*, (1914), Arthur Smith lists the five "noxious animals": "the Snake, the Scorpion, the Frog, the Centipede, and the Lizard." Interestingly, the lizard is associated with thunderclaps.

2. *Failure* to startle to a dangerous object does, of course, discriminate one from the general run of beings (see Chapter 5).

3. In a poll of readers of *The Lansing State Journal*, "The Born Loser" was judged the most popular and the most often read of the 23 cartoons carried, ahead of "Peanuts," which was second and "Garfield," which also frequently contains startles and which was third (June 8, 1987).

4. In cartoons, another frequent icon for startle is a hat flying off vertically or off to one side.

5. See, for example, the account in Chapter 8 of a Malay informant's blurting out "Allah!" after being startled.

6. There is no "Lord!" or "Lordy!" in the Spanish original, which reads: "'Qué bárbaro,' dijo, sinceramente asustada, y fue todo lo que pudo decir." (Gabriel García Márquez, 1967, *Cien Años de Soledad*, p. 28) ["'How barbarous,' she said, sincerely having received a *susto*, and that was all that she could say."] For a discussion of *susto*, see Chapter 4.

7. See the Macbeth entries under "Guilty" in the previous chapter. Shakespeare's use of startle in *Macbeth* is quite wonderful. Earlier in the play, startles have revealed Macbeth's secret ambition and his guilty conscience. Now his failure to startle turns out to be equally significant. Context, the circumstances under which he startles or fails to, identifies the significance intended.

REFERENCES

Adams, D. (1990). *The long dark tea-time of the soul*. New York: Simon & Schuster, Pocket Books.

Addison, J. (1713). "Cato," in *Bartlett's Familiar Quotations* (1955). Boston: Little, Brown.

Aretaeus of Cappadocia. (ca. A.D. 100–200). In D.W. Goodwin & S.B. Guze (Eds.). (1984), *Psychiatric diagnosis* (3rd ed). New York: Oxford University Press.

Arnold, E. (1882). *The light of Asia*. Boston: Roberts Brothers.

Austen, J. 1818/1971. *Persuasion*. In R. W. Chapman, (Ed.), *The Oxford illustrated Jane Austen*. Oxford: Oxford University Press.

Bellow, S. (1984). *Him with his foot in his mouth and other stories*. New York: Harper & Row.

Benedict, R. (1934). *Patterns of culture*. Boston: Houghton Mifflin.

Benson, E.F. 1935/1984. *The worshipful Lucia*. New York: Harper & Row.

Bird, I. 1879/1982. *A lady's life in the Rocky Mountains*. London: Virago Press.

Burton, R. 1885/1932. In Bennet Cerf (Ed.), *The Arabian nights' entertainment; or, The book of a thousand nights and a night*. New York: Blue Ribbon Books.

Carroll, L. 1893/1965. *Sylvie and Bruno concluded*. In *The works of Lewis Carroll*. London: Hamlyn.

Cellini, B. 1560/1961. *The autobiography of Benvenuto Cellini*. New York: Dodd, Mead.

Chute, C. (1985). *The beans of Egypt, Maine*. New York: Warner Books.

Collins, W. 1868/1903. *The moonstone*. New York: Century.

Conrad, J. 1915/1918. *Victory*. Garden City, NY: Doubleday, Page & Co.

Defoe, D. 1719/1968. *The life and adventures of Robinson Crusoe*. Boston: Houghton Mifflin.

Dickens, C. 1837/1948. *Posthumous papers of the Pickwick Club: New Oxford illustrated Dickens*. Oxford: Oxford University Press.

Dickens, C. 1859/1908. *A tale of two cities*. New York: Merrill.

Dillard, A. (1974). *Pilgrim at Tinker Creek*. New York: Bantam.

Dinesen, I. 1953/1988. *Babette's feast: And other anecdotes of destiny*. New York: Random House.

Doctorow, E.L. (1985) *World's fair*. New York: Random House.

Everett, M. (n.d., early 1900s). *Startling experiences*. Chicago: The Educational Company.

Fauconnier, H. 1931/1965. *The soul of Malaya* (Eric Sutton, Trans.). Kuala Lumpur, London: Oxford University Press.

Flaubert, G. 1857/1991. *Madame Bovary* (F. Steegmuller, Trans.). New York: Quality Paperback Book Club.

Foot, D. (1955). Introduction to *Hard times. New Oxford illustrated Dickens*. London: Oxford University Press.

García Márquez, G. 1967/1987. *Cien años de Soledad*. Bogota: La Oveja Negra.

García Márquez, G. 1985/1989. *Love in the time of cholera* (E. Grossman, Trans.). New York: Penguin.

García Márquez, G. 1967/1970. *One hundred years of solitude* (G. Rabassa, Trans.). New York: Harper & Row.

Goffman, E. (1963). Behavior in public places. Glencoe, IL.: Free Press of Glencoe.

Hawthorne, N. 1851/1960. *The house of the seven gables*. New York: Dell.

Holmes, O.W. 1858/1955. *The autocrat of the breakfast table*. New York: Heritage Press.

Horace. ca. 70 B.C./1964. *The odes of Horace* (J. Michie, Trans.). London: Rupert-Davis.

Hughes, R. 1929/1976. *A high wind in Jamaica*. St. Albans, England: Triad/Panther.

Issa. In R.H. Blyth. 1800/1949. *Haiku* (Vol. 1). Tokyo: Hokuseido Press.

Kenkabo. In R.H. Blyth. 1930/1960. *Japanese life and character in Senryu*. Tokyo: Hokuseido Press.

Keilor, G. (1987). *Leaving home*. New York: Viking.

Krieger, L.C. *The mushroom handbook* (2d ed.). In V.J. Marteka (Ed.). (1980). *Mushrooms, wild and edible: A seasonal guide to the most easily recognized mushrooms*. New York: Norton.

Lakoff, G. (1987). *Women, fire, and dangerous things*. Chicago: University of Chicago Press.

Lawrence, D.H. 1915/1976. *The rainbow*. New York: Penguin.

Lawrence, D.H. 1920/1976. *Women in love*. New York: Penguin.

Marquis, D. 1922/1939. *The best of Don Marquis*. Garden City, NY: Garden City Books.

Morgan, L.H. (1877). *Ancient society*. New York: Holt and Company.

Mukerji, D.G. (1923). *Jungle beasts and men*. New York: Dutton.

Murasaki, S. ca. 1020/1977. *The tale of Genji*. (A. Waley, Trans.). New York: Knopf.

Murdoch, I. (1983). *The philosopher's pupil*. New York: Viking.

O'Hanlon, R. (1984). *Into the heart of Borneo*. New York: Vintage Books.

Orwell, G. 1934/1962. *Burmese days*. New York: Time Books.

Proust, M. 1913/1928. *Swann's way* (S. Moncrief, Trans.). New York: The Modern Library.

Pym, B. (1981). *Jane and Prudence*. New York: Harper & Row, Perennial Library.

Rossner, J. (1975). *Looking for Mr. Goodbar*. New York: Simon & Schuster.

Saint Exupery, A. de. (1943). *The little prince* (K. Woods, Trans.). New York: Reynal and Hitchcock.

Santaro. In R.H. Blyth. 1930/1960. *Japanese life and character in Senryu*. Tokyo: Hokuseido Press.

Sengai. In L. Stryk (Ed. and Trans.), 1800/1985 *On love and barley: Haiku of Basho*. Honolulu: University of Hawaii Press.

Shiki. In R.H. Blyth. ca. 1890a/1952. *Haiku* (Vol. 2). Tokyo: Hokuseido Press.

Shiki. In R.H. Blyth. ca. 1890b/1954. *Haiku* (Vol. 4). Tokyo: Hokuseido Press.

Shiki. In R.H. Blyth. ca. 1890c/1964. *A history of haiku* (Vol. 2). Tokyo: Hokuseido Press.

Smith, A. 1914/1965. *Proverbs and common sayings from the Chinese*. New York: Dover.

Steinbeck, J. (1962). *Travels with Charley*. New York: Viking.

Sterne, L. 1759/1983. *The life and opinions of Tristram Shandy*. London, New York: Oxford University Press.

Stevenson, R.L. 1884/1981. *Treasure Island*. New York: Scribner's.

Stevenson, R.L. 1879/1924. *Travels with a donkey in the Cevennes*. London: Macmillan.

Swift, G. (1983). *Waterland*. London: Heinemann.

Tyler, A. (1985). *The accidental tourist*. New York: Knopf.

Tylor, E.B. (1871). *Primitive culture: Researches into the development of mythology, philosophy religion, language, art and custom*. London: J. Murray.

Vonnegut, K. (1976). *Slapstick: Or lonesome no more*. London: J. Cape.

White, K.S.A. (1979). *Onward and upward in the garden*. New York: Farrar, Strauss, Giroux.

White, L. (1949). *The science of culture: A study of man and civilization*. New York: Farrar, Strauss.

White, T.H. (1946). *Mistress Masham's repose*. New York: G. P. Putnam's Sons.

White, T.H. (1977). *The book of Merlyn: The unpublished conclusion to The once and Future King*. Austin: University of Texas Press.

Wister, O. (1902). *The Virginian*. New York: Macmillan.

Wolfe, T. (1987). *The bonfire of the vanities*. New York: Farrar, Strauss, Giroux.

Wordsworth, W. 1800/1935. "Strange fits of passion I have known." In Sir Ifor Evans (Ed.), *Selections from William Wordworth*. London: Methuen Educational.

Yakamochi. (ca. A.D. 760) In A. Waley (Trans.). 1919/1946. *Japanese poetry: The "Uta."* London: Humphries.

Part II

LATAH AND OTHER STARTLE-MATCHING SYNDROMES

7

ATTENTION CAPTURE AND THE STARTLE-MATCHING SYNDROMES

We can no more decide what we pay attention to than we can decide whom we will love.

Jerome Barkow, *Darwin, Sex, and Status*, 1989, p. 117

RCS: *Tell me what it feels like after you've been startled.*
MH: *It's such an intense thing, and I feel like I'm so aware—you know, I just feel like all my resources are zeroed in at this one moment.*

Mary Haskell, 1977, interview

THE CAPTURE OF ATTENTION

I write this on a bright summer day, sitting on a bench and looking at a brightly lit green scene with trees, flowers, a path, and butterflies. Intermittently, a red-winged blackbird, song sparrows, and goldfinches sing or call. The bench is hard and a bit uncomfortable, and I feel it in my back and buttocks. Sitting here with drifting thoughts, I find my attention drawn repeatedly to a deep blue clump of delphiniums. In a visual world of mostly green, over and over again my eyes are attracted to that intense blue. After a while I realize that I am staring and that I have become less and less aware of the other sights, sounds, and kinesthetic sensations equally available to me. My attention has been both drawn to and filled by this one stimulus, the blue delphiniums. However, although my attention is held by the delphiniums, other stimuli claim it from time to time, and when I want to I can direct it elsewhere.

At other times stimuli are more compelling. Sometimes one's attention may be so captured by a stimulus that it is difficult or impossible to turn away. A suddenly appearing truck or tiger may do this or a very powerful or sexually attractive person, or something awesome. I have suggested the term "attention-capture" to denote this experience (Simons, 1980); other terms used for it include "enthrallment" and "fascination," especially in their adjectival forms: "enthralling" and "fascinating." "Arresting" and "spellbinding" are also sometimes used. A person whose attention has been captured is in some contexts said to be "rapt."[1]

"Enthrallment" is a revealing term. The word "thrall" is derived from old Germanic terms for slaves, bondsmen, and servants. "To enthrall" is defined in *Webster's New International Dictionary* (1960) as:

> 1. To hold in thrall or reduce to the condition of a thrall. 2. To charm or captivate; to hold spellbound.

Only the second derived meaning is in current usage, but it holds within it the first: one whose will is not free, who is subject to the commands of another. "Spellbound" is defined simply as "Bound as or by a spell; fascinated." "To fascinate" in turn is defined (again in *Webster*) as:

> 1. To bewitch, to enchant, to cast a spell over [marked as obsolete]. 2. To grip the attention of, especially so as to deprive of power to move, act or think for oneself; to hold spellbound, as by some irresistible charm, as a serpent *fascinates* its prey. "Bunsby dropping like a *fascinated* bird into the jaws of Mrs. Max MacStinger," G.B. Shaw. To allure and hold intent, especially by qualities that charm, etc.

Many of the stimuli that capture attention may also induce startles, depending on whether one comes upon them gradually or abruptly. Other attention-capturing stimuli rarely startle; for example, repetitive rhythmic sounds or motions: ocean waves, fountains, certain kinds of drumming, and the back-and-forth motion of mechanical devices.

Something may capture attention not because of its properties but rather because of its significance, just as it may be the significance rather than the properties of a stimulus that induces a startle. This significance may be idiosyncratic or it may be shared, sometimes widely within a culture, sometimes ubiquitously in many cultures. Although there are enormous commonalities, what attracts or captures the attention of one person is not always something that would attract or capture the attention of another. Both trait and state characteristics of the subject are important in determining whether attention-capture will occur, and if it does, how enthralling that capture of attention will be.

Attention-Capture May Paralyze

Attention-capture paralysis must be familiar to everyone: Surely everyone has been stopped in his or her tracks by some attention-capturing stimulus at least once, and memorably. As in the case of the term "startle," attention-capture-induced paralysis is also often referred to metaphorically. The dictionary excerpt above gives both an actual example of fascination and an example of its metaphoric use.

An example of a metaphoric use is Abraham Lincoln's 1862 exhortation to the American Congress in which he used the phrase "we must disenthrall ourselves" in a call to action. An overwhelmingly complex and frightening situation had paralyzed the country's ability to react:

> The dogmas of the quiet past are inadequate to the stormy present. The occasion is piled high with difficulty, and we must rise with the occasion. As our case is new, so we must think anew and act anew. We must disenthrall ourselves, and then we shall save our country. (Abraham Lincoln, November 24, 1862)

Space and the fact that I have not extensively collected literary references to attention-capture permit the inclusion of only a few exhibits of attention-capture paralysis and of attention-capture's other common sequelae. Those that follow were selected to suggest the cultural consensus on attention-capture's form and properties. Note the variety of contexts in which the concept is used.

In the first, the stimulus is an enthralling sound, a powerful countertenor voice:

> He sang now with his full voice, with all its high weird slightly husky penetrating force. . . . The sound of his voice filled the garden and made it resonate like a drum. . . .
>
> The effect on the revellers was indeed that of an enchantment. They became, of course, instantly silent. . . . And they stood where they were, as still as statues, some even in the attitude in which the music had surprised them, kneeling on one knee or holding up a hand. (Iris Murdoch, 1983, *The Philosopher's Pupil*, p. 395)

In the next exhibit, a sports writer describes the effect on her of catching sight of a monster trout. The fish is a great prize and has some affinities as a stimulus with snakes and creepy-crawlies.

> A dark specter in the shadow of the bridge, hovering a foot or so above bottom. . . . His tail moved methodically back and forth, otherwise he was motionless.
>
> He was monstrous. We froze for a moment, mouths partly open, rod and reel hanging forgotten in our hands. Then our

senses returned. (Deb Pozega Pierce, "Grit and a Hollow Victory,"
Lansing State Journal, July 7, 1980)

The next exhibit is "appalling." Following the awful bellowing of a
cow, Erland and a cowherd come across a bear devouring a cow. Appalling
sights often startle, but they may also capture attention even without startling. The stimulus is

> a shaggy mass that turned into a bear with red hot opened maw.
> . . . Then the man snatched Erland's [spear] from him, for he stood
> palsied [paralyzed] by horror. The heifer lay there still living, but
> udder and thighs were eaten away. (Sigrid Undset, 1920, *Kristin
> Lavransdatter, II* [original in Norwegian], p. 73)[2]

Attention-capture, startle, and fluster can also be induced by high
degrees of beauty or sexual attractiveness. Gustave Flaubert, for example,
refers to this phenomenon in describing the effect on an adolescent boy of
looking at Madame Bovary:

> For he would be standing there, his hands at his sides and his eye's
> staring, as though a sudden revery had tied him to the spot with a
> thousand strands. (Gustave Flaubert, 1857, *Madame Bovary* [orig-
> inal in French], p. 305)

In the next exhibit, from a newspaper cartoon in two panels, such a
beauty devastates a group of young soldiers:

> In the first panel one of the soldiers is asked, "Did Miss Buxley [a
> young woman of unusual beauty] just walk by here wearing a
> bikini on her way to the pool?" In the second we see that he is
> standing with his foot in a bucket of paint. The seven other sol-
> diers shown in the panel are all stupefied, startled, or otherwise
> massively affected. One has fallen down a ladder, one who had
> been aiming a sledgehammer at a stake held by another has missed
> it and instead hit his helper on the head, etc. ("Beetle Bailey,"
> *Lansing State Journal*, April 30, 1979)

We deduce that Miss Buxley has indeed come by. A recent feature in
the London *Sunday Times* cites both actual and metaphoric examples of
this, a visit to London by the "legendary beauty," Elizabeth Taylor:

> Nor is it a simple case of the aura of celebrity and money. Eliza-
> beth [Taylor] has much more going for her than that.
>   Faced with her legendary beauty, brave men—and women—
> crumble, as we saw all week. . . . Captains of industry trip over
> their feet, intellectual giants mumble their words, studio heads

spill their drinks. So I suppose I should have been more understanding on Tuesday when London ground to a halt . . . because
Liz Was Having Lunch. (Sally Burton, *The Sunday Times* [Lon-
don], November 10, 1991)

ATTENTION-CAPTURE MAY INDUCE APPROACH

When attention is captured, it is not only mental activity that is affected.
Sometimes all movement ceases, as in most of the examples above, but
sometimes the person whose attention has been captured orients to and
moves irresistibly toward the arresting stimulus. In classical mythology,
the singing of Orpheus was so enthralling that even trees, rocks, and rivers
were drawn toward it. The Sirens of the Mediterranean used their beauty
and the beauty of their singing to fascinate seamen and draw them onto the
reefs, and in a similar fashion the Lorelei worked the Rhine. The affected
seamen were not merely distracted; they were drawn, steering their vessels
into, rather than away from, these attention-capturing ("captivating,"
"attractive"[!]) beings.

The fact that attention-capture may induce approach has been used
by modern writers as well. In the following exhibit, Lucia, the never-
daunted heroine of a series of novels popular in the 1930s, is learning to
ride a bicycle:

> A little way in front of her, a man near the edge of the road, with
> a saucepan of tar bubbling over a pot of red hot coals, was doctor-
> ing a telegraph post. Then something curious happened to the
> coordination between Lucia's brain and muscles. The imperative
> need of avoiding the fire pot seemed to impel her to make a bee-
> line for it. With her eye firmly fixed on it, she felt in vain for that
> powerful brake, and rode straight into the fire pot, upsetting the
> tar and scattering the coals. (E. F. Benson, 1939, *Trouble for Lucia*,
> pp. 107–108)

A little while later, Lucia again rides by the spot. Again she sees the
saucepan of boiling tar and the pot of red hot coals, indubitably something
to avoid. However, somehow without wanting to—in fact, wanting
intensely not to—Lucia finds herself irresistibly steering directly toward it.

> Telegraph post after telegraph post flitted past her, and then she
> caught sight of the fire pot again. Lucia felt that he was observing
> her, and once more something curious occurred to her coordina-
> tions, and with it the familiar sense of exactly the same situation
> having happened before. Her machine began to swoop about the
> road; she steadied it, and with the utmost precision went straight
> into the fire pot again. (Benson, 1939, p. 108)

As Lucia is just learning to bicycle, it is probably her intense concentration on the novel task that makes her vulnerable to attention-capture in the story that she tells. The anecdote ends with her counseling another bicycling neophyte:

> Just remember not to look at anything you want to avoid. (1939, p. 119).

This example is fictional and humorous, but real-life examples occur too, and tragically. A World War II memoir, for example, tells of bomber pilots on practice runs diving straight into their targets on the ground, and suggests that this was probably because they were "fascinated." (Hynes, 1988, p. 136)

ATTENTION-CAPTURE MAY INDUCE MATCHING

Someone whose attention has been captured may cease all movement or may move irresistibly toward the enthralling stimulus. Two other behaviors that sometimes follow the capture of attention are matching and obedience. "Matching" means copying movements one has just seen or repeating sounds one has just heard (usually, but not always, words). In the literature aimed at neurologists and psychiatrists, matching of movements is called "echopraxia" and matching of sounds (words), "echolalia." The matching of movements can be quite precise and may occur so shortly after the behavior being matched as to appear simultaneous unless viewed in slow motion on film or videotape. The matching of sounds occurs promptly but usually perceptibly trails the model.[3]

As considerable recent work has shown, matching in one form or another is a regular feature of a great variety of human social interactions. Newborns match heard speech rhythms with micro-movements of body parts (Condon & Sander, 1974), and beginning at 12 to 21 days of age they match observed facial expressions and manual gestures as well (Meltzoff & Moore, 1977). Later socialization and language acquisition entail considerable immediate matching of what is seen and heard. Studies of the interactional synchrony of adult speakers and listeners also reveal considerable behavioral matching in tempo and rhythm.

At the Michigan State University Interaction Analysis Laboratory, I have been collecting examples of gross motor matches. Searches through videotapes of interacting groups frequently revealed unconscious matches. A prime example is that of two men videotaped in the course of a seminar, who matched each other's awkward arm position (arms together up and behind the head) and who intermittently performed hair grooming movements in perfect synchrony for over a half minute. Subsequent inquiry revealed that they were close co-workers, junior and senior colleagues who expressed positive feelings for each other. At the time, neither had been aware of the matching.

In an experiment, a teacher whose exercise class had closely followed her model performance made certain grooming movements we had specified during rest periods. An examination of the videotape made of this session revealed that many of these were matched by her pupils. Though such matching is widespread, it only occasionally comes to awareness as, for example, when an alert newspaper photographer took a sequence of pictures showing Joseph Califano, then Secretary of Health, Education and Welfare, listening to a speech by President Jimmy Carter and repeatedly matching his postures and gestures.

In an autobiographical account of her work as a mission doctor in Africa, Louise Jilek-Aall told how villagers who had never seen anyone remotely like her before were fascinated by the sight of her. When she combed her hair, they matched her every movement (1979, p. 31).[4] D. Carleton Gajdusek described similar behavior in his account of first contacts with South American Indians and with Melanesians (quoted in Yap, 1974, p. 97).

Like attention-capture-elicited approach, the matching of sounds and movements that is elicited by attention-capture is also a resource used by authors in literary contexts. For example, in the novel *Possession*, after using the words "startling" and "shocking," A. S. Byatt describes a mirror match. The vividness and precision of her writing makes it an easy match with which to empathize:

> Roland looked at Maud. The pale, pale hair in fine braids was wound round and round her head, startling white in this light that took the colour out of things and only caught gleams and glancings. She looked almost shockingly naked, like a denuded window-doll, he at first thought, and then, as she turned her supercilious face to him and he saw it changed, simply fragile and even vulnerable. . . . . Both put their hands to their temple, as though he was her mirror. (A. S. Byatt, 1990, *Possession*, p. 282)

"The Snow Queen," one of the most beloved of Hans Christian Andersen's fairy tales, contains an example of verbal matching. Suitors for a princess find her palace awe-inspiring, and standing enthralled before the princess herself—a young woman of high status and power, beautiful, and a great prize—all they can utter is a repetition of the last word that they heard the princess say:

> [Suitors for the princess] could all talk well enough when they were out in the street, but when they came through the palace gate and saw the guards in their silver uniforms, and the footmen in gold all the way up the stairs, and the great halls all lit up, they were dumbstruck; and when they stood before the throne where the princess was sitting, they could find nothing to say except the last word she had spoken herself, and she wasn't really interested

in hearing that again. It was just as if everybody there had got snuff on the stomach, and had fallen into a stupor until they came out into the street once more—they could talk alright again then. (Hans Christian Andersen, 1845, *Hans Andersen's Fairy Tales* [original in Danish], p. 234)

ATTENTION-CAPTURE MAY INDUCE OBEDIENCE

Sometimes when a person's attention has been captured, he or she may obey forcefully given commands, all the while aware and often protesting. This phenomenon is usually called "automatic obedience." Automatic obedience means being unable to refuse to obey a command that one might reasonably wish to refuse, issued by someone without the authority or power to compel obedience. "Automatic" may not be the best term for the phenomenon, but it's not clear what would be better.

Obedience requires a command, and as someone must issue that command, it involves the action of another person in a way not required of "movement-arrest," "approach," or even "matching." Under what circumstances might someone issue a command? Someone who issues a command to a person whose attention has been captured must (1) know that some people whose attention has been captured will obey commands while in a fascinated state, (2) know that the person targeted is susceptible in this way, (3) want to elicit obedience from that person in that setting at that time, and (4) believe that doing so will not have significant negative consequences to himself or herself. He or she who commands must know how the trick works and on whom, and must want to work it. All this means that obedience will be less frequent and widespread than the other sequelae of attention-capture. Exhibits illustrating automatic obedience are discussed later in this chapter.

STARTLE MAY INDUCE ATTENTION-CAPTURE

As a number of museum exhibits in Chapters 5 and 6 assert, startle may induce attention-capture, especially in someone who startles readily and strongly. When some persons are startled frequently, startles become easier and easier to elicit, and previously innocuous stimuli become startling ones. At the same time, the responses to startling stimuli become more violent and often more stereotypic. When one is startled, what one had been thinking of vanishes and is replaced by some strong and compelling new perception, often a perception of something dangerous (Fig. 7.1). This is useful in interactions with predators, with conspecific antagonists, and with other unpleasant surprises such as falling trees or avalanches, and it may be the reason for its evolutionary selection. There is no definitive way of confirming or rejecting such speculations about selection pressures.

After a startle, attention does not necessarily fix on the startling stimulus or its source, but may fix instead on that portion of the environment

ROSE IS ROSE/ *Pat Brady*

Figure 7.1 The startling object, in this cartoon a dead wasp, may completely fill one's atttention. ROSE IS ROSE reprinted by permission of United Feature Syndicate.

most strongly marked from background. That which is fixed on is often something visible, even though the startling stimulus may have been auditory or kinesthetic. It may be noteworthy because of physical properties such as size, contrasting color or lighting, rapid movement (especially toward the subject), unanticipated proximity, and so on. Objects may also become strongly marked and hence attention-capturing through learned associations, which may be either idiosyncratic or widely shared within a cultural group.

For everyone, the experience of being startled is the experience of being flooded with a specific and irresistible altered state. For most people, recovery is usually rapid even from a strong startle, but some persons who startle readily and violently find themselves recovering slowly, trapped in an altered state for a significantly longer period. During this time, attention undirected by conscious thought searches for a salient object on which to fix. Here are two descriptions by American hyperstartlers of the heightened attention to a particular stimulus that a startle may induce:

RCS: Tell me what it feels like after you've been startled.

MH: It's such an intense thing, and I feel like I'm so aware—you know I just feel like all my resources are zeroed in at this one moment. (Mary Haskell, 1977, interview)

Yeah, now that thing, that thing out of the corner of my eye, that was a strange sensation because it was a double startle and I felt like I was acutely aware of it. It looked like, not glowing, but I felt that under normal circumstances maybe I wouldn't have noticed it. It was really small. (Karen Ellis, 1977, interview)

The next exhibit is a first-person account of a prolonged episode of attention-capture. A hyperstartler tells of being fascinated by a fireworks display:

It was the centennial celebration of the opening of the Golden Gate
Bridge. One of my friends has an apartment one block away from
the bridge. . . . So we were virtually under the fireworks display,
which lasted for almost an entire hour continuously. . . ; about 15
of us there. And after the celebration was over they began teasing
me because I had spent the entire hour screaming at the top of my
lungs, just yelling, just staring out at the fireworks. And while I
recall being excited by it, I did not recall that anything that I was
doing was any different than anybody else. But when I asked them
what did they do, they explained to me that they were just going
"Whoo!" and "Aaah!" and walking back and forward just watching
it, but they were able to hear me above everything that was going on.

As they explained it to me, all I was doing was staring at the
lights, at the fireworks. My attention was not diverted to anything
else, anything going on in the room.

At the same time they were showing on the TV in the house
what was going on outside. There was music on in the house, people were going back and eating things and drinking. But they said
that all I did was stand by the window for the entire hour looking
out. I remember that whole hour looking at the fireworks, seeing
them vividly. But to be honest I was surprised when they told me and
began to tease me, "My God, Frank, you were just screaming the
whole time through." But I didn't know I was doing anything special
at that time until they told me. (Frank Gordon, 1983, interview)

Although Mr. Gordon considered himself conscious and aware during
the episode, he had no recollection that his behavior differed in any way
from the activities of others in the same setting. The claim of amnesia for
behaviors performed while attention has been captured has often been considered spurious and self-serving both by subjects' contemporaries and by
scholars, but this account, in which no subjective benefit is apparent, has
the ring of truth.

THE STARTLE-MATCHING SYNDROME

Hyperstartling with matching, "automatic obedience," and "naughty talk"
constitute the main features of what has been called "the startle-matching
syndrome" (Simons, 1985). Societies exist in which play with startle is so
frequent an aspect of daily social interaction that this extreme form of
hyperstartling is familiar to everyone. In many of these societies, hyperstartling is induced by repetitive startling much as it was in Aunt Sally in
Chapter 3, and people who are known to startle readily and violently are
teased daily. The role of startle in such societies will be examined in some
detail in the next three chapters. But even in Western industrialized societies there exist small pockets of interacting people who play the startle
game ferociously. This usually occurs in places where the ordinary West-

ern social rules for moderating the teasing of one person may be sus-
pended—for example, in dormitories and barracks and on factory floors. In
such settings the full syndrome with matching and obedience may develop.

Here are two reports by anthropologists of Americans who not only
hyperstartle, but who, in the prolonged enthralled period after being startled, also match and obey. The first is taken from letters sent between Pro-
fessors Hal Vreeland and David Aberle. They were passed on to me by Professor Aberle, when he learned of my interest in hyperstartling Westerners.
Many years ago, he had observed and written about similar play with
hyperstartling persons in Mongolia (Aberle, 1952). The second is a transcription of an interview with Professor Henry Harpending. Both of the
people they describe hyperstartle, match, and obey commands.

Because much of the point of commanding a vulnerable hyperstartling
person is to demonstrate his or her helplessness to resist, the commands
issued often are to perform dangerous, improper, or degrading acts. In the
accounts that follow, both subjects are induced to perform sham copulation
with an unwilling female co-worker and one is said to expose his penis
when commanded to do so. After being startled one man matches the "It's
no fucking good!" he has just heard, and the other matches the gestures of
hitting himself on the head and of wiping paint or grease across his face.
Both men protest ineffectively, but neither is able to resist obeying the
commands.

Neither the matching nor the obedience is quite perfect, automatic,
or simple. The first subject, "Gus," is able to modify the "fucking" he hears
to "fushin'" in his response, and the commands "Whip it out!" and "Give
it to her!" are ambiguous enough to require central processing. Thus the
matching and obedience must involve not only reflex activity but also some
cerebral activity. How this system appears to work will be discussed in
Chapter 11.

Case 1. "Goosey Gus": Factory worker, Maryland

> Owen tells me that he has already scooped me regarding the char-
> acter I encountered one day while working on a drill press in the
> machine shop. This fellow, known affectionately as Goosey Gus,
> worked three presses away from me and responded beautifully to
> either a goose or a poke in the ribs. As soon as the guy next to me
> told me about Gus, I took note, and perceived that he fitted neatly
> into the general syndrome which you described in your article. All
> you had to do was poke Gus and he would say or do almost any-
> thing requested of him.
>
> Two amusing stories were passed on to me. One day a middle-
> aged woman who works next to Gus was bending way over, fishing
> something out of a box. One of the men poked Gus and said "Give
> it to her Gus," whereupon Gus rushed over and proceeded to go
> through the motions of copulation. Ordinarily Gus is very retiring
> and never swears. On another occasion, one of our top company

engineers came into the shop to inspect a part that was being machined, but not up to snuff. Someone near Gus poked him and whispered "It's no f. . kin' good," whereupon Gus held up the part to the engineer and said "It's no fushin' [*sic*] good." Afterwards he was extremely regretful of his actions. He is apparently the butt of continual and unmerciful stimulation; somehow he has managed to keep on a fairly even keel through 15 years of this torment by his fellow workers. (Vreeland, 1952, letter)

I never learned anything more about Gus, assuming that Ascher would do a much better job. He is now a man of about 55 to 60 years of age, heavy-set and paunchy. Unless stimulated, he was very quiet, in contrast to the rowdies working with him. On several occasions I heard him protest when he saw one of his friends obviously working up to another prank, but he seemed incapable of defending himself against an imminent attack except by verbal protest (with no cussing) and by backing away and trying to shove the aggressor back from him. (Vreeland, 1953, letter)

Case 2. Factory worker, New York State

HH: I grew up in upstate New York. My uncle was, until he retired, the manager of a plant that fabricates sheet metal in Zeeburg, Connecticut, an aircraft company, but it does sheet metal fabrication. He supervised perhaps one hundred men. One of the men was a source of humor for this plant, and I've seen him a couple of times and I've heard a number of anecdotes from my uncle. What I've seen is my uncle . . . this was when I was a teenager. . . . My uncle at one point walked up behind this man and said (and the man wasn't aware of him, the man was working at a table), and he said, "Fuck her in the ass, fuck her in the ass." And the guy immediately started going into pelvic thrusting movements, put his arms out, and his head moved around, and these were really sexual movements. Then my uncle touched him on the shoulder and shook him a little bit, and the man gave a little shake, turned around and said, "God damn you, Gerald!"

      Another thing I've seen is my uncle from a distance away yell at the guy, get his attention, and then staring at him hit himself on the head. And this fellow repeated it. And everybody turned and laughed, of course, as this fellow was hitting himself on the head.

RCS: Do you mean that he did what he saw?

HH: He did what my uncle was doing.

RCS: When you said your uncle called to get his attention, do you remember if it was sudden, startling to get his attention, abruptly?

HH: He was 25 yards away, as I remember and he yelled his name in a loud voice, "Hey Jack!" The guy turned around and my uncle stared at him and did this, and apparently this was one of the standard kinds of humor in that plant.

RCS: Did you see those two incidents yourself?

HH: Yes, sometime around 1965.

RCS: Do you know any other stories, not witnessed by you, that you heard about funny things or other things that this man did?

HH: The same kinds of things. Apparently they could go up and just give him suggestions, "Whip it out, whip it out," and he would.

A terrible story, which is probably true given the level of interaction at this plant of doing something like I described with hitting him on his head only reaching down and making a grasping motion with the hand—my uncle or the instigator would do this—and the fellow would put his hand in paint or grease and then wipe it on his face.

RCS: Wipe it on his face because he saw someone else make the motion?

HH: Because someone else made the motion; yes. Just with air, but this fellow would reach in a grease pan or paint. . . . And I also heard described that this fellow would always come out of it, shake his head, look around, and be kind of shame-faced and a little bit angry at what they'd done to him.

RCS: Shame-faced and angry, and you're pantomiming a dazed look.

HH: Yes, dazed, exactly.

RCS: Did he have a nickname?

HH: Not that I remember, no. (Harpending, 1985, interview)

Although there is no registry for cases of startle-elicited matching or obedience, isolated reports of their occurrence pop up regularly in various scholarly and popular writings. The next account was published by Hardison in the *Journal of the American Medical Association*. The subject is a Georgia housewife who hyperstartles, flings objects, emits naughty talk, matches, and obeys after being startled. She also responds with a jump (a startle?) and naughty talk when tickled. In his report, Hardison (1980) says that he has collected descriptions of four additional American hyperstartlers who obey commands after being startled.

Case 3. Housewife, Georgia

I was raised in a small southern rural community. I was 17 years old when my girlfriend confided to me that her mother was goosey. I was astonished that this reserved, kind, intelligent woman responded when startled or tickled by jumping in the air and shouting curse words that I had not thought possible for her to utter.

To my further amazement, she responded to sudden loud commands by repeating the command while performing the order. If, for instance, she was suddenly told: "Stir your tea with your finger!" she would shout: "Stir your tea with your finger!" while stirring her tea with her finger. She appeared to be normal in every other way, but she could not prevent these remarkable responses when poked or startled. Her daughter was not goosey. (Hardison, 1980, p. 70)

Cases 4–6. Transport driver, farm laborers, South Africa

In 1902, Andrew Gilmour published an account of three cases he had encountered in South African "natives":

In all three (subjects) sudden auditory, tactile or visual stimuli produced the diseased condition. Sudden and unexpected sounds caused them to imitate these sounds, while words, musical notes, etc., were accurately repeated by the men. A sudden touch appeared to make them lose control of themselves, while all movements of the experimenter were copied without fear of consequences. . . . In the three cases mentioned above no influence of religion or of superstition could be traced and no native name could be found applied to the disease. (Gilmour, 1902, p. 20)

What Gilmour means by his final comment is that the cases he observed, like those of the Americans who startle-match, cannot be explained simply as culturally prescribed behavior. However, in certain cultures, both Western and non-Western, the behaviors and experiences constituting the startle-matching syndrome are intimately enmeshed in a whole complex of beliefs, values, and customs. How the syndrome is played out in these settings is the subject of the next three chapters.

NOTES

1. Attention is focused intentionally in a similar manner in meditation and (probably) in hypnosis.

2. Ohnuki-Tierney reported an actual parallel instance in a case of *imu* (see Chapter 10). In her example the stimulus was the memory of an appalling sight:

For example, in the case of a male *imu* whose initial occurrence of *imu* took place at the sight of a writhing reindeer which he had shot, he immediately entered the state of *imu* when someone asked, "What happened to the reindeer you shot?" (1980, p. 101)

3. Both the matching that is seen in everyday life and the matching that may follow attention-capture occur in three forms: parallel homologs in which the matcher's right side follows the model's right; mirror homologs in which the

matcher's left side follows the model's right; and analogs in which functionally equivalent behaviors are performed by model and matcher in markedly different ways (see Simons, 1977).

4. When the Lorelei presented herself to sailors, she also combed her hair. I wonder if there is something in grooming activity (or manipulation of long hair) that is especially attention-capturing.

REFERENCES

Aberle, D.F. (1952). Arctic hysteria and *latah* in Mongolia. *Transactions of New York Academy of Sciences, 14,* 291–297.

Andersen, H.C. 1845/1984. *Hans Andersen's fairy tales* (L.W. Kingsland, Trans.). Oxford: Oxford University Press.

Barkow, J.H. (1989). *Darwin, sex, and status.* Toronto: University of Toronto Press.

Benson, E.F. 1939/1987. *Trouble for Lucia.* New York: Harper & Row.

Byatt, A.S. (1990). *Possession.* New York: Random House.

Condon, W.S., & Sander, L.W. (1974). Neonate movement is synchronized with adult speech. *Science, 183,* 99–101.

Flaubert, G. 1857/1991. *Madame Bovary* (F. Steegmuller, Trans.). New York: Quality Paperback Book Club.

Gilmour, A. (1902). Latah among South African natives. *Scottish Medical & Surgical Journal, 10,* 18–20.

Hardison, J. (1980). Are the jumping Frenchmen of Maine goosey? *Journal of the American Medical Association, 244,* 70.

Hynes, S. (1988). *Flights of passage.* New York: Simon & Schuster.

Jilek-Aall, L. (1979). *Call Mamma doctor.* Saanichton, BC, and Seattle, WA: Hancock House.

Lincoln, A. 1862/1957. Speech delivered November 24, 1862. In P.M. Angle (Ed.), *Abraham Lincoln's speeches and letters, 1832–1865.* New York: Dutton.

Meltzoff, A.N., & Moore, M.K. (1977). Imitation of facial and manual gestures by human neonates. *Science, 198,* 75–78.

Murdoch, I. (1983). *The philosopher's pupil.* New York: Viking.

Ohnuki-Tierney, E. (1980). Shamans and Imu: Among two Ainu groups—Toward a cross-cultural model of interpretation. *Ethos, 8,* 204–228.

Simons, R.C. (1977). Matching behavior—Considerations of form and incidence. Symposium: *Methodological and Theoretical Considerations in Human Ethology.* Annual meeting of the Animal Behavior Society/International Society for Human Ethology, Pennsylvania State University, University Park.

Simons, R.C. (1980). The resolution of the *latah* paradox. *Journal of Nervous and Mental Disease, 168,* 195–206.

Simons, R.C. (1985). Sorting the Culture-bound syndromes. In R.C. Simons & C.C. Hughes (Eds.), *The Culture-bound Syndromes.* Dordrect: D. Reidel.

Webster's New International Dictionary. (1960). Springfield, MA: G.&C. Merriam.

Undset, S. 1920/1946. *Kristin Lavransdatter II.* New York: Knopf.

Yap, P.M. (1974). In M.P. Lau & A.B. Stokes (Eds.), *Comparative psychiatry: A theoretical framework.* Toronto: University of Toronto Press.

8

LATAH
The Paradigmatic Startle-Matching Syndrome

If a door banged, Aunt Sally jumped and said "ouch!" if anything fell, she jumped and said "ouch!" if you happened to touch her, when she warn't noticing, she done the same. . . . So the thing was working very well, Tom said he never see a thing work more satisfactory. He said it showed it was done right.

Mark Twain, 1884, *The Adventures of Huckleberry Finn*, p. 261

If we don't poke and startle them they don't become latahs. If we keep poking at a normal person he'll become a latah. It doesn't take long. After five days, little by little by little, a person's reason just takes off!

Pawang Lumun, Field notes, 1978

LATAH: THE MALAY FORM OF THE STARTLE-MATCHING SYNDROME

The best known of the culturally labeled and elaborated versions of the startle-matching syndrome is the one found in Malaysia and Indonesia, where it is called *latah*.[1] The origin of this term is not known; although a number of etymologies have been suggested, none are convincing. *Latah* is often said to be the Malay word for "nervous" or "ticklish" (e.g., Adams, 1951; Gimlette, 1939), but "jumpy" would be closer, though still not exactly equivalent. In Malay, *latah* denotes both hyperstartling with any of its usual sequelae, such as naughty talk or striking out, and the full startle-matching syndrome with matching and obedience. In ordinary Malay speech the same term is used both for the condition and for the person who manifests it, though the dictionary term for such a person is *pelatah*, the prefix *pe-* signifying "one who."

158   rough equivalent

Figure 8.1   Pictured is the family of Sidang Hussain bin Dalip, which took me in as an adopted family member. Sidang Hussain is standing in the center, flanked by sound recordist Betsy Shipley and the author. Research assistant Jaafar Omar is at the extreme left. Photograph by Gunter Pfaff.

For most of a year I visited Malay villages asking indigenous informants if they knew of any *latahs*. In Melaka, Selangor, and Negri Sembilan, the Malay States in which I worked, *latahs* were common, and there was a good consensus among the villagers as to who they were. I talked with villagers, *latahs* and non-*latahs*, about the condition of being *latah*, both abstractly and as exemplified by the *latahs* they knew or knew about. I recorded what I was told, either in the form of field notes written on the spot or as tape recordings that were subsequently transcribed and analyzed.

It turned out that not only *latah* persons but also episodes of *latah* were common. Further, virtually everyone in the community participated in the complex of behaviors concerning *latah*, either as a *latah*, an elicitor of *latah* episodes, or as a spectator, and even spectators regularly got involved. Living in one of the villages, Kampung Padang Kemunting, much of the time and participating in the ongoing social life of the village, I also had many opportunities to witness episodes of *latah*, to observe the lives of those identified as *latahs*, and to talk informally with *latahs* and other villagers not only about *latah* but also more generally about other aspects of life in the village (Fig. 8.1).

After the general nature of what was happening and how it seemed to work began to become more clear, I made a list of topics on which I especially wanted information from *latahs* and another list of information I especially wanted from their non-*latah* peers.[2] In talking with informants, the technique used was not simply to follow the list, asking questions serially. Instead, I would begin by making it known that I was studying *latah* and would appreciate any information my informant could offer. I would then follow offered leads, referring to the lists toward the end of our talk to remind me of topics we had not discussed. By that time I would usually have a reasonable idea of what the informant was trying to tell me and how he or she wanted me to think about it, and thus I could choose the topics that might be especially informative to pursue in the remainder of that interview. No informant discussed all topics; often circumstances permitted only a few of the questions to be explored in depth. It was also often possible to stimulate discussion of topics that were situationally relevant in settings in which a full interview would have been impossible.[3]

In addition to talking with people about *latah*, I carefully watched every episode of *latah* I came across, recording my observations on the spot in the form of field notes. I also filmed a few of these episodes on super 8-mm sound film (this being before the days of easily portable field video recording). The grant from the H.F. Guggenheim Foundation, which supported my fieldwork, provided funds for a cameraman and sound recordist to join me for a 6-week period to obtain a more extensive 16-mm film record of *latah* for closer study back in the United States. While they were with me, we filmed a number of interviews as well.[4]

As in most ethological studies, the initial investigative strategy was observational and inductive. If one looks at a sequence of interaction again and again, attending at different times to different features and scrutinizing them, one notices things. Repeatedly viewing films of the same episodes, sometimes a few seconds of interaction again and again, clarified how events were sequenced; it also confirmed and rejected hypotheses about what was happening, and suggested new hypotheses not previously considered.[5] It was also possible to compare film data from two culturally distinct groups in Malaysia with film data from the Philippines, Japan, Thailand, and the United States. And what appeared on the films could be compared with notes of field observations and the interview materials.

The picture of *latah* that grew out of what I saw was quite consistent with what I had been told in the course of my residence in the village. It is this picture of *latah*, derived from observations, interviews, and the study of audiovisual recordings of *latah*, that is presented here.

A COMPOSITE DESCRIPTION OF *LATAH*

Latahs are persons who startle far more readily and far more violently than their non-*latah* peers, a fact readily apparent both in direct observations and on the films. When asked how they can tell who is a *latah*, Malay informants invariably cite an excessive startle response as the major identifying criterion (Fig. 8.2). As one informant, 'Tok Ahmad bin Ngah, explained:

Figure 8.2   When an empty film can is dropped behind four villagers who
volunteered for this experiment, only Cik Muniah, a *latah*, startles. (Still from
film *Latah*)

> If someone comes slowly from behind and we don't know it and
> we don't catch sight of him and he pokes us quickly in the ribs it's
> like this [demonstrates a violent startle]. That is called "*latah*." If
> we want to know if someone is *latah* or not, that's how we tell.

Latahs do everything that other hyperstartling people do elsewhere.
They may strike out at objects or others, assume overlearned defensive postures, or say improper or idiosyncratically stereotyped things. Not only are
their startles to minimal stimuli more physically violent than those of their
peers (the movements that characterize startle are magnified and exaggerated), they are also more violent psychologically in that the disruption of
ongoing attentional processes, which startle always causes, is for them
more extreme. After a series of startles, a *latah*'s speech and behavior may
become quite disorganized.

In addition, after being startled some *latahs* experience strong attention-capture, focusing on salient aspects of their perceptual fields and nar-
rowing and locking attention on them. *Latahs* may call out the names of
what they see or repeat or approximate sounds they have just heard. They
may match movements of objects or of other persons with movements of
their own bodies. As with persons whose attention has been captured generally, *latahs* will sometimes obey imperiously given commands. The usual
technique for eliciting obedience is to lean close, raise the voice in a characteristic manner, and to make pointed gestures. Doing so is part of the

behavioral repertoire of persons raised in Malay culture, learned in childhood from watching others do so.

When a just-startled *latah* is confronted with a looming gesticulating
person imperiously commanding, "Dance! Dance!," it is not surprising
that he or she usually dances. Cik Alimah binti Mamad, one of the villagers, described how this process works. The specific stimulus can vary, as
long as the *latah* is startled.

> When she's sitting quietly we can take a piece of wood and bang it,
> or we can poke her in the ribs over and over and she'll become
> *latah*. She gets startled! Then if we order her to hit or dance, she'll
> hit or dance. And she'll do whatever we tell her to do with what
> she's holding. Whoever is in front of her will be hit. That's what a
> *latah* does!

Both obedience and matching are shaped by the actions of others, and,
like matching, obedience always follows closely in time the stimulus which
initiates it. If one tells a just-startled *latah* to throw her fish on the ground
tomorrow she will not do so.

Informants emphasize that what sets off this remarkable chain of
behaviors is being startled. When one *latah*, Cik Rahmah, told me:

> If someone pokes and startles me and orders me to do something
> I won't know what I'm doing. I might even take off my clothes!

her husband, Encik Yusof bin Kecut, felt constrained to clarify:

> She only gets flustered if she's poked and startled. If we were just
> to tell her normally to take off her clothes, she wouldn't do it. But
> if she were poked and startled first she might.

Very infrequently, I was told of someone with strong *latah* having his
or her attention captured by the motion of some inanimate object or the
behavior of an animal and matching it without ever having been startled.
I never saw an instance of this, but Professor Wolfgang Pfeiffer, who studied *latah* in Java, saw it (personal communication).[6] I also occasionally
came across anecdotal reports of persons showing attention-capture behaviors simply from being in the presence of someone of especially high status. I never saw this happen either but believe it possible.

Informants frequently told me that virtually anyone could be made
into a *latah* if startled by others frequently enough. As one *latah*, Cik Layut
Ali, explained, if startled enough, a Westerner might develop *latah* too:

> At first, one is merely startled. One sees a centipede, or a snake,
> or a coconut leaf falls, and one is startled. Then someone sees that

happen. Later when he sees me again perhaps he'll poke me in the ribs. After a while something can happen. Take an ordinary person like Betsy[7] here—if she's startled—Whenever you see her you poke her in the ribs. After a while she'll get very flustered! She'll say whatever comes out. If you tell her to dance, she'll dance. If you poke her in the ribs whenever you see her, she'll do this too. That's what it's like.

Many non-*latah* informants also told me that they believed that it was this repetitive poking that caused persons to become *latah*. For example, Cik Layut Ali's husband, Pawang Lumun, an indigenous healer, once explained:

If we don't poke and startle them they don't become *latah*. If we keep poking at a normal person he'll become a *latah*. It doesn't take long. After five days, little by little by little, a person's reason just takes off! ["akal naik!"]

Thus, when I asked the headman of the village[8] in which I lived if this could happen to him, he answered that it might, though it would require that he be actually startled, and he did not startle easily.

INTERVIEWER (RCS): If someone poked you in the ribs every day, would you become a *latah* or not?

SIDANG HUSSAIN: If it were done face to face like this [demonstrates] I think not, but if it were done from behind and over and over I think I'd become a *latah* too. But not if I caught sight of the person doing it.

In actuality, it is those persons who have been observed to startle especially readily and violently who are selected for the kind of frequent and repetitive startling by others that defines them as *latahs* and leads to the development of the syndrome's more dramatic manifestations. One *latah*, Hajah Misah Bani, described how this sequence had happened to her: first being observed hyperstartling, then being intentionally startled by others with increased frequency, and finally developing full-blown *latah*:

It began when my mother died. I was very sad. I was sitting quietly like this, thinking my mother is gone. Someone came from behind. He grabbed me and said, "What's up?" I was startled! My body trembled like this. My mind went blank. When my body stopped trembling he did it again. I picked up a stick and hit him. I couldn't think—how could I? Later, wherever I went people liked to watch me. They thought I was just pretending. They poked me in the ribs over and over until I became ill!

The overwhelming majority of *latahs* are women. When asked why, villagers often told me that it is because women have less *semangat* than do men. *Semangat* is usually translated as "soul substance"; it is something that if weak or insufficiently present makes one susceptible to a wide variety of afflictions and influences. To assert that women have less *semangat* is more or less equivalent to asserting that "women belong to the weaker sex." Although in actuality Malay women are probably as healthy as men and seem as often to be of strong, forceful character, this is a widespread Malay belief.

However, "less *semangat*" was not the only explanation for the difference in incidence by gender that I received. Malay informants also often gave a second explanation, which was not cosmological and inferential like "less *semangat*," but which was based on their own observations and experiences. They said that women were more often *latah* because they were startled more often by others than men were. Both men and women preferred to startle women because they could do so with impunity, which was not always the case when one startled men. This explanation makes a great deal of sense. It is not only consistent with my observations of interactions in the villages, but as will be discussed more fully in Chapter 11, it also explains why in cultures in which men receive more frequent startle-teasing it is men who develop most of the cases of the startle-matching syndrome. In these excerpts from interviews, two informants, one man and one woman, neither of them *latah*, give both these explanations:

SIDANG HUSSAIN: Women's *semangat* is a bit weaker than men's. Men have rather stronger *semangat*. You see, even their physical strength is greater than women's. So that if a man becomes *latah* when people poke him suddenly in the ribs he might become strong. For that reason people fear his striking back. But people don't fear women much because they're weaker.

CIK ASPAH BINTI SIDEK: Many more women than men are *latah*; women's *semangat* is weaker than men's. And people are afraid to poke and startle men. Even other men don't like to do it to each other. It's women who like to poke each other. When they're sitting around, someone pokes someone, someone else pokes someone else. Women are shy about poking men.

INTERVIEWER (RCS):   Shy or afraid?

CIK ASPAH: Shy. Well, shy and afraid too.

Women do seem to like to poke each other here; I saw a considerable amount of this poking, and not only of *latahs*. Some typical examples were recorded in field notes:

Observed startle at a bazaar: A woman standing next to me waiting for a certain kind of snack to be steamed. A woman friend came up and poked her from behind. After she stiffened and let out an "Ah!" her friend told her that she was waiting for her to leave and this finished the incident. She is not a *latah*. (Field notes, January 31, 1978)

I just watched Rashima, a young matron, sitting with someone who I believe is her best friend. They repeatedly reached behind each other to startle one another. There was much giggling. The next day I saw Rashima waylay and startle Zaiton, a pretty adolescent, who jumped and squealed. None of the three women is a *latah*. (Field notes, January 1, 1978)

The stylized sharp poke in the ribs (giving the *cucuk*) is part of a larger pattern of playful touching from which even Betsy Shipley was not exempt:

Betsy told us that Cik 'Pah would often give her a little swat on the behind when she adjusted her sarong or sometimes just when she went by, never in direct view of us menfolk, though occasionally Gunter or I might glimpse it out of a corner of an eye. I once saw Cik 'Pah give Cik Tah, a massive woman of about 55, a playful swat too. Only once did I see a similar swat being given by a man to another man. (Field notes, January 23, 1978)

In this social context, the poking of *latahs* seems less intrusive and less distressful. Here, playful touching, teasing, and startling are often used as social lubricants.

In the course of play with a *latah*, persons other than the *latah* were often also mocked or teased indirectly. Cik Layut's husband had lost a leg to a shark and consequently had a wooden leg. After she was startled, one of the commands frequently given to her was "Walk like your husband!"—that is, imitate his limp. A startled *latah* was often commanded to hit or to do something silly to some specified person present or to say something silly about him. This was, for example, an acceptable way to tease me, as recorded in the next excerpt from field notes:

Jaafar [my principal Malay research assistant] and I briefly interviewed Gayah, her son Yusof, and some of her friends. She seems a soft-spoken, sensible woman who answered our questions clearly and thoughtfully. Afterwards, unasked, some of her women friends startled her by reaching behind and grabbing at her. In the course of perhaps two minutes she was startled by being grabbed or poked from behind perhaps ten times. Each time she'd briefly match whatever they said.

Often the model given to her to match was something silly, e.g., "Jangut bikin tali ambil air." ("Beard make rope [to] take water" or "That beard would make a good well-bucket rope.") Each time she repeated what had been said there was much laughter, in which she joined. (Field notes, December 4, 1977)

The reference was to my full beard. It was not the *latah* who suggested the comment. At the time the fieldwork was done, beards were uncommon in the village.

As in the incident above, not only the *latah* but also those playing with her may use the occasion to say or do something otherwise not permitted — for example, to mock or tease someone usually considered socially superior and therefore exempt. As Raymond Lee has noted:

> Role reversals in *latah* and possession hysteria involve the temporary denial and ridicule of assigned female positions in Malay [social] structure. . . .
> Low-status subjects are temporarily allowed to mock their superiors who, in turn, must accept with goodwill their status degradation. (Lee, 1981, p. 239)

Under ordinary circumstances the comment made about my beard would have been a highly improper thing for the person offering it as a model to say. As a social and cultural phenomenon, *latah* includes not only the person manifesting the syndrome but also those interacting with the *latah* and even spectators.

Even in the city we noted a very high frequency of playful swats, pokes, and startles. In this social context, spouses and other family members cannot do much to protect *latahs*; *latahs* are considered fair game. As Encik Yusof bin Kecut explained:

> I don't believe there's anything we can do. We can't scold much because this kind of teasing is considered acceptable. But if it's too extreme we can scold a little.

One informant, for example, who eloquently and passionately expressed her indignation about the treatment her *latah* sister once received, objected only to what she considered an outrageously excessive command, not to the fact of the startle-teasing itself. She was indignant that the people who were teasing her sister went too far, not that her *latah* sister was subjected to startle-teasing:

> It happened to my sister at a wedding. People kept startling her with pokes in the ribs, over and over. After she became *latah*, they ordered her to eat and she ate; they ordered her to dance and she danced. They ordered her to do all sorts of things and she did whatever they ordered. Finally, someone ordered her to take her clothes off, and she did that too. She didn't know what was happening so she just stripped off.
> When she took her clothes off, the people around her were embarrassed, and her children were embarrassed too. One of her children got angry. He gave her a stick and told her to hit the per-

son teasing her. But instead of hitting him she smashed all the dishes and plates. Her children were furious, and they took her home.

When she came to her senses she was ashamed. It wasn't right or fair to do what they did to her, ordering her to strip! Startling her should have been enough. When she's that flustered she doesn't know what she's doing. Whatever they ordered she did, like a person without shame.

Although they may be embarrassed, *latahs* are not considered either morally or legally responsible for what they do after being startled. 'Tok Ahmad bin Ngah, a man in his seventies, told a story which he had heard when he was a boy:

A long time ago I heard a story. It happened when the British governed here. When the British were here there was a court in Pengkalan Balak. Major Bawal was the judge. He was responsible for sentencing. One time a *latah* was holding a knife when someone came up from behind, startled her with a poke, and ordered "Stab!" Right away she stabbed, and she stabbed a man to death! When the victim died, she was arrested by the police.

A while later when the time for the trial came, she was taken to court. During the hearing the judge asked, "Why did you kill that man?" She said, "I didn't know what I was doing. When I killed him I didn't know anything! I'm a *latah*, and someone poked me and startled me. I didn't intend to kill anybody. I lost my reason because I was startled by a poke in the ribs and when I was ordered to stab, right away I stabbed. Because of that I plead not guilty."

Wow!

About a week later came the trial. To prepare for it, the judge ordered a plank to be studded with nails, about ten nails. Then the plank was positioned with the point of the nails facing up. The judge said, "Now we'll test whether you're a real *latah*." A policeman came up behind the *latah* and poked her in the ribs, and he shouted, "Slap those nails!" Right away the old lady slapped down on those nails, and blood began to gush from her hand. The judge had to agree. "Truly, this woman is a real *latah*. This old woman is not guilty; the guilty one is the person who poked her."

So the woman who poked the *latah* was the one who was sentenced to be hanged.[9]

A similar test was described in William Fletcher's 1908 "Latah and Crime":

In order to investigate the question of "volition" with regard to crime in a person subject to pronounced *latah* the following experiment was carried out. A woman named J—— was admitted to the General Hospital, Kuala Lumpur, suffering from sarcoma of the breast. She was very *latah* and said that she had been so since the death of one of her children, which had taken place rather suddenly a few years ago and was a great shock to her. J—— was in a small room with two other Malays. This room communicated by a short passage with a ward in which there was a large number of Tamil patients. She could not see the ward from her bed in the little room.

On the particular day on which the experiment was carried out there was a drizzling rain, and, as is their custom in such weather, the Tamil patients were curled up on their beds entirely covered by their blankets. One of these patients was aroused and sent out into the veranda. The outline of the body was then reproduced under the blanket by means of a pillow and a folded raincoat. The appearance was indistinguishable from that presented by the real patients as hidden under their blankets in the beds near.

J—— was then summoned from her room and told that there was a rich Tamil woman covered with jewelry asleep on one of the beds. The bed with the raincoat was then pointed out to her. Suddenly a large amputating knife was thrust into her hands and a command was shouted at her, "Kill that woman and steal her jewelry." J—— rushed at the bed and with great force drove the knife into the blanket and the raincoat underneath. Hardly had she struck before she uttered a cry of remorse and threw herself back with a look of horror on her face. The command "Kill!" ("Potong!") [actually "Cut!"] was shouted at her, and again she fell to hacking the raincoat with her knife. (Fletcher, 1908, p. 255).

It will be apparent by now that a major element in the complex of behaviors and beliefs constituting what the Malay informants defined as "*latah*" is the behavior of people other than the *latah* herself or himself. To a great extent, it is the behavior of others toward potential *latahs* that results in their developing *latah*, and it is the behavior of others toward *latahs* that largely determines the behaviors that *latahs* perform. It is also the behavior of others that defines the interactional status of *latah* and their social roles. One can tell who is a *latah* from observing the behavior of others toward her:

Early in the evening at a joget [dance party] I saw a large, assertive, obviously "prominent" man of about 45 suddenly grab from behind and push an old woman of about 60. He said something to her and she responded with a few words which I could not hear. That was all; I saw no unusual motor behavior, and if she said something naughty I didn't hear it.

Later in the evening I saw a girl of perhaps eleven come up to her and push at one of her breasts, then with both hands push her strongly backwards. The woman responded only with annoyance, scolding the girl and pushing her roughly away. Unlike the male elicitor, the little girl did not attempt to catch the old lady by surprise. Bystanders whom I asked confirmed what I had deduced from the behavior of the prominent man and the girl: that the old woman was a *latah*. (Field notes, December 7, 1977)

Sometimes when I asked why someone was considered a *latah* I was told not what the *latah* did but rather how others behaved toward him or her. For example, we saw Rashima, a woman in her early twenties, poke Matt Ali, a man in his fifties, as he passed by her at a wedding, and later we saw an older woman poke him too.

When I asked Rashima how she knew Matt Ali was a *latah* she responded, "When he comes to the store other people poke him, so I also try to poke him too." Later, in response to the same question asked in a different form, she said, "Since I see other people poking him, I do the same." ["*Tengok orang lain cucuk, saya ikut.*"] When asked who, she answered "many people" and gave her two younger sisters [girls in their teens] as examples. When I persisted in asking why she chose to poke him rather than anyone else she simply explained, "Other people are not *latah* like he is."[10] (Field notes, January 1, 1978)

When I asked if being *latah* was a marriage impediment I was told that it was not, at least for women, which is consistent with my observations. However, although in the scholarly literature being a *latah* is usually said to be inconsequential, it is quite an affliction for some, especially for heterosexual men. Some men develop patterns of social avoidance, something especially unfortunate in a village of frequent feasts and gatherings.

Rashima's mother told Jaafar that now when Matt Ali comes to the store he appears fearful and there is a twitching of his body as if he anticipates someone coming at him from behind. Earlier, he himself had told us that he was particularly teased when at the *kedai* [the small sundry shop] where he comes to buy supplies or a cup of coffee. He doesn't come to the shop so frequently now. As much useful social interaction takes place at the *kedai*, this is a real social handicap. (Field notes, January 1, 1978)

I was once asked by Jaafar why people are ashamed of being *latah* and sometimes also ashamed of having *latahs* in their midst. This question came up not infrequently in talks with others as well, although always indirectly and with extreme delicacy, openly acknowledged to me only by those with whom I was especially close. I believe that the shame has at least four sources: (1) evidencing lack of control of biological functions is often associated with shame; (2) the actual behaviors performed are usually improper by ordinary standards of etiquette; they often evoke contemptuous laughter and are "*kasar*";[11] (3) if there is naughty talk, one is vulnerable to the accusation that one's thoughts are on sexual matters; and (4) being known to be a *latah* gives others license to act toward one in ways generally considered disrespectful.

> At dinner yesterday, Dato Sidang was sitting, holding a heavy pitcher. As he reached across to return it to its place, he accidently bumped it very slightly against a bowl of rice. With a smooth swing thus interrupted, his arm was thrown off balance and he exclaimed, "Allah!" He appeared to be startled. I asked him if he had said "Allah" with or without thinking. He smiled and answered, "without," and that it had just popped out. He added that this happens to him occasionally and to others in similar circumstances. I said I thought *latah* was like this, but stronger. He responded that in such unthinking moments a person said whatever sort of thing dwelled in his mind. If he was a person whose thoughts were filled with God one kind of thing; if his mind were elsewhere, those things. (Field notes, December 11, 1977)

Though people have license to startle *latahs* virtually any time, there are some situations in which it is especially culturally appropriate to tease them in this way.[12] One of these is the time when a Malay groom is being escorted in a processional to meet his bride to be. This is an impressive ceremony. Wearing considerable expensive finery (in the villages I visited, it was often rented), the groom is ceremoniously escorted to the home of the bride accompanied by a party of rhythmically drumming and chanting young people. In Kampung Padang Kemunting the procession usually passed through specially constructed gates elaborately decorated with leaves and colored paper, often with showers of Roman candles and other fireworks on either side of the path. It is a happy, highly social, and visually and auditorily arresting spectacle. Advised to watch for *latah* behavior, Jaafar saw the following incident:

> Last night, as the groom was being drummed in, Jaafar noticed a woman of about fifty standing in the crowd and sham drumming in the air. Looking down he saw her woman companion repeatedly *cucuking* her in the side to keep her going. Jaafar said that this *cucuking* was almost continuous during one halt of the groom [a little less than a minute] and was done by touching her repeatedly in different places with her hand. When the drummers moved forward the stimulator stopped and the *latah* stopped. The *latah* matched the drumming, hitting her palm on the edge of an imag-

inary drum, following the rhythm well. She is considered *latah* but not strongly so. (Field notes, December 25, 1977)

Another culture-typical time for the elicitation and display of *latah* behavior is the cleanup period after a wedding feast has concluded. This is the time for much lighthearted play among the women who are doing the cleaning up. It takes place on the last day of the ceremonials, after two or three weeks of intensive preparation, cooking, cleaning, and serving. It is also at the close of a period of intensive visiting, when houses are packed with relatives and friends. During this final cleanup there is much good-natured playful teasing, and the women who have been doing the work have special license to tease. I saw, for example, a woman swinging a sopping rag in an extravagantly playful manner, throwing water in all directions over people as she walked through the cleanup area. Her doing so was met with big smiles, much laughter, and some reciprocal water throwing. I was told that family males are also splashed and that sometimes men and women are chased by others to be daubed with the oily blacking that has accumulated at the bottom of pots. In this context the teasing of the *latah* seems less aggressive and more a friendly and playful part of a generally happy time; no one is allowed to keep his or her dignity.

Though all are hyperstartlers, *latahs* differ widely in the number and extent of *latah* behaviors that being startled characteristically elicits from them. In discussing such differences many Malay informants used the terms "*latah sedikit*" ("a little *latah*") and "*latah kuat*" ("strong *latah*"). Although these terms do not have precise boundaries, they generally differentiate those who are merely hyperstartlers who characteristically say something naughty or strike out from those who sometimes also match or obey.

Some persons identified as *latah* only startled extremely readily and extremely violently, never matching sounds or behaviors and never obeying commands. Instead, they merely blurted out something blatantly silly, improper, or otherwise inappropriate or assumed stereotyped defensive postures. Most non-*latah* informants believed that under certain circumstances they too might do similar things. It was the ease and reliability with which strong startles could be elicited from some persons, the frequency with which they were observed to startle, and the reliability or stereotypy of the naughty talk, assumption of defensive postures, or throwing or dropping objects that led others to classify them as *latahs*. Westerners would call people with *latah sedikit* "very jumpy," and very jumpy Westerners like Ms. Gould and Aunt Sally would in Malaysia be considered "*latah sedikit*." I have called this milder form of *latah* "immediate-response *latah*" because its manifestations are limited to those that can be part of the startle response itself. However, in Malaysia, because hyperstartlers are so often repetitively startled by others, immediate-response *latah* often develops into attention-capture *latah* with matching and obedience, and the potential for that progression was often mentioned in discussions about it.

When interviewed, some persons (mostly men) indigenously classified as "*latah sedikit*" denied being *latahs*, even when I myself had seen or had collected convincing witnessed accounts of their being treated as *latahs* by others and of their behaving in ways most villagers would categorize as *latah*. When interviewed, they would explain that their problem was merely that of being a bit jumpy ("*mudah terperanjat*"). Another criterion they sometimes cited was that, unlike *latahs*, they could inhibit their responses if they knew when the stimuli were coming. They explained that although others might treat them as *latahs*, they really were not.

In the following (edited) excerpt from an interview, Jaafar is interviewing Matt Ali, who strenuously denies being a *latah*:

MA: It's like this, they only say that I'm *latah*. Some people just tell lies. . . . Regular *latahs* can be found, but as for me, I'm not one. . . . The true definition of *latah* is like this: If someone comes from behind and we ordinary people don't know they're there and if he pokes us suddenly, we get startled. Now as for those who are called *latah*, the same thing can happen when they are poked from the front. I'm not a *latah*. I'm not. If the stimulus comes from the front, nothing happens [laughs].

J: What happens if *you* are startled?

MA: If startled I say whatever speech comes out.

J: Whatever speech?

MA: Only a little most of the time. And at first. The second time it won't happen again. . . . If you come hidden, from behind and poke, anyone would be startled! He might say anything. It's like that.

J: So if it's repeated a second time, you . . .

MA: Nothing more happens. Nothing!

J: Nothing more happens?

MA: There isn't another startle.

J: You can be startled once, but not twice.

MA: Once, but not twice. That's why when I already knew that someone was behind my back . . . like we're standing now . . . how could I be startled? . . . Right! A second time, whatever happens. I won't be startled again, when I already know someone is behind me.

J: But if a person is *latah*, if the startle is repeated a second time . . . ?

MA: Not only two times, he'll do that ten times. That's what is called a *latah*. I know. Formerly I had an uncle like that but he died.

Thus, at the mild end of the response continuum the question of whether one is a *latah* or not depends on where one draws the boundary. Different people drew the boundary in different ways:

> Cik Gayah gave the usual story of being easily startled, and her son and husband said that when she is startled when alone—for example, by a coconut falling—she'll have an excessive reaction, saying "*Loseh!*," a meaningless word, or words which sound Arabic but which also have no meaning. They deny that she ever says vulgar words, though Jaafar, a careful and trustworthy observer, had heard her say "*Butol!*" ["Prick!"] some days earlier, and I had heard her say "*Loseh! Buntut!*" ["*Loseh!* Ass!"] the day of the interview. Sometimes when startled she drops things. She believes that when this started about 20 years ago, it was only an excessive startle reaction, which later progressed to imitation and obedience as she was startled with increasing frequency by people who observed her vulnerability.
>
> To illustrate how she believed the process to work she cited her son Yusof, now thirty-six. For ten years he has been easily startled ["*mudah terperanjat*"] which he admits to, although he does not consider himself *latah*. Cik Gayah says that his youngest daughter occasionally *cucuks* him just to watch his reaction. Other children *cucuk* him also, and he was identified to us as a *latah* by many when we surveyed the village. However, Cik Gayah, whose *latah* is quite strong, considered him only an incipient *latah*. She said that if this keeps up he will become a *latah* too. "That's how I got to be *latah*." (Field notes, February 19, 1978)

We were told that in the previous year Encik Yusof once ate a block of dried shrimp paste (a very unappetizing substance) after being startled and commanded to do so at a wedding. I saw children, including the children of his extended family household, startle and tease him. Nevertheless, to us he acknowledged only that he was easily startled ("*mudah terperanjat*"). He told us that Cik Mah's son, who is also considered *latah* by kampung village people (and was so identified to us by many when we made the kampung survey), considers himself to be only "*mudah terperanjat*" also. Clearly, this is a less prejudicial way of looking at things. "*Latah*" is a role and a status, "*mudah terperanjat*" merely a physiological condition.

One option open to anyone being treated as a *latah* is to acquiesce to that social role as defined in Malay society and play it for all it is worth, accepting the frequent startle teasing that goes with the role with good grace and writing off as ultimately inconsequential the intrusion into personal dignity and personal space to which *latah* are subjected. This is a frequent and happy solution for hyperstartlers living in a society in which they will be frequently teased and in which angry protest would gain neither support nor sympathy (Fig. 8.3).

Figure 8.3   In an episode of *latah* in which Hajjah Misah is teased and commanded, she gets off some good hits at her tormentor as part of her performance.
These were not gentle swats, either. (Still from film *Latah*)

It will be remembered how Ms. Gould (in Chapter 2) integrated the
fact of hyperstartling into her life in a positive way. It served for her as a
social lubricant, lessening the gap that her intelligence, forceful personality, social class, and good looks might otherwise have engendered between
her and many of the people with whom she worked. Similarly, a *latah* is not
purely a victim. Being a *latah* or behaving as if one were in a *latah* state can
be a social asset rather than a social liability. Some of the *latah* episodes I
saw appeared to be proceeded by sham startles rather than actual ones, and
sometimes the matching, obedience, and disorganized speech and behavior seemed to be deliberately performed as well. I believe that in these
episodes I saw persons who comfortably accepted their condition and status purposefully define voluntary behavior as that of a *latah* in a *latah*
episode (Fig. 8.4).

To play out this role, some *latahs* may perform long sequences of
absurd-appearing behavior, even in the absence of adequately startling
stimuli, acting as if they were in the typical altered state of a truly startled
latah. Malays themselves often question whether a given performance is
real *latah* or if the person behaving as a *latah* is merely pretending.[13] Analytically, it is useful to separate these unstartled performances from the
episodes of immediate-response *latah* and attention-capture *latah* which
provide the behaviors on which the enacted ones are modeled.

I saw only some of the women *latahs* perform in this way, and the only
men I saw so performing were homosexual transvestites. Homosexual
transvestites have a defined and accepted role in rural Malay life. At village

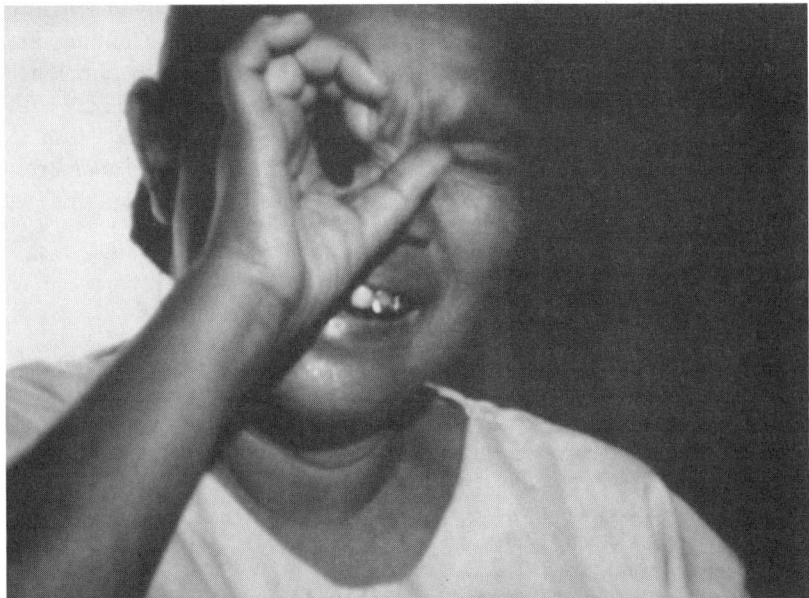

Figure 8.4 In an episode of *latah*, Cik Muniah mocks Gunter Pfaff, the cameraman, by screwing up her face and grimacing through a viewfinder made of her thumb and fingers. During episodes of *latah*, *latahs* have license to mock those about them, regardless of relative social status. (Still from film *Latah*)

dances, for example, they were popular dance partners and no stigma (or special comment even) resulted from dancing with them. People often giggled and smirked when discussing them, but there was no noticeable homophobia. There is a significant incidence of *latah* among them, and in some of the cases I saw and was told of, the *latah* performances seemed somewhat histrionic. Heterosexual men who are *latah* strongly resist entering the *latah* state and neither clown nor perform.

Westerners describing personal observations of *latah* in the scholarly literature usually classify *latah* episodes or *latah* persons along some dimension of readiness of elicitation and severity of response, sometimes separating out those who match and obey from those who do not. Ellis (1897), for example, described "those whose symptoms are paroxysmal outbursts [often with coprolalia or striking out at another]" and "mimetic [cases]." Abraham (1912) used the terms "impulsive" and "mimetic," and Adams (1951) classified the episodes he saw as "mild attacks," "severe attacks," and "very severe attacks." Note that Abraham's and Adams's classifications are of episodes; one person might at different times have "attacks" (episodes) of different types. Ellis, who believed that his two forms of *latah* were most likely two different diseases, classified persons by the most extreme of the episodes they performed.[14]

My own classification (Simons, 1980) is of episodes, with "immediate-response *latah*" as the name of the category for episodes of hyperstartling with or without throwing, dropping, striking out, or naughty talk; "attention-capture *latah*" for those episodes in which matching or obedience occur; and "role *latah*" for episodes of purposeful, unentranced play with the *latah* role. Although not all *latahs* match or obey, and not all *latah* episodes include matching or obedience, most of the accounts of *latah* I collected featured these phenomena prominently. The implications of this fact are discussed in the next chapter.

NOTES

1. Properly speaking, throughout this and subsequent chapters I should continue to say "Malaysia and Indonesia" because the startle-matching syndrome is found in both nations and no one has demonstrated that variations between its presentations in the two is greater than the variation among its presentations within either. However, as this would soon become awkward and as I worked only in Malaysia, I will refer to *latah* as the "Malaysian form" of the syndrome. "And Indonesian" should be inferred.

2. See Appendix, pp. 249–252.

3. Because the choice of informants was casual and opportunistic, and because no attempt was made to sample experience or opinion in any systematic way, a tabulation of the responses would be misleading. In another area of Malaysia, Robert Winzeler used his own version of the topic lists in a more systematic way (see Winzeler, 1988).

4. In addition to its use as research data, this film record with additional relevant footage has been edited into a 38-minute film, *Latah: A Culture-Specific Elaboration of the Startle Reflex*, available in film and video formats from Indiana University Audio-Visual Center, Bloomington, Indiana 47405-5901. (See Appendix, pp. 254–262.)

5. Much of the most revealing viewing was done at sessions of the Michigan State University Interaction Analysis Laboratory. This was a group of professionals and students who met weekly to study films and videotapes of interpersonal events recorded from naturalistic settings in the course of a wide variety of research projects (e.g., dinner-table conversations, the introduction of a pet into a nursing home, childbirth in Yucatan). Often an entire 3-hour session would be spent repeatedly viewing a few minutes of interaction.

6. Watching rhythmic movement is the way an attention-captured state is induced in a story of a man who, forced to match movements, threw his baby into the air and failed to catch it. This story is discussed at some length in Chapter 8.

7. This was Betsy Shipley, the research project's sound recordist, who, along with her husband, Gunter Pfaff, our cameraman and film editor, lived in Kampung Padang Kemunting during the 6-week shooting of the film record. Significantly, for her example Cik Layut chose the one woman in our party, though Gunter and I were also present.

8. The headman, Sidang Hussain bin Dalip, and his family took me in and, by vouching for me, enormously facilitated the community's acceptance of my inordinate curiosity about *latah*. As Malays conceptualize intimate relationships largely in family terms (Banks, 1983; Provencher, 1971), after some months he suggested that we define our relationship, which persists, as that of brothers. Since that time,

we have addressed each other as "elder brother" and "younger brother," he being the elder.

9. A Siberian version of this story, recorded by Shirokogoroff, is given in Chapter 9, p. 190. The anthropologist Vivian Garrison once kindly sent me an American version. In it there is no command, only the startle with the stabbing occurring as a result of unplanned striking out.

> [A second story I heard] involved another man, a woodcarver, who also was "goosey." One day while he was whittling something, someone goosed him, and the woodcarver just stabbed the man who goosed him with the knife with which he had been carving. [The narrator] did not remember what happened to the man as a consequence. (Garrison, 1986, personal communication)

10. Rashima and her mother told me that Hussain Dorani had been like this for only the last 2 years, which is what he had told me also. When I asked what he did after being startled, they said that he always gave the same verbal response, "Celaka!" which means "accident" or misfortune" and which is often used when an English speaker might say, "Damn it!" When quizzed intensely about what else Hussain Dorani had ever been seen or heard to do, Rashima and her mother agreed that he does not use improper language, that he does not obey or match, but that he always has an exaggerated startle response with shoulders well up, and that he sometimes assumes a defensive pose with arms raised, characteristic of *bersilat*, the Malay art of self-defense.

11. "Coarse, crude, unrefined," a major conceptual category here. The opposite is *"halus"*: "proper, dignified, graceful, refined." H. Geertz has insightfully discussed this aspect of *latah* behavior in a much-cited paper (1968).

12. I believe that there are at least a few times culturally specified as inappropriate for startle-teasing as well, though I have only minimal data on this point. In the village in which I lived, startling a *latah* while actual feasting was going on was considered bad form, though it was sometimes done. While in the Philippines, I learned that midwives, who often display the startle-matching syndrome there, are not to be intentionally startled when they are delivering babies.

13. P. M. Yap made the same observation, noting: "The diagnosis of established cases presents no problem, but where mild, abortive cases are concerned, it is often difficult to separate the genuine cases from those which are basically histrionic and exhibitionistic in nature" (1952, p. 537). The films help. However, some of the unentranced episodes I saw and filmed were not "mild" and "abortive" but rather were lengthy, elaborately constructed, and intense.

14. Intensity of response and the serial recruitment of elements are not, of course, the only dimensions along which *latah* episodes can be classified. Professor Woon Tai-Hwang of the University of Malaysia told me of hearing the terms *latah gembira* and *latah marah* used in Selangor villages, terms that refer to the affective tone of the episodes ("happy *latah*" and "angry *latah*").

REFERENCES

Abraham, J.J. (1912). *Latah* and *Amok. The British Medical Journal, 1*, 438–439.

Adams, A.R.D. (1951) *Latah* and *Amok. The British Encyclopedia of Medical Practice* (2d ed.), Vol. 8, pp. 1–9.

Banks, D.J. (1983). *Malay kinship*. Philadelphia: Institute for the Study of Human Issues.

Caudill, W., & Lin, Tsung-yi. (1969). *Mental health research in Asia and the Pacific.* Honolulu: East-West Center.

Chapel, J.L. (1970). *Latah, Myriachit,* and *Jumpers* revisited. *New York State Journal of Medicine, 70,* 2201–2204.

Chiu, T.L., Tong, J.E., & Schmidt, K.E. (1972). A clinical and survey study of *Latah* in sarawak, Malaysia. *Psychological Medicine, 2,* 155–165.

Clifford, Sir Hugh C. (1898). Some notes and theories concerning *Latah* (pp. 186–201). *Studies in brown humanity.* London: Grant Richards.

Clifford, Sir Hugh C. (1897). *In court and kampong.* London: Grant Richards.

Clifford, Sir Hugh C. 1926/1970. *In days that are dead.* Freeport, NY: Books for Libraries.

Clifford, Sir Hugh C. 1916/1927. *The further side of silence.* Garden City, NY: Doubleday, Page, and Co.

Djamour, J. (1959). *Malay kinship and marriage in Singapore.* London School of Economics Monographs on Social Anthropology. London: University of London Press.

Ellis, W.G. (1897). *Latah,* A mental malady of the Malays. *Journal of Mental Sciences, 43,* 33–40.

Firth, Ray. 1966/1975. *Malay fishermen, their peasant economy.* New York: Norton.

Firth, Rose. (1966). *Housekeeping among Malay peasants.* London School of Economics Monographs on Social Anthropology No. 7. London: Athlone.

Fletcher, W. (1908). *Latah* and crime. *Lancet, 2:* 254–255.

Galloway, D.J. (1922). A contribution to the psychology of *Latah. Royal Asiatic Society of Great Britain & Ireland, 85,* 140–150.

Geertz, H. (1968). Latah in Java: A theoretical paradox. *Indonesia, 5* (Ithaca, Cornell), 93–104.

Gilmour, A. (1902). *Latah* among South African natives. *Scottish Medical & Surgical Journal, 10,* 18–20.

Gimlette, J.D. 1939/1971. *A dictionary of Malayan medicine* (p. 141). New York: Oxford University Press.

Hairul, A. & Khan, Y. (Eds.). (1977). *Kamus Lengkap.* Petaling Jaya: Pustaka Zaman.

Kline, N. (1963). Psychiatry in Indonesia. *American Journal of Psychiatry, 119,* 809–815.

Lee, R.L.M. (1981). Structure and anti-structure in the culture-bound syndromes: The Malay case. *Culture, Medicine and Psychiatry, 5,* 233–248.

Murphy, H.B.M. (1973). History and the evolution of syndromes: The striking cases of *Latah & Amok.* In M. Hammer, K. Salzinger, & S. Sutton, (Eds.). *Psychopathology.* New York: John Wiley.

Nash, M. (1974). *Peasant citizens: Politics, religion, and modernization in Kelantan, Malaysia.* Papers in International Studies, Southeast Asia Series, Columbus Ohio University Center for International Studies.

Neki, J.S. (1973). Psychiatry in South-East Asia. *British Journal of Psychiatry, 123,* (574), 257–269.

Peacock, J.L. (1968). *Rites of modernization.* Chicago: University of Chicago Press.

Pfeiffer, W.M. (1968). New research findings regarding *Latah. Transcultural Psychiatric Research, 5,* 34–38.

Pelzer, K. J. (1971). *West Malaysia and Singapore: A selected bibliography.* New Haven, CT: Human Relations Area Files.

Pfeiffer, W.M. (1966) Psychiatric peculiarities in Indonesia. *Transcultural Psychiatric Research, 3,* 116–119.

Provencher, R. (1971). *Two Malay worlds*. Berkeley, CA: Research Center for south and southeast Asia Studies. Monograph No. 4.

Shirokogoroff, S.M. (1933). Psychological conditions of groups investigated. *Psychomental complex of the Tungus* (pp. 241–260). London: Kegan Paul.

Simons, R.C. (1980). The resolution of the *Latah* paradox. *Journal of Nervous and Mental Disease, 168* (4), 195–206.

Simons, R.C. (1983a) *Latah* II—Problems with a purely symbolic interpretation. *Journal of Nervous and Mental Disease, 171*, 168–171.

Simons, R.C. (1983b) *Latah* III—How compelling is the evidence for a psychoanalytic interpretation? *Journal of Nervous and Mental Disease, 171*, 178–181.

Simons, R.C., & Hughes, C.C. (Eds.). (1985). *The culture-bound syndromes*. Dordrecht: D. Reidel.

Simons, R.C., & Pfaff, G. (1983). *Latah: A culture-specific elaboration of the startle reflex* [16mm film, color, optical sound, 38 min]. Distributor: Indiana University Audiovisual Center.

Swettenham, F.A. (1895). *Malay sketches* (pp. 64–82). New York: Macmillan Collier.

Swift, M.G. (1965). *Malay peasant society in Jelebu*. London: Athlone.

Twain, M. (Samuel L. Clemens). 1884/1979. *The adventures of Huckleberry Finn*. New York: Signet.

Van Loon, F.H.G. (1927). *Amok* and *Latah. Journal of Abnormal and Social Psychology, 21*, 434–444.

Wagner, N.N., & Eng-Seong, T. (Eds.). (1967). *Psychological problems and treatment in Malaysia*. Kuala Lumpur: University of Malaya Press.

Wilson, P. (1967). *A Malay village and Malaysia*. New Haven, CT: Human Relations Area Files.

Winstedt, R. (1950). *The Malays: A cultural history*. London: Routledge and Kegan.

Winzeler, R.L. (1988). *Malaysian conceptions of Latah and healing*. Prepared for Symposium on Cultural Dimensions of Healing in S.E. Asia. Association for Asian Studies Meeting, San Francisco.

Yap, P.M. (1952). The *Latah* reaction: Its pathodynamics and nosological position. *Journal of Mental Science, 98*, 515–564.

Yap, P.M. (1951). Mental diseases peculiar to certain cultures: A survey of comparative psychiatry. *Journal of Mental Science, 97*, 313–327.

Yap, P.M. (1969). The culture-bound reactive syndromes. *Mental Health Research in Asia and the Pacific*, 34–52.

9

EXPLAINING *LATAH*
The Importance of Descriptive Detail

Tell me, ye learned, shall we for ever be adding so much to the bulk—*so little to the* stock? *Shall we for ever make new books, as apothecaries make new mixtures, by pouring only out of one vessel into another?*

Lawrence Sterne, 1759, *The Life and Opinions of Tristram Shandy*, pp. 342–343

You've made it into a story, and stories are false.

Iris Murdoch, 1978,
The Sea, The Sea, p. 335

Most early descriptions of *latah* in the Western scientific and popular literatures were written by colonial administrators and medical officers. Resident in Malaysia and interacting daily with Malays in many settings, their opportunities for observation were extensive. They were not, however, unbiased observers. As Littlewood and Lipsedge (1989) have pointed out, accounts of culture-bound syndromes such as *latah* were used, often intentionally, to help justify the domination by a colonial power of a colonized people.

Sir Hugh Clifford, who produced seven engrossing books about his experiences as a colonial administrator, wrote extensive descriptions of both *latah* and *amok*. In the preface to *The Further Side of Silence*, Clifford made his aim explicit:

Thus at a preposterously early age I was the principal instrument in adding 15,000 square miles of territory to the British dependencies in the East; and this fact forces me to the conclusion that my share in the business stands in need of some explanation and defence, if readers who are not themselves Britishers are to be persuaded that I am not merely a thief upon a rather large scale. The stories and sketches contained in this book supply me with both. (Clifford, 1916, p. x)

Clifford's rationale, which he could expect most readers who were themselves "Britishers" to share, was simply that:

> In common with most Englishmen who have travelled widely and who have marked things for themselves with a seeing eye, I hold that the British Empire is the mightiest agent for good that God in His infinite wisdom has ever brought into being in this His world. (Clifford, 1916, p. 155)

In Clifford's books, the illustrations as well as the texts portray the subject people as "primitive" and violent. For example, many of the dramatic woodcuts in the 1927 deluxe edition of *The Further Side of Silence* show angry Malay men brandishing weapons or distressed Malay beauties in various states of undress. The captions to these woodcuts include: "As a cat treats a maimed mouse," "My fill of stabbing and killing," and the now classic, "She fought like a wildcat."

In the early literature, this colonial perspective was overtly racist; for example:

> And in that instant it flashed across his mind that never again would it be possible for him to be afraid of Mûruts or of any other natives. The consciousness of the racial superiority of the white man over the brown had come to him with the force of absolute conviction. (Clifford, 1916, p. 71)

Writers unblushingly referred to "the more primitive mental development of the Malay race," and most early explanations of *latah* cite "race" explicitly to explain why *latah* was to be found in Malaya and not in Great Britain:

> "*Latah*" is to be found in quite a number of races and. . .these are all situated within the tropical or sub-tropical belt, and are all more or less in the infancy of civilization. (Galloway, 1922, p. 141)

However, despite their racial biases, colonial administrators and medical officers were in a good position to observe behavior. Although Hugh Clifford believed in the racial superiority of the English, he saw clearly enough that *latah* was some sort of exaggerated startle response and that the state of a Malay in an episode of *latah* was not radically different from that of a severely startled Englishman. In *Studies in Brown Humanity*, he set forth this understanding clearly and succinctly:

The man who is the victim of a sudden fright or nervous shock
loses for a moment all control over his body as completely as does
the Malay on whom *latah* has won its firmest grip. The difference
which exists between him and the *latah* man is only one of degree
and that difference may often be more trifling than that which sep-
arates one *latah* subject from another. Imagine a start or a "jump"
infinitely prolonged and you have the *latah* state about which so
much has been said and written. (1898, p. 196)

Anyone who desires to really account for this affliction must, I am
convinced, begin by analyzing and examining and explaining the
pathology of the common start or "jump," to which we are all in a
lesser or a greater degree subject. This must be the starting point.
(1898, p. 197)

Clifford noted that *latah* episodes were not always intentionally induced
and that the matching that *latahs* performed was involuntary:

A complete stranger by startling a *latah* man or woman can induce
the condition of which I speak accidently and without exercising
any effort of will. (1898, p. 189)

[I]n this extremity [the *latah* state] it [the *latah* person's body]
seizes upon the first moving object that catches its sight and follows slavishly every movement which it makes. (1898, p. 200)

He contrasted the *latah* state with hypnosis, which he believed
involved submission to another person's will:

That there is no question of a weak will surrendering itself to some
stronger brain is amply proved by the fact that a *latah* person will
mimic the swaying motion of wind-shaken boughs just as readily
as the actions of a human being. (1898, p. 200)

Clifford suggested that the universally observed absence of *latah* among
preadolescent children was most likely a matter of neurophysiology:

It is easily conceivable that the seed of the affliction may have no
chance of coming to maturity, so to speak, until the nerves of the
boy or girl have passed the rudimentary stages. (1898, p. 199)

Attributing the proximate mechanism of *latah* to easily elicited, violent,
and prolonged startling, Clifford postulated that perhaps this jumpiness was
an effect of the tropical climate. Clifford believed that Europeans living in
the tropics generally became progressively more "jumpy" (his word), and
that they suffered from a general weakening of the will. He suggested that,
although to a certain extent these changes "may be the effect of any tropical
climate upon the system of a European," there might be something special

about the climate of the Malay peninsula and archipelago that was especially conducive to their development. Believing in the inheritance of acquired characteristics, Clifford offered the hypothesis that Malays were particularly susceptible to *latah* because of their long exposure as a people to the local climate. Others have also postulated climatic factors, either the tropics generally, something about the climate of the Malay archipelago especially, or since other forms of startle-matching have been reported from the arctic (see Chapter 10) extremes of climate (e.g., Shirokogoroff, 1935, p. 245).

Clifford presented his hypotheses cautiously; he did not rule out the possibility that psychological factors are relevant, but he said that his observations led him to conclude that

> *Latah* is an affliction which cannot so easily be explained by psychology, and undoubtedly it is a matter which must largely be treated as a question of pathology. (1898, p. 189)

This view of *latah* as a Malay manifestation of pathological startle was also held by a considerable number of subsequent investigators, both psychiatric and anthropological. Excellent reviews of this literature can be found in Adams (1951), Pfeiffer (1971), Winzeler (1984, 1988), and Yap (1952), to which I refer interested readers.[1] However, as the years have passed, alternative explanations that explicitly deny the central role of startle or indeed of any physiological alteration in determining the form of *latah* behaviors have gained increasing currency. Instead, most contemporary explanations of *latah* consider it to be merely a Malay custom whose features are adequately explained by the symbolic significance of matching, obedience, and coprolalia. Other contemporary reinterpretations of *latah* explain that *latah* behaviors result from training to imitate, from social reinforcement, or from an assortment of psychoanalytic factors. These reinterpretations of *latah* do not stem from new observations that differ from those reported earlier but rather are the result of the adoption of modes of conceptualization currently popular in the disciplines of psychological anthropology and cross-cultural psychiatry. What follows is a representative sampling.

LATAH RESULTS FROM TRAINING TO IMITATE

> *Latah* is widespread in the Indonesian-Malay culture area. *Latah* in Java may relate to the fact that Javanese are trained so much through bodily imitation (as opposed to verbal instruction). Javanese children's hands are repeatedly prodded into position by parents until they learn how to gesture properly. Javanese students are taught to play the gamelan [musical instrument] by having their hands manipulated by the teacher until complex compositions have been learned. Almost no verbal explanations are given. (Peacock, 1968, pp. 159–160)

LATAH SYMPTOMS ARE CULTURALLY DERIVED SYMBOLS USED BY DISTURBED PERSONS TO EXPRESS PSYCHOLOGICAL PROBLEMS

Thus it appears that *latah* is an unusually clear-cut example of how the form of a set of symptoms may be determined primarily by a cultural tradition, a tradition which persists because of its congruity with basic themes in the wider culture. . . . The way which culture could be said to "provide" a ready-made set of symptoms to a psychologically disturbed person may be better understood when a symptom is viewed as a kind of symbol, as a symbolic act by means of which a person can express his psychological dilemmas outwardly. (H. Geertz, 1968, p. 101)

LATAH RESULTS FROM SOCIAL REINFORCEMENT OF *LATAH* BEHAVIOR

The social aspect is apparent in that *latah* never occurs in social isolation.[2] We are dealing with an instrumental or operant learning situation for sexual/aggressive behavior where social attention is the reinforcement. (Chiu, Tong, & Schmidt, 1972, p. 162)

LATAH IS BEST EXPLAINED PSYCHOANALYTICALLY

[T]here are seven main factors contributing to the development of a typical case of *latah*. . . : 1. Repressed wishes probably of an infantile sexual character. 2. Stimulus generalization leading to nonsexual stimuli being misinterpreted as sexual. 3. A masochistic tendency resulting in a failure to defend against the provocative stimuli. . . . 4. Dissociative child-rearing practices. . . . 5. The rewarding of hypersuggestibility in adults. 6. Suppression of lengthier dissociations or trance states through which the repressed wishes could obtain fuller expression. 7. An inflexibility of impulse control that leads to exaggerated startle reactions. . . . (Murphy, 1976, pp. 16–17)

LATAH IS A WAY OF ASSERTING AND LEGITIMATING CULTURAL NORMS

If cultural rules and symbols are constructed objects to which values are attributed, then it is logical to conclude that symptoms of mental illness in particular cultures are really value judgements of how individuals should *not* behave. . . . Role reversals in *latah* and possession hysteria involve the temporary denial and ridicule of assigned female positions in Malay [social] structure. (Lee, 1981, p. 239)

To conceptualize *amok*, *latah*, and possession hysteria as anti-structures in Malay society implies that they are not unique phenomena requiring a special vocabulary for description and analysis. Rather, they can be treated as instances of the many anti-structures that provide bases of contrast for the legitimation of structure in any society. (1981, p. 245)

LATAH IS A WAY OF ASSUMING A POWERFUL TRANSCENDENT ROLE

Latah involves mimesis and obscenity, both of which are a surrender of the self. There is a muddling of the distinctions between subject and object, or self and other. This kind of muddling is precisely a sign of transcendence. The folkloristic accounts of encounters between *latah* women and tigers indicate what powers may accrue to such a person. . . . *Latah* is consistent with the behavior of beings in Malay-Javanese mythology and artistic culture and fits into basic ideas about the nature of the self; this I think is the best explanation for its existence that we are likely to achieve. (Kenny, 1978, pp. 226–227)

LATAH IS A MALAY WAY OF EXPRESSING MARGINALITY

One of the most extreme of these more contemporary reinterpretations is a latter formulation of Michael Kenny, who has written a half-dozen papers on *latah*. Kenny contends that

The *latah* pattern can be fully explained in terms of its meaning [marginality] within specific social and cultural contexts. (1983, p. 160)
    I do not deny the universality of the startle reflex, but it seems basically irrelevant to the understanding of *latah*. (1983, p. 166)[3]

LATAH IS A CONSCIOUS DECEPTION

Agreeing with Kenny on the irrelevance of the startle reflex, Robert Bartholomew concluded that *latahs* are engaged in conscious deception:

Performers are engaged in conscious, ritualized social gain through the purported exploitation of a neurophysiological potential. The latter process is essentially irrelevant, akin to sneezing or yawning. It is concluded that *latah* is a social construction of Western-trained universalist scientists. (1994, p. 331)

A Puzzle

I spent much time trying to puzzle out why what seemed so clear to those who first reported on *latah* was so at variance with what most modern authorities on the subject now believe. The more I considered, the more it seemed that much of the difference lay in the significance given to the myriad brief, prosaic startle-events—usually without matching or obedience—which occurred so frequently in the lives of *latahs* but which never appeared in the anecdotal "case reports." It was the case reports that were providing most of the scholars now writing about *latah* with their pictures of what *latah* was like. The explanations they offered worked only as long as one took solely the more dramatic symptoms of *latah*, the matching, obedience, and "coprolalia" to be that which needed explanation.

Even when they had visited areas in which *latah* was endemic, most contemporary interpreters had not actually lived in a village in extensive daily contact with resident *latahs* but rather had had startle-induced matching and obedience demonstrated to them.[4] The prosaic, brief startles that are so much a part of the everyday existence of a *latah* are private rather than social events. They were seldom reported because they were seldom seen, and because even when they were seen they did not lend themselves to telling in the form of brief, interesting anecdotes. And when I looked at the stories most often cited by modern interpreters of *latah*, I found an interesting bias: They are all good stories. The problem is that good stories suppress the merely prosaic ones, which are considerably more frequent. The request to tell about *latah* elicits good stories that take on a life of their own, becoming "that which is to be explained." For illustration, here is an exceptionally long-lived *latah* story that has been repeatedly reinterpreted.

The Unfortunate Cook

An early description of *latah* was published by H.A. O'Brien in 1883 in the *Journal of the Royal Asiatic Society, Straits Branch*:

> I have met a man several times lately who is a very strong *latah* subject. He is cook on board a local steamer, and is naturally (alas, for human nature!) the butt of all the crew, who daily and almost hourly exercise their clumsy wit—the wit of sailors *plus* orientals—at his expense. All this skylarking, however, had a tragical ending the other day, which illustrates the point of which I am speaking.
>
> This cook was dandling his baby forward one day; one of the crew came and stood before him with a billet of wood in his arms, which he began nursing in the same way as the *latah* was nursing his baby. Presently he began tossing the billet up to the awning, and the cook tossed his child up also, time for time. At last, the sailor opened his hands wide apart and let the wood fall upon the

deck, and the cook immediately spread out his hands away from the descending child, who never moved again after striking the boards. (O'Brien, 1883, p. 150)

Two years later, in 1885, this story was quoted and discussed by Gilles de la Tourette in the famous paper describing the syndrome that now bears his name. An abbreviated version then appeared in *The British Journal of Psychiatry*, 13 years after de la Tourette's paper:

> Mr. O'Brien also described a case of *latah*, the finale of which has become historical in these parts. A Malay cook on board a local steamer, the butt of the crew on account of his disease, was daily subjected to their clumsy wit. One day as this cook was dandling his child one of the crew came and stood before him with a billet of wood in his arms, which he began to toss up to the awning and catch again. The cook tossed his child up also, time for time. At last, the sailor opened his hands wide apart and let the wood fall upon the deck. The cook immediately imitated him, missed the catch, and allowed the child to fall heavily upon the planks, from which it was picked up quite dead. (Ellis, 1897, p. 35)

The Ellis version retells O'Brien's story almost verbatim, though the matching which O'Brien described: "At last, the sailor opened his hands wide apart and let the wood fall upon the deck, and the cook immediately spread out his hands away from the descending child. . ." is merely noted by Ellis: "The cook immediately imitated him. . . ."

Fifteen years later, Abraham (1912), in *The British Medical Journal*, presented this story to a yet wider audience. He did not attribute it to either O'Brien or Ellis, even though elsewhere in the same paper he cited both and attributed a second anecdote, set off in quotes, to O'Brien. The story of "The Unfortunate Cook" he merely referred to as "classical." Here it is as told by Abraham:

> The cook of a coasting steamer had his baby brought to him when the ship was in port. He was known to be intensely devoted to, and proud of, the child. It was also known to his shipmates that he was *latah*. When he was nursing the baby, in his arms on deck, one of the Malay crew came along with a billet of wood, which he pretended to nurse in his arms, like a baby. Next he began to toss the billet of wood in the air, catching it again as it fell, knowing that the unfortunate *latah*, absolutely unable to resist, would be fascinated into imitating him. This the poor victim did do, tossing his precious baby up towards the awning and catching it again, loathing and dreading to do so, yet compelled by his *latah* state to absolutely keep time with his tormentor. Suddenly instead of catching his billet, the sailor opened his arms and let it fall on the

deck. Unable to resist, the miserable father did likewise. The baby fell heavily on the deck and never regained consciousness. (Abraham, 1912, p. 438)

Abraham tells the story in an improved, more "literary" style. In his story the cook has explicit psychological attributes: He is "intensely devoted to, and proud of," the child, "fascinated" by the sailor's actions, and experiences "loathing and dread." There is one new piece of potentially significant data: The matching, which in O'Brien's and Ellis's versions is merely "time for time" (i.e., one toss by the shipmate, one toss by the cook), becomes in Abraham's version "absolutely keeping time with his tormentor" (i.e., moving simultaneously, or close to it). This is what generally occurs when *latahs* match, and 29 years after its first telling, the story has been expanded to include it. Ellis's only explicit moral judgment is that the cook is the "butt" of the crew, whose wit is "clumsy." To Abraham the cook is an "unfortunate *latah*," and a "poor victim," a stronger and more explicit moral stance.[5]

As Abraham says, the story had by this time become "classical." This is so in several senses. It is like a classical Greek drama in which a protagonist with a Fatal Flaw encounters Malignant Fate: The Unfortunate Cook could not resist opening his hands even when to do so meant the death of his beloved child. It is also classical in the sense of "old," known to many and told often in various versions. It continues to be cited as a description of *latah* and it continues to be retold and reinterpreted—for example, by Raymond Prince and Françoise Tcheng-Laroche as one of three case histories in a recent paper, "Culture-Bound Syndromes and International Disease Classifications" (1987). It was also cited prominently and discussed by Beiser (1987) in his commentary on their paper.

Like many early British stories, "The Unfortunate Cook" makes a political point. In it O'Brien deprecates "oriental wit," and elsewhere in the paper he speaks of *latahs*' "entire absence of [sexual] 'virtue' and moral self-restraint (seldom a prominent characteristic of Malay belles)," this last being purely and simply an outrageous slander. Why then is this old story still so often cited? I believe there are two reasons. First, of course, is the story's intrinsic dramatic interest; it's a very good tale. But second, and more importantly, "The Unfortunate Cook" has become a classic illustration of the thesis that the matching of *latahs* is both involuntary and absolute.

Contemporary Malay Anecdotes of *Latah* Episodes

It is not only Europeans who, when asked about *latahs*, tell dramatic stories. In the seven tales one Malay woman told me, a *latah* put herself in danger, a baby was almost killed because of proximity to a *latah*, two *latahs* injured themselves, one seriously, and one *latah* killed a baby. Many of the accounts of *latah* that I heard from other informants were equally dramatic, and a number of the more dramatic stories were related to me by several informants. In many the word *bahaya* ("danger") was used or the *latah* was said to have done something radically unsafe—for example, played with a cobra or failed to flee a tiger. All but five of the 23 Malay stories of *latah* that I collected systematically told of death, injury, or danger. In this set of systematically collected accounts, there were five deaths (all of *latahs*), one self-injury, and four injuries to others. In one story a girl is disfigured when her *latah* father throws water, which he had been boiling for tea, into her face. In another a male *latah* who has been commanded to climb a coconut tree and act in a reckless manner is stung by bees and falls to his death. One of the stories ends with *two* dead *latahs*:

> A Malay woman called Mak Cik Esah bin Daud, popularly known as Mak Cik *Latah*, a midwife in a village, aged about fifty years old, was very gentle, polite, humble, and generous. One day in Kampung Sri Langkan there was a woman giving birth in great need of a midwife. Kampung Sri Langkan was far away and lacking in good transportation and facilities; roads there were for bicycles and pedestrians only. Nevertheless, the woman's husband went to get the midwife at about one A.M. He had walked about two miles to the midwife's house in a dark night and through a slight drizzle. [The midwife is informed and agrees to attend the birth.] On reaching home a large crowd was already gathering. Kassim's wife and the midwife carried out their duties subsequently.
>
> There was also a *latah* named "Timah" among the crowd. While Cik tensely performed her daily routine job, Timah saw the long umbilical cord, and, thinking it to be a snake, retreated in fear. The midwife followed suit, and they both began to strike out at each other. As it happened, the midwife was holding a knife and she stabbed Timah's abdomen. They exchanged cuts, stabbing each other and causing confusion and unnecessary bloodshed. Neither would give way. Finally, however, without knowing what she was doing, Timah stabbed herself and collapsed. When day dawned, the relatives who watched were mystified and confused.
>
> Hence, that is the story of two *latahs* who succeeded in killing each other. When Timah was stabbed by the midwife, people became speechless and despondent. Therefore, to prevent danger, those who know a *latah* should not startle her or disturb her unnecessarily. That's all of the story of the *latahs*, midwife Esah and Timah, which ended up with them killing each other.

That's strong stuff. The *latah*'s predicament provides several sources of peril. The danger may result from matching as in "The Unfortunate Cook" and in a story I heard several times in which a *latah* mother who was watching the actions of a frog held her baby under the water whenever the frog went under until it finally drowned. The danger may result from automatic obedience, as in the story told in Chapter 8 in which a *latah* who was holding a knife stabbed a man to death when someone poked her in the ribs and commanded: "Stab!" And it may also result from sudden unplanned defensive responses, similar to those described by American hyperstartlers in Chapter 2, by Garrison in an American anecdote cited in the notes to Chapter 8, and by Shirokogoroff, who described startle-matching in Siberia:

> One day he [the subject] was sitting alone, with his small son, in the wigwam [*sic*]. A knife fell down in front of him (evidently the knife had been in the hanging hunting belt). He seized it and thrust it into his son's body. (1935, p. 248)

However, despite their frequency in stories, fatal encounters are not the usual outcomes of *latah* episodes. Although I regularly asked about injuries or deaths that people present had actually witnessed, only one informant ever told me that he had actually seen a fatal encounter, and his story was not convincing. All other accounts were at least secondhand. Why then are such stories so frequent in Malay accounts of *latah*? I think that it was largely because they make the point about the absolutely compelled nature of *latahs'* matching and obedience and because they were such good tales.[6]

There is a third reason why Malay accounts of *latah* so emphasized danger: the great value Malay culture places on self-control in all circumstances. (Firth, 1975; Provencher, 1971) In Malay culture it is considered dangerous not to be in control of one's behavior, and it is also considered dangerous to be in the presence of someone not in control. In Malay culture, *latahs* typify people unable to control their actions. When I was introduced to village headmen to obtain permission to study in their villages, one of my assistants sometimes explained that my study would benefit the community because I would lessen the danger to and from *latahs*, this despite the fact that in reality *latahs* are not dangerous at all.[7]

Prosaic Episodes of *Latah* That Do Not Make Good Stories

Some kinds of events make better stories than do others. Predictions and premonitions that come true, for example, are more likely to be recounted than are failed predictions or premonitions that turn out to be empty. Some things are simply more interesting than others and have been used to make stories in many cultural contexts: the acquisition, misuse, and loss of power; sexual attraction when consummation is beset with difficulties, for example. "The Unfortunate Cook" is a good story. What motivated the crewman to do a dreadful thing like that, and how was it played out afterward? Because it is a story with a beginning, middle, and ending, it is not hard to imagine even more dramatic expansions than Abraham's. Most of the other frequently told, reprinted, and cited descriptions of *latahs*, like

"The Unfortunate Cook," make the point of how absolutely and uncondi-
tionally a *latah* may be forced to match or obey. Stories of *latahs* disrobing
in public are frequent for similar reasons; these too are engaging stories
that make the same point.[8]

However, unlike the dramatic anecdotes most frequently told to me
and most frequently cited in the *latah* literature, most episodes of *latah* do
not readily make good stories. *Latahs* are merely easily startled people who,
like American hyperstartlers, are startled frequently by chance occurrences. They startle more easily than others, and their startles are stronger,
sometimes resulting in attention-capture. *Latahs* told me, and my own
observations confirmed, that even in social contexts most of their startles
are brief, prosaic, and "unstoryable."[9]

Underreported Elements of the Syndrome

In the literature about *latah*, many characteristic and recurrent features are
seldom reported and have no common names. One such feature is a behavior I have called the "Get-It-Off-Me" response. When startled, some *latahs*
perform frantic brushing-off movements or, if they are sitting, rapid up-
and-down movements of the feet. I have seen this done by American
hyperstartlers, by *latahs*, and by persons with the startle-matching syndrome in the Philippines. It was recorded in the films of hyperstartlers
from Malaysia, Thailand, and Japan and was reported in a case of startle-
matching in Holland (Jenner, 1990, p. 195). Both the brushing and the
movement of the feet are automatic, unlearned maneuvers that are highly
effective against most creepy-crawlies. Such immediate and unreflective
responses are not only theoretically important but are also important in the
actual day-to-day survival of people in rural Southeast Asia, most of whom
regularly encounter poisonous snakes, scorpions, centipedes, and hornets
as part of their ordinary experience. However, some *latahs* and other hyperstartlers perform such movements even to sudden startling loud sounds.
With the exception of the Dutch case cited above, the Get-It-Off-Me
response has gone unreported in the *latah* literature and therefore has not
been treated as something needing explanation.

Another frequent yet rarely reported aspect of *latah* behavior is a tic-
like vocalization I call the "Eh!" response. This is the utterance of a sharp
"Eh!" once or several times at intervals of a few seconds, sometimes
inserted into ongoing speech. *Latahs* said "Eh!" only during the course of
latah performances, never at other times in their everyday behavior or
speech. "Eh!" was often uttered with a slight jump as if it were a startle-
eliciting stimulus, a startle response, or both. Whether it functions to
induce the neurophysiologic state associated with *latah* or whether it is
only communicative, a signal to onlookers that what they are seeing is to
be taken as part of a set of *latah* behaviors, I do not now know. I suspect that
at different times either or both may be the case.[10] These "Eh!" vocalizations are included in the transcription of a *latah*'s speech in Yap's important

paper (1952, p. 534), but they are not discussed. Unlike Yap, I had not noticed them in the field but only became aware of their frequent occurrence while studying our film records of *latah* at the Interaction Analysis Laboratory. With the single exception of Yap's transcript, they have not been mentioned in the *latah* literature.

Yet another response with no name is a special case of matching: the extraction from ongoing speech of several words recently uttered by either the subject or by someone else in her hearing, not the last words spoken. Although this behavior occurs not infrequently in the speech of *latahs*, it too never appears in the anecdotes that are analyzed in much of the contemporary literature on *latah*.

> Jaafar had been talking with Mak Cik Rahama at her house for about twenty minutes before I joined them. Two friends, her children, and her husband were present. After I joined them, we talked about genealogies. After about ten minutes a friend poked Rahama from behind and she jumped (she had been sitting), stretched out her left arm, and repeated in a loud, "startled" voice four words extracted from the innocuous genealogic information she had just been relating to us. (Field notes, March 12, 1978)

To be an adequate interpretation of the *latah* syndrome, a formulation must explain not only the dramatic matching, obedience, striking out, and amusing behaviors that make for good stories, but also *latah*'s prosaic aspects. It must also explain the regular but rarely reported features of episodes such as delayed matching of words extracted from ongoing speech, "Eh!" behavior, and the "Get-It-Off-Me" response.

Limitations of Verbal Descriptions

All descriptions of behaviors or events are by logical necessity incomplete as decisions must always be made about how much of the setting is to be included, what the units described will be, how extensive they will be in time, what blocks of time will compose the unitary elements that are combined to constitute the narrative event, and, of course, what the elements are that are considered significant and interesting to any audience. With all accounts, especially accounts made to foreign investigators, there is always the question of how the narrator wants the anecdote and the indigenous people to be judged. An outsider's capacity to understand culturally meaningful features of the event described is also assessed by his or her informants, and narratives may be further colored by assumptions about what he or she wants to hear and by estimates of his or her fluency in the local language. Conversely, they may be colored by the narrator's fluency in the language of the investigator. Although stories often reveal attitudes and values especially clearly, parsing stories may give a quite misleading idea about the nature of the class of events of which they tell.

It was a great advantage to have actually lived in a Malay village. What people told me in the long equatorial evenings was of enormous help in understanding what I had seen and heard during the working day, and what I had seen and heard helped me to understand and interpret what I was being told. I remember, for example, an outspoken young woman who waxed indignant over the inconsiderate behavior of others to *latahs*. She was the only informant who called tormenting *latahs* a sin ("*dosa*"). But at times in telling *latah* stories she giggled, and I had seen with my own eyes her participation in the teasing of *latahs*. I also saw the passionately articulate woman whose indignantly related story of her sister's humiliation at a wedding is quoted in Chapter 8 participate vigorously in some heartless *latah* teasing of the very same sister.[11]

Advantages of Audiovisual Recordings

A film or videotape record permits a kind of study not available to the observer of the live event. With a live event, one can consciously attend to only a few aspects at a time, and while dramatic and attention-attracting events are taking place, less dramatic events of equal or greater significance may go unnoticed. With film or video, concurrent events can be attended to in different viewings, attending on each viewing to a particular aspect of interest, with detail amplified by large-screen projection or slow motion. The time scale of live observation is too brief to discern, for example, whether or not a *latah* who claimed to have been startled actually had been. Did she blink? How long was the interval between the stimulus and her response? Such data are, however, available in the film record.

Episodes of *Latah* in the Film *Latah*

In addition to descriptive and interpretive talk about *latah* by indigenous informants, the film *Latah* contains 22 scenes from 13 different episodes of *latah* performed by seven persons who acknowledged being *latahs* after being so identified by their peers. Five of these *latahs* are women and two are men. Six of the scenes, all brief, are episodes of *latah* shown in their entirety. The other 16 scenes are segments of the remaining seven *latah* episodes. A few of the scenes are shown twice. The scenes were edited for a variety of expository purposes—for example, a 10-minute role *latah* performance that was cut to three contiguous scenes, separated by fades to indicate the passage of time. Independent of anything I or others say in or about the film, these 22 scenes constitute a data source available for anyone to analyze independently.[12]

Because they are so similar to the episodes of *latah* I witnessed almost daily, I believe that the episodes shown in the film are both typical and representative of the reality of *latah* in the village of Kampung Padang Kemunting. In addition, I believe that they are reasonably typical and representative of the *latah* syndrome as seen throughout Malaysia. However, just as there are significant differences in the named variants of the startle-matching syndrome engendered by culturally specific constructions and constraints, it seems likely that even within Malaysia there are subcultural variations in episode patterns.

Although the episodes of *latah* in the film are representative of the kind of events informants told me of and that I saw, they, like episodes described in oral narratives or in print, were chosen to illustrate specific aspects of *latah* or to make specific points. Though the range of events is well represented (there is at least one of most kinds of *latah* events), both the frequency and the distribution of these events are skewed toward prolonged, socially generated, and highly socially modified episodes. This is also true of the corpus of film from which the episodes shown in *Latah* were selected.

Because reels of 16-mm film only record 10 continuous minutes, and because we had a limited supply of film, most of the *latah* episodes we shot began with a startle induced by another person on a prearranged signal. Our procedure was to discuss the research in some detail with each *latah* subject. As I had been living in the village for some months and inquiring about *latah* widely, most people already knew me and knew about the project. The cameraman, sound recordist, and I made social visits to *latahs'* homes, during which we were always served something to drink and often something to eat with our hosts. We brought our equipment and left it in view for curious inspection while we chatted. During these visits I would ask if there was any objection to sometime setting up an occasion when the *latah* would unexpectedly be startled and filmed. We filmed only those subjects who consented, most but not all of the *latahs* we asked. Refusals, of course, were not random; men refused more often than did women.

With the exception of two instances described more fully below, filming was always to some degree a social event. Such social episodes are therefore overrepresented, and the brief spontaneous episodes of hyperstartling, sometimes with momentary attention-capture, which are actually vastly more frequent in the lives of *latahs*, are underrepresented in the film. It is for this reason that the few scenes of brief, unplanned, spontaneous startle that we were fortunate enough to capture on film are especially interesting.

Because they were brief, unstaged, and unpredictable, these were the most difficult scenes to capture on film, even though they were the kinds of *latah* episodes I saw most frequently. Given the debate about the nature of *latah* in the literature, they are among the most revealing of all the *latah* footage. Some of these scenes are brief, excessive startles occurring in the course of long *latah* episodes. One *latah*, Hajah Misah, startles when someone innocently offers her a long cylindrical log to pound betel on; it is presented from the side when her attention is distracted elsewhere. Cik Mah startles when a friend motions toward her face in an attempt to indicate that she should close her eyes and quiet down. Dancing at a wedding, Cik Maimun Husain startles violently when a flashbulb goes off. Two startles to the noise of intentionally dropped film cans are brief as is the startle of Rahama, who when unexpectedly poked in the side merely jumps a bit, says "*Puki!*" ("Cunt!"), then laughs in an embarrassed way. A poked *latah* says "*Konek lebam!*" ("Soft boy's prick!"), then "Eh!" with apparent embarrassment.

Two other brief episodes occur when a *latah* is accidently startled by a chance occurrence; we refer to them as "the fish startle" and "the boat startle." Both of these episodes were unplanned. We got them on film only because we happened to be on the beach filming one of the subsistence activities (rice and coconut cultivation, fishing, and mat making), which, like the sheer beauty of the village, the film shows without comment.

The "fish startle" occupies only a few seconds and is not explicitly commented on in the film. However, it was so interesting to us that we spent a significant number of very limited postproduction dollars on it. The money went to create an "optical pan," so that what one now sees is the enlarged center of the original footage. The effect is that of the telephoto we would have used on the spot had we had any inkling of what was about to happen.

In the "fish startle," Cik Mah, a *latah*, is picked up in the course of a long wide-angle pan of the beach. Although she has been coming down to the boats daily for fresh-caught fish all her life, when a fisherman holds up a long, thin fish, which dangles from his hand in a sinuous curve, Cik Mah startles violently, jerking back and raising her arm abruptly. There is no more to the incident, no matching, no obedience, no silly talk or behavior, and no social interaction around its occurrence.

The "boat startle" begins with Cik Mah watching a young fisherman scooping prawns from the floor of his boat into a clear plastic bag. As he attempts to drop some prawns into a 5-gallon red plastic container, it tips and falls to the bottom of the boat with a clatter. Cik Mah is just out of camera range, but we hear her voice saying "*O gali-ya!*" ("Oh, dig-ya!," an idiosyncratic phrase the significance of which I never discovered) when startled by the sound and sight of the spilling container. After a pause of a few seconds, she resumes speaking in a normal voice. The fisherman looks up at her and says, "Ay!," raising his right hand. Cik Mah responds with a loud "Ay!," matching his movement with her left hand (a mirror homolog), which had been outstretched toward him and the prawns. Then, as he continues to gesture with his right hand, she matches his movement with her right (a parallel homolog) (Fig. 9.1).

When he returns to sorting the prawns, she again moves her right arm, converting what had been a match to the standard deprecatory emblem,[13] which means, "Oh never mind, that isn't anything." She looks somewhat sheepish, and she begins to coil the bow painter (rope) and lay it in the bow as she speaks to him in a normal voice. Ignoring her, he turns to some other fishermen and says: "*Joget, dia joget*": "As for dancing, she will dance" or "If one dances, she will dance."

Cik Mah's final response, the deprecatory shake, can be thought of as exemplifying the exact opposite of role *latah*. Instead of acknowledging her infirmity and expanding and playing with it, she seems to be attempting to

Figure 9.1   The "Boat Startle." Accidentally startled when a bucket of prawns overturns, a *latah*, Cik Mah, matches the hand gestures of the fisherman whose action startled her. (Still from film *Latah*)

normalize and minimize what she had done by redefining it. Most of us have done something parallel at times, turning the wave to someone who turns out not to be an acquaintance into a head-scratch or the unnecessary adjustment of a hat. Unskillful attempts at such repair[14] are often parodied by comedians, especially those who specialize in portraying the timid or incompetent. The significance of this brief scene is that it is a record of a *latah*'s attempt to minimize and pass off as unremarkable her matching response. Matching, like other components of the startle-matching syndrome, may be not only played up; it may also be played down.

Although such events as the fish and boat startles are very frequent in the lives of *latahs,* they never get made into stories. None of the widely accepted cultural or social explanations of *latah* explain them. When Cik Mah startles to the spilling prawns and to the fish, she is not by any stretch of the imagination expressing repressed sexual impulses or symbolizing her marginality. The boat and fish startles demonstrate that much of what sets the *latah* apart is simply her readiness to startle, her experience as a chronic condition of that state of hyperresponsiveness to insignificant stimuli that most of us know only when excessively tired, preoccupied, wary, or high on caffeine.

CONCLUSIONS

It is less useful because it is less informative to endlessly reinterpret the previously collected "classical" accounts of *latah* than to investigate, using

modern methods and standards of data collection, the actual lives of contemporary *latahs*. There is a probably apocryphal story of a medieval
philosopher bewailing the fact that we shall never be able to know how
many teeth a horse has, since the pages in Aristotle containing this information had been lost.[15] However in the case of *latah*, we have written
descriptions of many observations and also a film record.

Stories are useful exemplars of the points they were selected to make.
True or not, they tend to describe extreme cases and do not adequately
depict the range of *latah* events. It is too easy to theorize about the matching, obedience, and "coprolalia" which stories feature. "Training to imitate" might appear to explain why *latahs* match, and "repressed sexual
impulses" might seem a reasonable explanation for *latahs*' naughty talk, but
what about all the other odd things they do and say? If one proposes a formulation that explains only a single manifestation of *latah*, one must suggest others to explain its other manifestations. However, multiple manifestations are often parts of a single episode or are performed by the same
latah subject at different times. It is this whole range of behaviors and experiences of *latah* that must be explained. Any explanation of *latah*, no matter how consistent with a cherished theory, is not an adequate explanation
if it fails to account for all of the behaviors seen and what is actually experienced by the participants.

It is the details of actual behaviors and experiences that solve the mystery, that tell the true story. Details generate questions and provide
answers; they narrow the range of possible interpretations. When one has
competing explanations, an empirical approach with attention to observed
detail narrows the possible explanations in a way that theory cannot. As the
level of abstraction increases, increasingly disparate events are included in
any category. The more general the description of the phenomenon being
studied, the greater the number of hypotheses that can explain it. The more
detailed the description, the fewer the hypotheses that adequately explain
the mass of observed facts.

Though a "most true" hypothesis is always hard to prove, the examination of minute descriptive detail often allows one to chose a "least false"
hypothesis. For any hypothesis, one must ask which observations would
it account for, which are consistent, which inconsistent with it? A mass of
data which it fails to account for or with which it is inconsistent should be
fatal to a theory. A good explanation must explain all or most of the data,
not just a convenient selection.

Finally, the explanation of *latah* as a consequence of excessively easy
and violent startling is, after all, quite congruent with the indigenous
understanding of *latah*. It is what *latahs* and the villagers who live with it
most often say. It is therefore ironic to find this explanation attacked by so
many Western scholars as merely "biomedical," reductionistic, and anti-
thetical to indigenously held beliefs and values.[16] Which of the explanations cited in this chapter is closest to the indigenous view? When in a systematic survey Winzeler asked Malay informants about Kenny's allegation

that being a *latah* was associated with a powerful transcendent role, he found that "nothing that I was able to learn from any of the very large number of *latah* persons I interviewed in detail, or from other informants, supported the notion that *latah* persons might be thought to have special powers by virtue of being *latah*. . . . Basically everyone thought this was a silly idea" (1988, p. 8).

The point that a neurophysiologic interpretation of *latah* is more congruent with the indigenous explanation than with most contemporary symbolic formulations was made most clearly in an eloquent letter I received from David Hufford. His explanation of "Old Hag," a culture-bound syndrome from Newfoundland, as a cultural elaboration of the neurophysiology of sleep paralysis[17] engendered violent criticism in the anthropological literature similar to that with which my papers on *latah* were originally received. Hufford observed:

> One of the several similarities between your work and mine, and the response to it from various sectors of the academic community, is the fact that your explanation of *latah* is actually much more congenial to indigenous explanations than are the standard ethnopsychiatric explanations.
>
> Most often, academic psychodynamic and anthropological approaches have reacted to local traditions by providing what are essentially competing interpretations or meanings in the broadest sense of those words. They have then implied that those interpretations were somehow explanations, although generally they are not. That is why they are generally incapable of producing predictions or of being falsified. Explanations, using the term in a narrow sense, are reductive, empirical, logical, and therefore confirmable and disconfirmable. Explanations also do not generally compete with meaning systems. . . .
>
> The traditional academic interpretations of the beliefs of various cultures are really much more aggressive and hostile to local systems of meaning than are neurophysiological ones because they say "Here is what your experience really means." No matter how many times that statement is couched in terms of respect for the "creativity" and "subjective reality" of the local meaning system, it is always implicit that in ontological terms the local system is in an inferior position to the academic system of interpretation. And furthermore, such academic interpretations are usually in direct logical conflict with the local system, although this conflict is frequently hidden through the extensive use of metaphor and symbolic language. . . .
>
> Maybe that is what intrigues me about this gradually developing picture of superior congeniality between our approach and those indigenous explanations for the matters under discussion than is implicit in traditional psychodynamic and anthropological approaches. It is primarily on the matter of congeniality and

respect that the traditional approaches have based their fundamental claim to being the proper interpreters of culture. (David
Hufford, 1990, personal communication)

In addition to the data presented in this and the preceding chapter,
there is a second line of evidence that supports the hypothesis that *latah* is
the playing out in a Malay cultural context of the behavioral and experiential potential inherent in the neurophysiology of the startle reflex. This
evidence is the similarity of the descriptive features of *latah* to the behaviors of persons like those discussed in Chapter 7 who do not come from a
cultural context in which any of the usual ethnopsychiatric or anthropological explanations of *latah* could possibly apply. The next chapter
describes more of these *latah*-like startle-matching syndromes from other
cultures. The striking cross-cultural similarity of behaviors, down to the
smallest details, provides a second and logically independent line of evidence for their neurophysiological shaping.

NOTES

1. Both the altered neurophysiology of startle in *latahs* and the cultural contexts in which *latah* occurs are discussed in the papers by Yap and Pfeiffer. Interested
readers are referred especially to Yap's dated but insightful and prescient work.
2. The context makes it clear that by "social isolation," Chiu et al. (1972)
mean "when the *latah* is alone." This assertion is simply wrong.
3. In fairness to Kenny it should be acknowledged that his most recent paper
on *latah* concedes that "both Europeans and locals agree that 'shock' or 'startle'
is an important factor in the genesis of *latah*." (1990, p. 125) This concession, however, does not alter his purely culturological interpretation or his dismissal of the
argument for the relevance of neurophysiological factors as "simplistic" (Kenny,
1990, p. 138).
4. Geertz and Bartholomew, however, did spend considerable time in Malay
villages, and Peacock spent much time in rural Indonesia. Why their explanations
of *latah* fail to take into account its full range of features remains puzzling.
5. Moral evaluations are understandably often included in descriptions of
startle-teasing. In Chapter 7, Vreeland described the exploitation of Goosey Gus's
vulnerability as "unmerciful," and he uses the terms "torment," "aggressor," and
"rowdies." Similarly, Harpending says "a terrible story" and "given the level of
interaction at this plant."
6. In retrospect, I believe that I and others who collected tales for me must
have shown special interest in the "good stories" too.
7. When the subject of danger from *latahs* came up in this way, I would
explain that my study was at that time an investigation only, that any practical benefit was uncertain and at best far off. My guide's comment did, however, properly
raise the question of whether my study could be of any benefit to the *latahs* being
studied or to their communities, an issue to be discussed in Chapter 11.
8. The film *Latah* contains scenes of informants relating incidents of both
killing and disrobing. These are structured as stories, with beginnings, middles,
and endings.

9. This useful term and concept comes from unpublished lectures by the late Harvey Sachs, the analyst of conversations.

10. Tanner (unpublished) has suggested that this "Eh!," which she observed in Indonesia, may be a vocal tic associated with the neurophysiologic disturbance that shapes other manifestations of *latah*. I do not believe this is correct, but it is an interesting possibility.

11. Both the indignation and the teasing are shown in the *Latah* film.

12. The film also contains five scenes of *imu*, a startle-matching syndrome of the Ainu people in Japan, discussed in Chapter 10, and one scene of an American hyperstartler.

13. Ekman differentiated what he referred to as "emblems" from direct expressions of emotion and from other kinds of gestures, defining them as "those nonverbal acts which have a direct verbal translation, a dictionary definition consisting of a word or two or perhaps a phrase, which is known to all members of a culture or subculture" (Ekman, 1973, p. 181).

14. "Repair" is a term used by Jordan and Fuller (1975) to describe the work done by participants in an interaction after some "glitch" has occurred to make the flow of the interaction smooth and nonproblematic once again and to excuse and justify the preceding irregularity.

15. This line of reasoning stems from the Platonic concept of real essences whose manifestations in the world are only shadows. I do not believe that this is a position most of those writing about *latah* in the anthropological and psychiatric literature would choose to take explicitly.

16. For example, to quote Kenny:

> The consequences of adopting this or any other biomedical formulation are potentially great in that they may blur the human content of the phenomena. I can only repeat what was said in 1898 by one of the earliest, and still one of the best commentators on *latah* [Sir Hugh Clifford]: "It is doubtless difficult for a medical man to always bear in mind that a patient is a human being in the first instance, and a 'case' purely incidentally." (1983, p. 166)

Clifford, however, as the quotes given earlier in this chapter amply demonstrate, did believe *latah* to be a special case of neural pathology. In the passage cited above, Clifford was criticizing neurophysiological interpretations of *amok*. For other strong negative opinions about the propriety of including neurophysiologic considerations in the explanation of *latah*, see also Murphy (1983), Winzeler (1984), Karp (1985), and Bartholomew, (1994).

17. See Hufford, 1976 and 1982.

REFERENCES

Abraham, J.J. (1912). *Latah* and *Amok*. *The British Medical Journal, 1*, 438–439.

Adams, A.R.D. (1951). *Latah* and *Amok*. *The British Encyclopedia of Medical Practice* (2d ed., Vol. 8, pp. 1–9).

Bartholomew, R.E. (1994). Disease, disorder, or deception? Latah as habit in a Malay extended family. *Journal of Nervous and Mental Disease, 182*, 331–338.

Beiser, M. (1987). Commentary on "Culture-bound syndromes and international disease classifications." *Culture, Medicine, and Psychiatry, 11*, 29–33.

Caudill, W., & Lin, Tsung-yi. (1969). *Mental health research in Asia and the Pacific.* Honolulu: East-West Center Press.

Chapel, J.L. (1970). *Latah, Myriachit,* and *Jumpers* revisited. *New York State Journal of Medicine, 70,* 2201–2204.

Chiu, T.L., Tong, J.E. & Schmidt, K.E. (1972). A clinical and survey study of *Latah* in Sarawak, Malaysia. *Psychological Medicine, 2,* 155–165.

Clifford, Sir Hugh C. (1897). *In court and kampong.* London: Grant Richards Press.

Clifford, Sir Hugh C. 1898/1927. Some notes and theories concerning *Latah* (pp. 186–201). *Studies in brown humanity.* London: Grant Richards Press.

Clifford, Sir Hugh C. 1916/1927. *The further side of silence.* Garden City, NY: Doubleday, Page and Co.

Clifford, Sir Hugh C. 1926/1970. *In days that are dead.* Freeport, NY: Books for Libraries.

Djamour, J. (1959). *Malay kinship and marriage in Singapore.* London School of Economics Monographs on Social Anthropology. London: University of London Press.

Ekman P. (1973). Cross-cultural studies of facial expression. In P. Ekman (Ed.), *Darwin and facial expression.* New York: Academic Press.

Ellis, W.G. (1897). *Latah,* a mental malady of the Malays. *Journal of Mental Sciences, 43,* 33–40.

Firth, Ray. 1966/1975. *Malay fishermen, their peasant economy.* New York: Norton.

Firth, Rose. (1966). *Housekeeping among Malay peasants.* London School of Economics Monographs on Social Anthropology No. 7. London: Athlone.

Fletcher, W. (1908). *Latah* and crime. *Lancet, 2,* 254–255.

Galloway, D.J. (1922). A contribution to the psychology of *Latah. Royal Asiatic Society of Great Britain & Ireland, 85,* 140–150.

Geertz, H. (1968). *Latah* in Java: A theoretical paradox. *Indonesia, 5* (Ithaca: Cornell), 93–104.

Gilmour, A. (1902). *Latah* among South African natives. *Scottish Medical & Surgical Journal, 10,* 18–20.

Gimlette, J.D. 1939/1971. *A dictionary of Malayan medicine.* Oxford: Oxford University Press.

Hairul, A., & Khan, Y. (Eds.). (1977). *Kamus Lengkap.* Petaling Jaya: Pustaka Zaman.

Hufford, D.J. (1976). A new approach to the "Old Hag." In W.D. Hand (Ed.), *American folk medicine* (pp. 73–85). Los Angeles: University of California Press.

Hufford, D.J. (1982). *The terror that comes in the night.* Philadelphia: University of Pennsylvania Press.

Jenner, J.A. (1990). *Latah* as coping. *International Journal of Social Psychiatry, 36,* 194–199.

Jordan, B., & Fuller, N. (1975). On the nonfatal nature of trouble: Sense-making and trouble-managing in *Lingua Franca* talk. *Semiotica, 13,* 11–31.

Karp, I. (1985). Deconstructing culture-bound syndromes. *Social Science and Medicine, 21,* 221–228.

Kenny, M. (1978). *Latah:* The symbolism of a putative mental disorder. *Culture, Medicine and Psychiatry, 2,* 209–231.

Kenny, M. (1983). Paradox lost: The *Latah* problem revisited. *Journal of Nervous and Mental Disease, 171,* 159–167.

Kenny, M. (1990). *Latah:* The logic of fear. In W. J. Karim, (Ed.), *Emotions of culture: A Malay perspective.* Singapore: Oxford University Press.

Kline, N. (1963). Psychiatry in Indonesia. *American Journal of Psychiatry, 119,* 809–815.

Lee, R.L.M. (1981). Structure and anti-structure in the culture-bound syndromes: The Malay case. *Culture, Medicine and Psychiatry, 5,* 233–248.

Littlewood, R., & Lipsedge, M. (1989). *Aliens and alienists*. London: Unwin Hyman.

Murdoch, I. (1978). *The sea, the sea*. Middlesex: Viking Penguin.

Murphy, H.B.M. (1973). History and the evolution of syndromes: The striking cases of *Latah* & *Amok*. In M. Hammer et al. (Eds.), *Psychopathology*. New York: John Wiley.

Murphy, H.B.M. (1976). Notes for a theory on *Latah*. In W. Lebra (Ed.), *Culture-bound syndromes, ethnopsychiatry, and alternate therapies* (Vol. 4). Honolulu: University of Hawaii Press.

Murphy, H.B.M. (1983). Commentary on "The resolution of the *Latah* paradox." *Journal of Nervous and Mental Disease, 171*, 176–177.

Nash, M. (1974). *Peasant citizens: Politics, religion, and modernization in Kelantan, Malaysia*. Papers in International Studies, S.E. Asia Series No. 31. Athens, Ohio: Ohio University Center for International Studies.

Neki, J.S. (1973). Psychiatry in South-East Asia. *British Journal of Psychiatry, 123*, 257–269.

O'Brien, H.A. (1883). *Latah. Journal of the Royal Asiatic Society, Straits Branch, 11*, 143–153.

Peacock, J.L. (1968). *Rites of modernization*. Chicago: University of Chicago Press.

Pelzer, K.J. (1971). *West Malaysia and Singapore: A selected bibliography*. New Haven, CT: Human Relations Area Files.

Pfeiffer, W.M. (1966). Psychiatric peculiarities in Indonesia. *Transcultural Psychiatric Research, 3*, 116–119.

Pfeiffer, W.M. (1968). New research findings regarding *Latah. Transcultural Psychiatric Research, 5*, 34–38.

Pfeiffer, W.M. (1971). Die *Latah*-artigen reaktionen. In *Transkulturelle psychiatrie* (pp. 80–125). Stuttgart: Thieme.

Prince, R., & Tcheng-Laroche, F. (1987). Culture-bound syndromes and international disease classifications. *Culture, Medicine, and Psychiatry, 11*, 3–19.

Provencher, R. (1971). *Two Malay worlds*. Research Monograph No. 4. Berkeley, CA: Center for South and Southeast Asia Studies.

Shirokogoroff, S. M. (1935). *Psychological conditions of groups investigated. Psychomental complex of the Tungus* (pp. 241–260). London: Kegan Paul.

Simons, R.C. (1980). The resolution of the *Latah* paradox. *Journal of Nervous and Mental Disease, 168*, 195–206.

Simons, R.C. (1983a). *Latah* II—Problems with a purely symbolic interpretation. *Journal of Nervous and Mental Disease, 171*, 168–171.

Simons, R.C. (1983b). *Latah* III—How compelling is the evidence for a psychoanalytic interpretation? *Journal of Nervous and Mental Disease, 171*, 178–181.

Simons, R.C. (1987). A feasible and timely enterprise. *Culture, Medicine, and Psychiatry, 11*, 21–28.

Simons, R.C., & Hughes, C.C. (Eds.). (1985). *The culture-bound syndromes*. Dordrecht: D. Reidel.

Simons, R.C., & Pfaff, G. (1983). *Latah: A culture-specific elaboration of the startle reflex* [16mm, film color, optical sound, 38 min.]. Distributor: Indiana University Audiovisual Center.

Sterne, L. 1759/1983. *The life and opinions of Tristram Shandy*. Oxford: Oxford University Press.

Swettenham, F.A. (1895). *Malay sketches*. New York: Macmillan Collier.

Swift, M.G. (1965). *Malay peasant society in Jelebu*. London: Athlone.

Van Loon, F.H.G. (1927). *Amok* and *Latah. Journal of Abnormal and Social Psychology, 21,* 434–444.

Wagner, N.N., & T. Eng-Seong. (Eds.). (1971). *Psychological problems and treatment in Malaysia.* Kuala Lumpur: University of Malaya Press.

Wilson, P. (1967). *A Malay village and Malaysia.* New Haven, CT: Human Relations Area Files.

Winstedt, R. (1950). *The Malays: A cultural history.* London: Routledge and Kegan.

Winzeler, R.L. (1984). The sudy of Malayan *Latah. Indonesia, 37,* 77–104.

Winzeler, R.L. (1988). *Malaysian conceptions of latah and healing.* Prepared for Symposium on Cultural Dimensions of Healing in S.E. Asia. Association for Asian Studies meeting, San Francisco.

Yap, P.M. (1951). Mental diseases peculiar to certain cultures: A survey of comparative psychiatry. *Journal of Mental Science, 97,* 313–327.

Yap, P.M. (1952). The *Latah* reaction: Its pathodynamics and nosological position. *Journal of Mental Science, 98,* 515–564.

Yap, P.M. (1969). The culture-bound reactive syndromes. In W. Caudill & Tsung-Yi Lin (Eds.), *Mental health research in Asia and the Pacific* (pp. 34–52). Honolulu: East-West Center Press.

10

THE STARTLE-MATCHING SYNDROME IN OTHER CULTURES

The Jumper

Ba gor! I jomp an' jomp all tam'
Bot jos' can't halp dat—dere she am!
Cos' w'en som' fellaire he say "Boo!"
Morgee! I jomp an' holler, too.

Long tam', 'way back ma broder, Joe,
Hav' gon' roun' house, an' off she go.
—Go bang, r-rat clos' op side ma ear;
Sence w'en I ac'dis way—dat queer!
I tak' med'ceen—don't geet som' cure.
Gass I got jomp-ops now for sure.
An' mos' all tam' som' son er gon
T'ink mak' me jomp—wal, dat ban fon.

I'll tal yo' want'ing dat ban true—
Las' spreeng dey beeld dat r-ra'ltrack t'rough
R-rat pas' ma house, an' w'at yo's s'pose?
Dem ra'ltrack fellaires, wal, he goes
Sot pos' for whees-el side ma door,
An' den—wal, p'rap I didn't swore!
Wan tra'n com' pas' long jos' 'bout noon,
An' go "whoot-toot!" Wal, bamby, soon,
Wa'n't no whol' deeshes 'round—for why?
'Cos', sacre, I jomp op sky-high

An' keeck dat table 'roun' 'dat plac'
An' lat som' howl com' off ma face.
Dat vife he skeer mos' near on death,
An' all dem shildreen hol' deir breath
For saw deir fadder ac' lak' dat
An' geeve dose dinnaire wan beeg slat.

An' wan tra'n she go pas' on night,
Long 'bout de tam' I sle'p mos' tight.
An' w'en she whees-el, "Whoot-too-too!"
I jomp lak' wil' cat, I tal you.
I heet ma vife gre't beeg hard slams
An' black her eye mos' seexteen tam's.
Till las' she go off sle'p down stair,
—She say I worse as greezly bear,
Bot w'at yo' t'ink? I swore dis true,
I nevaire know w'at t'ing I do.

Wal, w'en t'ings geet bos' op dat way,
I ban saw ra'ltrack boss wan day.
I tal heem 'bout I poun' ma vife,
—Can't halp dat t'ing for save ma life—
An' he-he blor-rt, lak' wan gre't caff,
An' lean way back an' laff an' laff.
I don't saw nottin's dere for fon
'Bout havin' dat ol' ra'ltrack ron
Op pas' ma house an' hav' dem car
Mak' me bos' op ma home, ba gar!
I tol' heem dat bam-by dat soun'
Ban mak' me keeck dat whol' house down.
"I'll tal yo' w'at," say he bam-by,
—He wap' hees eye off lak' he cry—
"I'll tol' yo' w'at dees ro'd weell do:
We'll send op our construckshong crew,
We'll beeld, to show dat we hain't mean,
Wan good, beeg cage an' pot yo' een."

Ba gar! Dat all I geet off heem!
—I weesh dey not fin' out dat steam!
Holman Francis Day, *Pine Tree Ballads*, 1902, pp. 251–253

The distribution of persons who not only hyperstartle but who also match and obey is quite curious. Although occasionally such a person may turn up almost anywhere, there are places in the world besides Malaysia and Indonesia where they are quite frequently encountered. People who exhibit the startle-matching syndrome appear to be numerous in Southeast Asia, but significant numbers of them can be found in an assortment of rather diverse cultural contexts as well—including Siberia, Lapland, Yemen, Japan (among the Ainu), and in North America along the eastern portion of the border between Canada and the United States. In each of the places where the syndrome is abundant, it has been elaborated into a complex of experiences, behaviors, values, and beliefs that is explicit, recognized, and bears a name. Each culture-specific elaboration is colored strongly by the local culture, has a local name, and is embedded in local traditions.

Why the startle-matching syndrome should be found in such a strange assortment of geographically, ecologically, ethnically, and culturally diverse sites has long been a great puzzle.[1] However, if one understands how the elements of the syndrome are determined by the neurophysiology associated with startle and attention-capture, the puzzle is solved. All of the places where persons with the startle-matching syndrome are numerous are places in which the potential for the development of attention-capture phenomena inherent in the startle reflex has been culturally exploited and elaborated. In all of these places, hyperstartlers, once identified, are assigned a status in the local culture which not only permits but which encourages others to startle them publicly and frequently. Just as in Malaysia and Indonesia and in the occasional case in the West, attention-capture phenomena such as matching and obedience develop from that inordinately frequent startling. Cultural and social factors explain not the *form* of the syndrome, which is everywhere pretty much the same, but rather its *geographic distribution*.

Central to the understanding of the startle-matching syndrome is the fact that all of the various culture-specific manifestations of the syndrome consist of sets of most of the same basic elements, culturally colored to be sure, but readily recognizable across cultures. This chapter presents a sample of the vast evidence supporting this assertion. For most of the sites other than Malaysia, I have only secondhand data from published materials (including films); for a few I have interviews with witnesses. For only one (the Philippines) do I have any personal observations. As in other chapters, excerpts from firsthand descriptions of the syndromes have been provided to help readers arrive at their own conclusions whenever such materials are available.

REPRESENTATIVE DESCRIPTIONS

A Report from the United States (State of Maine): Jumping

The subtitle of *Pine Tree Ballads*, the book in which "The Jumper" appears, is "Rhymed Stories of Unplanned Human Natur' Up in Maine." The poem is an example of a humorous ethnic monologue, a genre once popular in America. The poem pokes fun at its narrator, a male French Canadian hyperstartler; the rather difficult to read ethnic accent employed is alleged Canadian French-English. The railroad company has planted a new whistle-post right next to the narrator's home. When he complains that now the trains too frequently trigger his infirmity and asks for the post to be moved, his complaint elicits no sympathy. Although he explains that when startled he frequently strikes others near him, especially his children and his wife, whose eyes he has repeatedly blackened, the "rail track boss" laughs until the tears come out of his eyes and offers only to put him in a cage. The reader is expected to find the story humorous.

The paper generally cited as the first significant investigation of the Maine *"Jumpers"* to appear in print is by G. M. Beard (1880a), a late nineteenth-century physician. Having heard about the *Jumpers*, Beard traveled to Maine to see them for himself and to examine them systematically by performing what he referred to as "experiments" with them. Beard described what he did and saw in exceptional detail, and as the experiments were numerous and well thought out, Beard's writings are especially informative. In addition to seeing them hyperstartle, Beard saw Jumpers both match and obey. He musters considerable evidence to support his conclusion that the behaviors that follow their startles are involuntary—for example, from observations such as the fact that the blows which are struck on command are not tempered or moderated. He describes social performances and also what happens when Jumpers are startled accidentally or when alone. Here are some excerpts from the paper in which the descriptive data are most extensive:

I found two of the *Jumpers* employed about the hotel. With one of them, a young man twenty-seven years of age, I made the following experiments:

1. While sitting in a chair with a knife in his hand, with which he was about to cut his tobacco, he was struck sharply on the shoulder, and told to "throw it." Almost as quick as the explosion of a pistol, he threw the knife, and it stuck in a beam opposite; at the same time he repeated the order "throw it" with a certain cry as of terror or alarm.

A moment after, while filling his pipe with tobacco, he was again slapped on the shoulder and told to "throw it." He threw the tobacco and the pipe on the grass, at least a rod away, with the same cry and the same suddenness and explosiveness of movement.

When standing near one of the employees of the house, he was told to "strike," and he struck him violently on the cheek. I took this person into the quiet of my own room, only my friend being with me, in order that the experiments might be made without interruption or disturbance. I sat down by him, explained to him the object of my visit, conversed with him in regard to his family history and his own personal experience and observation of his peculiarity, and every now and then, during the conversation, I struck him without warning on the shoulder or on the back, or mildly kicked him; and every time he was so struck he moved his shoulders upward slightly, sometimes moving both the shoulders and the arms, with or without the peculiar cry. He knew that I was studying his case; he knew that the kicks and strokes came from me, and yet he could not avoid making a slight jump or motion, as though startled.

While holding a tumbler in his hand, standing near to him, I told him to "throw it." He dashed the tumbler with great violence to the floor, and then began deliberately picking up the pieces in a very quiet and patient way. Whenever I struck him quietly, easily, and in such a way that he could see I was to strike him, he made only a slight jump or movement; but when the strike or kick was unexpected, though very mild in character, he could not restrain the jumping or jerking motion; but the cry did not always appear. (Beard, 1880b, p. 171)

2. Another case in the house, a lad sixteen years of age, was not so bad as the other, but still presented all these phenomena: he jumped when he heard any sound from behind that was sharp and unexpected, and struck and threw when ordered to do so. The crowd around the hotel, partly for my benefit, kept him constantly teased and annoyed, so that when he approached he had a stealthy, suspicious, and timid look in his eye, as though he expected each moment to be jumped. (1880b, pp. 171–172)

This man, while playing with one of his mates, had thrown him to the ground; some one approached near and commanded "Strike him," and he struck him very hard and explosively, with both hands at a time.

When standing by a window, he was suddenly commanded to "jump" by a person on the other side of the window. He jumped straight up, half a foot off the floor, with a loud cry, repeating the order which had been given to him.

When the two Jumpers were close together, they were commanded to "strike": each struck the other simultaneously—not mild or polite, but severe and painful blows.

I experimented with him in the phenomenon of repeating language that was addressed to him. When the command was uttered in a quick, loud voice, he repeated the order as he heard it, at the same time that he executed it. When told to strike, he said "Strike" at the same time that he struck: when told to throw it, he said "Throw it" at the same time that he threw whatever was in his hand. It made no difference what language was used. I tried him with the first part of the first line of Homer's "Iliad," and with the first part of Virgil's "Aeneid," languages, of course, of which he knew nothing, and he repeated quickly, almost violently, the sound as it was uttered—"Menin Aida," the first part of the first line of the "Iliad," and "Arma-vi," the first part of the first line of Virgil. In order to have it repeated, it was necessary that the command should be very short, as well as quickly and strongly uttered. He would not repeat a whole line, or even half a line, but simply a word or two. (1880b, p. 172)

I can find no evidence that the presence of water or of fire will interfere, even in the slightest degree, with the motions which they are compelled to make. As has been made apparent by the above description, it is not necessary that the surprises should come from any human being; it is not necessary that they should be ordered to strike or to jump; and sound, from any source, that comes upon them with sufficient severity and suddenness, for which they are not forewarned and forearmed, may cause them to jump and to cry. One of those on whom I experimented told me that the falling of a tree in the woods, when unexpected, would have the same effect upon him. He said that one time he was so alarmed by a sudden crash of a tree that he not only jumped, but was perfectly entranced, so that he could not move, although the tree did not fall upon him. The explosion of a gun or pistol is almost sure to excite these *Jumpers*. The screech of a steam-whistle is especially obnoxious to them, few of them, so far as I have been able to learn, having been able to withstand it. On one of the lake-steamers in which I returned from the hotel, there was a *Jumper* who, when the screech was heard, jumped right up so that he nearly hit his head on the upper deck. (1880b, p. 173)

A Report from Siberia: *Miryachit*

None of the many papers on *miryachit* available to me contain as detailed behavioral descriptions as can be found in Beard's description of *Jumping*.[2] Most describe the experiences and behaviors of *miryachit* only briefly, the bulk of the paper being an extensive interpretation, usually cultural or psychological, often with frankly racist overtones. Although the following account is one of the more descriptive, it focuses almost exclusively on matching. Obedience, not mentioned here, is described in other accounts. The association of matching with hyperstartling is described, and it is emphasized that the act is reluctant and compelled.

In a very interesting account of a journey from the Pacific Ocean through Asia to the United States, by Lieutenant B.H. Buckingham and Ensigns George C. Foulk and Walter McLean, United States navy, I find an affection [*sic*] of the nervous system described which, on account of its known analogies, I think should be brought to the special notice of the medical profession. I quote from the work referred to the following account of this disease.

The party is on the Ussuri River not far from its junction with the Amur in Eastern Siberia: "While we were walking on the bank here we observed our messmate, the captain of the general staff [of the Russian army], approach the steward of the boat suddenly, and, without any apparent reason or remark, clap his hands before his face; instantly the steward clapped his hands in the same manner, put on an angry look, and passed on. The incident was somewhat curious, as it involved a degree of familiarity with the steward hardly to have been expected.

After this we observed a number of queer performances of the steward and finally comprehended the situation. It seemed that he was afflicted with a peculiar mental or nervous disease which forced him to imitate everything suddenly presented to his senses. Thus when the captain slapped the paddle-box suddenly in the presence of the steward, the latter instantly gave it a similar thump; or if any noise were made suddenly, he seemed compelled against his will to imitate it instantly, and with remarkable accuracy. To annoy him, some of the passengers imitated pigs grunting, or called out absurd names; others clapped their hands and shouted, jumped, or threw their hats on the deck suddenly, and the poor steward, suddenly startled, would echo them all precisely, and sometimes several consecutively.

Frequently he would expostulate, begging people not to startle him, and again would grow furiously angry, but even in the midst of his passion he would helplessly imitate some ridiculous shout or motion directed at him by his pitiless tormenters. Frequently he shut himself up in his pantry, which was without windows and locked the door, but even there he could be heard answering the grunts, shouts, or pounds on the bulkhead outside. He was a man of middle age, fair physique, rather intelligent in facial expression, and without the slightest indication in appearance of his disability. As we descended the bank to go on board the steamer someone gave a loud shout and threw his cap on the ground; looking about for the steward, for the shout was evidently made for his benefit, we saw him violently throw his cap, with a shout, into a chicken-coop, into which he was about to put the result of his foraging expedition among the houses of the stanitza [village].

We afterward witnessed an incident which illustrated the extent of his disability. The captain of the steamer, running up to him, suddenly clapping his hands at the same time, accidently slipped and fell hard on the deck; without having been touched by the captain, the steward instantly clapped his hands and shouted, and then, in powerless imitation, he too fell as hard and almost precisely in the same manner and position as the captain.

In speaking of the steward's disorder, the captain of the general staff stated that it was not uncommon in Siberia: that he had seen a number of cases of it, and that it was commonest about Yakutsk, where the winter cold is extreme. Both sexes were subject to it, but men much less than women. It was known to Russians by the name of *Miryachit*. (Hammond, 1884, p. 191)

A Report from Sweden (Lapland): *Lapp Panic*

The following frequently cited description of *Lapp Panic* contains the only account of the condition which I have so far been able to discover; I suspect that there are some treasures in Scandinavian languages which I have not been able to locate. Again, hyperstartling and matching are described; although obedience is not mentioned, the description is so sketchy that one cannot be sure whether or not it also occurs. As noted earlier, obedience is the only one of the responses requiring specific behavior on the part of other persons: issuing commands to a just-startled hyperstartler in a framed, forceful manner and at the right time. There surely must be many places where even though hyperstartling and matching occur, the local culture-typical way of interacting with hyperstartlers does not include issuing commands.

> From Swedish Lapland as well as from the Kola peninsula it has been reported that such fits may befall women who have been frequently harassed and frightened by mischievous boys. This nervous disposition must have been more widely spread in old times than it is now. According to Högström it appeared in men and women alike. He says that some Lapps are so easily scared that they suddenly swoon or behave as if they were out of their wits, and he continues:
>
> In the churches it has not only occurred that one has found the whole crowd in a swoon, but it has also happened that some of them have suddenly risen to their feet and started beating their neighbors. I have seen some Lapps behave in the same way in their tents when somebody has suddenly screamed, or a piece of live coal crackles. When they are thus frightened, they will jump to their feet, and do not mind if they have a knife or an axe in their hands, but hit the person who is next to them. I have also seen some of them imitate any quaint gesture of other people. If somebody else has twisted his mouth, pointed with a finger, danced or the like, they do all that in the same way: and when it is over they will ask whether they have behaved indecently, because they say they do not know what they have been doing. (Collinder, 1949, pp. 151–152)

A Report from Burma: *Young-Dah-hte*

There are only few published accounts of *Young-Dah-hte*, and they are very sketchy. The following is one of the more descriptive:

> A Burmese woman, aged 33, has been a patient in this hospital since 1928. . . .
>
> It would appear that she suffered from this condition before her admission as she says that it developed suddenly after seeing the blood of her murdered husband.[3]
>
> If she sees a person dance, she dances; if she is struck, she strikes the person by her side; if she sees one person kissing another, she kisses the person by her side; if tickled or startled she shouts and uses abusive languages. Another peculiarity about her is that if a question is put to her in a loud tone, she repeats the question, but if addressed in a normal manner she replies rationally. With the exception of this imitativeness and state of hyperacute suggestibility she has been classified as sane since 1930, but she is a woman of unstable temperament, easily irritable, quarrelsome and erotic. (Still, 1940, pp. 90–91)

A Report from Thailand: *Bah-tsche*

The southern border of Thailand is the northern border of Malaysia. Although there are great dissimilarities between Thai and Malay cultures, Thailand being for the most part Buddhist and Malaya Islamic, in southern Thailand, where the cultures overlap, *Bah-tsche* is called *la-tha*. (J. Westermeyer, 1982, personal communication) The following is an unpublished description by a Thai psychiatrist of some personal observations.

> My house is in a store in a marketplace. Usually we have people who grow vegetables, farmers, not very far from Bangkok. They bring their vegetables to this market and sell them; some of them conduct their business right in front of our house. A lady in her forties used to buy vegetables from the farmers in the market [to resell]. She usually put out her vegetables in front of our house or near the house. She has this reputation of having *bah-tsche*; it is a funny thing that she does once in a while. The kids or the people in the area come and make fun of her. When they sneak behind her and shout some words or make her startled, she would jump up and she would utter some vulgar words.
>
> The people would sneak behind her and ask her to do this and that. Usually they ask her to do what we call *ram wohng*, a kind of dancing. If one told her she would dance. If one said to do this she would. Some of them would ask her to take off her clothes, but I do not remember if she took off her clothes or not. Other people

would usually stop her and the scene at this point by just telling the people who command her to stop, or hold her and stop her from doing that.

Once the response is in progress she seemed very difficult to stop. She would do everything but at the same time beg that person to stop the command. People have fun in frightening her. They would ask her to do silly things. The words that she would utter sometimes were so funny! The words she'd utter would be related to the female genital organs or to the male genital organs, usually female. Sometimes she would do things to the point of exhaustion. These things could go on forever, but people usually stop in time.

When we have some kind of festival, at that time, she doesn't mind that much, seems to be willing to do so. She would be likely to at Thai New Year or *Song Kran*. People used to splash water on each other. If people would startle her she would get into dancing and let people do things to her and she wouldn't mind that much. At other times I saw her begging people to stop commanding her, to stop tickling her.[4] Usually the tickling would come with the commands; they would have to tickle her to continue. It's not just a command. They would start with the tickle, then they would command, they would repeat the tickling. They actually tickle her. Sometime they would just go near her and touch her and that will make her sort of frightened, and that's enough to make her frightened, or just touch her, and make some noise. Some do actually tickle her.

Basically those are the things that I saw. The last time I saw her was a few years before I came to the United States. That would have been when I was in medical school, six or seven years ago. She would have been in her late forties. Her daughter was a teenager at the time. I don't think that the daughter is afflicted with this condition. The daughter will ask or beg people to stop frightening her mother. That is usually enough to stop them. I believe that it is a hereditary condition; once a mother has it, it is thought that the daughter will have the potential for this condition, usually. I felt sorry at that time for her daughter, that she might have this same condition when she grows up. She's a pretty little lady. There is no special term for the person. *Bah-tsche* is usually an adjective but it can be a noun also, meaning the condition.

Maybe there are two extremes of the *bah-tsche*. [There are also] women, when you frighten or tickle them, they will utter a vulgar word, without imitating anything. That is very common, many people do that. One case I remember is not that old, a woman of between 20 and 30 who was working as a practical nurse on the ward. People would come up behind her and frighten her and she would use a lot of vulgar words. Sometimes it would come out like a train of words. It is quite funny to listen to. One of the most common things would be something like "falling down" or "falling down cunt" or some words literally meaning the "splitting of the vagina." If it were longer it might be "your vagina falling down into the water," that kind of thing. From any one person you would usually hear about the same words, like a mannerism. (L. Wongsarnpigoon, 1976, interview)

Videotapes of *bah-tsche* collected for me near Bangkok show hyperstartling, naughty talk, matching, obedience, and the Get-It-Off-Me response. The repetitive startling and teasing by onlookers were much like that which I had observed and filmed in Malaysia, but the dances and dance poses that the *bah-tsche* subjects performed when ordered to do so were, of course, Thai rather than Malay.[5]

A Report from Yemen: *Nekzah*

A number of cases of the startle-matching syndrome were reported from North Africa (Tripolitania, Somalia) and Arabia (Yemen) in the Italian colonial medical literature of the mid-1920s and 1930s. The most comprehensive of these reports was by Dr. Tommaso Sarnelli, who presented evidence that all the cases that had been reported from North Africa had been Arabs, and who reported his own observations of five cases that he studied in Upper Yemen. Dr. Sarnelli observed hyperstartling with matching, naughty talk, and involuntary striking out, as well as the license granted universally to anyone to startle those affected in order to evoke these behaviors. There is no report of those affected with *nekzah* being commanded by others. Translated excerpts from his report follow.[6]

Hagg Ahmed Et-Tawili, approximately 50 years old, is a drummer in the "tubulkhane" [military band] in Sanaa. . . . After I had spent some time with him chatting, I gave Muhsen, my assistant, the [small packets of] things he had asked for. He gave half of them to Tawili and kept the other half for himself. Suddenly he dropped them onto the ground. Then Tawili also dropped the packets he had been holding in his hands onto the ground. I pretended to be surprised and disappointed about his impolite action. The poor man, contrite and very sorry, begged me to forgive his involuntary action and declared his regret at not having been able to resist imitating Muhsen. At this point Muhsen abruptly shouted, "Ahmed!" and pretended to take his jacket off. [Tawili] gave the same shout and rapidly stripped off his jacket.

Later on I was informed by the escort and a few others that this wretched man was extremely popular in the town because a few wicked men have often driven him, by doing a few gestures, to take all his clothes off, to dive into the irrigation basins fully dressed, to throw his drumsticks away when he was on the point of drumming, and to throw anything else he had in his arms, light or heavy, even a child! (Sarnelli, 1934, pp. 753–754)

Abdallah ali Sciuubi [is] about 60 years old. . . . One morning he was on guard at the entrance of the "warscia" [the government weapons factory], when Cadi Abdallah El Amri, who is the Prime Vizier of the king and a person of great prestige throughout all of Yemen, arrived. Sciuubi had come to attention in salute, when just as the vizier was passing in front of him, a wicked comrade of his unexpectedly poked him on his back. The poor old man landed a solid back-of-the-hand on the chest of the minister! This action scandalized the people who were present. [When Sciuubi's condition was explained, the Vizier gave him a small coin and left him unpunished.] (Sarnelli, 1934, pp. 754–755)

Seyyed Mohammad El Barr, born in Hadramut, is a young man well-known in Sanaa because he is in the retinue of the children of the king. . . . It is well known that he reacts violently to every unexpected tactile stimulus and that he imitates every abrupt movement that he sees performed in front of him.

One night at my house . . . Seyyed El Barr came with a message. He was invited to join us, but before he had seated himself in front of Mr. Rascid Zog, Mr. Zog screamed and made as if to fall forward on the ground. With a similar scream [Seyyed El Barr] fell forward flat on his face onto the ground. (Sarnelli, 1934, pp. 756–757)

In the same [town of] Sanaa I also learned of the high frequency of this condition among the local women. For example, there is a well-known old noble lady who if she receives unexpected tactile or vocal stimulation reacts not only with a motor response but also with coprolalia. . . . (Sarnelli, 1934, p. 757)

Several of Dr. Sarnelli's cases were clearly distressed by their condition and had sought unsuccessfully for a cure. However, at least one apparently accepted his situation without distress: "because of it his very affectionate friends could amuse themselves" (Sarnelli, 1934, p. 753). Dr. Sarnelli reported that in Yemen the condition of *nekzah* was common.

Some Reports from Japan (Hokkaido): *Imu*

Imu, the startle-matching syndrome of the Ainu, the aboriginal people of northern Japan, has been much studied, especially by Japanese scholars. As is the case with a number of the forms of the syndrome, degrees of severity are recognized. Several accounts note that uttering a certain word or words is sometimes enough to precipitate an episode. Excerpts from accounts of investigations reported in 1936, 1964, and 1980 are presented below.

1. Among twelve cases examined by Sakaki, in five the morbid symptoms appeared immediately after a snake's bite; two cases got the first attack when seeing a snake; one patient when working in the fields was suddenly frightened by a rustle of grass which she believed to be caused by a snake; one patient was terrified while at work in the fields when she suddenly saw a big caterpillar and during following nights had horrible dreams. In one case the patient dreamed that she was bitten by a snake and in two cases it was impossible to find out the moment which could be directly connected with the beginning of symptoms.

The disease of *imu* is manifested by attacks which occur from time to time. The moment which brings forth an attack is everything which makes the patient afraid, especially if one of the words meaning a snake is pronounced (*"tokkoni," "ashtoma," " icombap,"* etc.), or a snake, or something which resembles the shape of a snake, is seen. Sometimes an attack can be produced by a word which is suddenly pronounced louder, a sharp sound, a word expressed with emphasis without connection with the topic of the conversation, and so on. (Winiarz & Wielawski, 1936, pp. 183–184)

When one of those above-mentioned moments occurs, it brings forth an attack of *imu*. . . . During a typical attack the sick woman assaults the persons in the environment by using physical force and cursing. Sometimes she runs away in panic. Symptoms of echopraxia, echolalia, and echomimia are shown besides. There is manifested automatic obedience or negative automatic obedience. (1936, p. 184)[7]

Besides the typical attacks, there are different forms of abortive fits. The woman who is suddenly frightened during her housework by a cry, will repeat it or for a few seconds she will imitate the movements of one of the persons present. (1936, p. 184)

2. A 64-year-old Ainu widow, the mother of four adult children. She was born in 1894 as the only child of Ainu parents. Until she was 15, she used the Ainu language in her daily life but has used Japanese ever since. She received no formal education. At the age of 20 she married. In her late 20's she became a widow and raised her four children by working on a farm. In the village, she is generally considered a sociable, hard-working and efficient woman.

During her childhood, she saw cases of *imu*, but no one from her family has had it as far as she recalls. Her first attack of *imu* occurred at the age of 57 when she was cutting grass and saw a snake. She had seen snakes before but had not experienced *imu*.

Since then, her *imu* became provoked by any kind of fright as well as by the sight of a snake. Village people at times teased her and induced her *imu* by giving her a sudden surprise. During these episodes she speaks in Ainu and can recall the events well later. Her own feeling about *imu* is that she does not feel ashamed or afraid of it, as, after all, she does not harm others and rather amuses them.

Her *Imu* Reaction: When a toy snake was thrust at her, she recoiled and tried to repulse it with her scarf.[8] For a while she stood stuporously. The interviewer invited her to come near him but she retreated. When ordered to go away, she advanced. Similarly she arose from the chair when asked to remain seated, but sat down at the order, "stand up." The gesture in which the interviewer drew a circle in the air with his fingers was skillfully copied by her. At the word *Tokkoni* ["snake"], she became angry and chased him with her scarf. Following a short period of no stimuli, she showed some shyness and apparently came to herself. (Kumasaka, 1964, pp. 736–737)

3. The Sakhalin Ainu see two distinct categories of *imu*. The first category involves a mild state in which an individual becomes surprised, but not necessarily frightened, and mumbles meaningless sounds. Each individual *imu* Ainu, when surprised, almost always utters the same nonsensical phrases, such as "Acikapahse," which has no meaning in Ainu. While in the field, I once stood up, bumped my head on a bare light bulb hanging from the ceiling, and uttered an English exclamation, "Oops." Those Ainu present thought that I was experiencing an *imu* state, since they had never heard the English expression, which was of course meaningless in either Ainu or Japanese. (Ohnuki-Tierney, 1980, p. 216)

Thus, for all the 77 Hokkaido Ainu *imu* individuals listed in Figure 1 by Uchimura, Akimoto, and Ishibashi (1938, pp. 10–13), the stimulus was the hearing of the word *tokoni* or seeing a snake, a toy snake, or a picture of a snake. Uchimura, Akimoto, and Ishibashi (1938, p. 46) report a case of a male Hokkaido Ainu who talked about a snake by referring to it as "a long worm" or "an abominable worm," without being incited into an *imu* state, until one of the investigators asked if he meant *tokoni*, using the Ainu term for snake, upon which he became seized with *imu*. Other items which serve as stimulus to some Hokkaido Ainu include a frog, an octopus, and a crab. (1980, p. 218)

An important category of stimuli is foreign objects that are newly introduced or otherwise unfamiliar to the individual. For example, metal washing pans newly introduced from the Japanese at the time of the investigation, or neon signs which an Ainu saw for the first time while visiting Tokyo served as stimuli (Uchimura et al.,

1938, p. 29) Unfamiliar objects also serve as stimuli for the Sakhalin Ainu, as in the case of a Sakhalin Ainu woman whose initial occurrence of *imu* took place at the sight of a Japanese domesticated cat which she had never seen before.[9] (1980, p. 218)

Some Observations from the Philippines: *Mali-mali, Silok, Balatong*

Mali-mali is the name of the startle-matching syndrome in Tagalog, *silok* in Ilocano, and *balatong* in Pampango. For ease of reference and because Tagalog is the national language of the Philippines, I will refer to the Philippine form of the syndrome simply as *mali-mali*, though indeed there may be unrecognized regional differences in the way it is understood and played out in a country as linguistically and culturally diverse as the Philippines.

While the previous accounts of startle-matching syndromes other than *latah* have all been secondhand or at a further remove, I was able to observe and talk with *mali-mali*s personally. Between 1977 and 1979 I spent about 3 months in the Philippines, divided between Manila, Los Baños, and the towns of Bay and Guagua. Most of the time was spent in Bay where I was assisted by Ms. (now Dr.) Josefina Nazarea Gutmann,[10] then on the faculty of the University of the Philippines at Los Baños. Dr. Gutmann is a native of Bay, and the local community was exceptionally open and helpful. I was similarly assisted in the Guagua area by longtime residents, Jesus and Lolita Cortez. Thus, though the period spent in the Philippines was short, I believe that it was possible to obtain a reasonably accurate picture of *mali-mali* as it occurs there. In Bay, Los Baños, and Guagua I observed *mali-mali*s in and out of *mali-mali* states, interviewed those who exhibited the syndrome and their families and neighbors, and collected some super 8-mm sound film footage of *mali-mali* episodes. What follows is a brief extract from these data.

Bay (pronounced "Bye") is a small town in the province of Laguna on the island of Luzon. Its inhabitants are mostly peasant fishermen and farmers who market their own produce. Those who are said to be "*mali-mali*" are mostly women but include a few older men. Most *mali-mali*s are women of relatively low status, in their thirties or older. The following interactions were observed in Bay:

1. A laundry woman when poked on her side would startle and utter such phrases as "*uten ng kabayo*" ("prick of a horse"). If the person poking her happened to be male, she would sometimes use the name of the person who poked her instead of "horse." Those who poked her were usually men of approximately her age or older. Sometimes younger children took over and prolonged interactions begun by adults.

2. A market vendor startled readily and strongly to unexpected sounds. After having been startled, she would utter words such as "*Ay pusa*"

(Oh cat) or *"utes"* (a "nonsense" word), which appear to be modified versions of *"puki"* ("cunt")[11] and *"uten"* ("prick").

3. An itinerant vendor who earns her living peddling goods around the town from a basket that she carries on her head was startled from behind by a man who commanded her to throw away her basket. Upon hearing the command, she snatched the basket from her head and thrust it at him. Everyone nearby laughed, but the woman merely sat down on the street and looked blankly at the people around her. She remained motionless for a few minutes, then picked up her things and walked away.

4. A fish vendor in the market was startled and commanded by a male customer to throw the fish she was selling. She responded by picking up the fish and throwing them on the ground two at a time. When she had thrown almost all of her fish, a schoolteacher in the crowd asked them to stop. The fish vendor stood motionless, stared at the people, covered her face with her hands, and began to weep.

5. In response to questioning about the responses of *mali-mali*s when alone, one informant told me of an incident that had taken place only a few days earlier. His mother, a *mali-mali*, was upstairs in his house, and he was downstairs. When he heard her call out a nonsensical phrase that he could not interpret, he looked up through an opening and saw that she had been reaching for something stored high up and a handkerchief had fallen on her head.

6. Aling Chayong, a widow in her sixties, lived in a small hut with her unmarried son. Her married daughter lived a few meters away with her own family. For many years, Aling Chayong had earned her living as an unlicensed midwife; she told us that she had assisted in the delivery of generations of babies in her own village and surrounding areas. She is well known locally both as a midwife and as a *mali-mali*. After having been startled, she says words such as *"Ay uten!"* or *"Ay puki!"* When alone, episodes are brief; in the presence of a crowd, episodes may last longer and include matching and obedience. When she assists in the delivery of a baby, others refrain from startling her intentionally.

Aling Chayong told us that she became a *mali-mali* during a wake. She was deep in thought about the dead child when a cat suddenly jumped from a window to her side. The sound and the unexpected appearance of the cat startled her violently. What happened next must have been a remarkable scene. Without conscious thought she picked up the dead child by the neck and ran with it as fast as she could, pursued by the mourners, led by the child's father. Ever since this wake she has been regarded by all as a *mali-mali*, and she now is frequently startled intentionally by the villagers to see what she will do.

7. Femia is a 40-year-old fish vendor at the town market. Like Aling Chayong, she told us that her *mali-mali* began at the wake of a dead relative. While she and a friend were dressing the body, somebody startled them from behind. Instantly and without reflection, they stood up and began dancing around the corpse. They only stopped when they noticed that a

crowd had started to gather to watch them. Ever since, she has been considered a "*mali-mali.*" She told us that this gave everyone license to make fun of her.

Femia is married to a fisherman and is the mother of four children. In the village in which she lives, husbands and wives generally work cooperatively to earn their living. Men usually go to sea at night, and at dawn women meet their husbands on the shore to help prepare the catch for market. It is the women's responsibility to sell the fish. If the catch is good, they take it to the market at San Pablo City, approximately 30 kilometers away. If the catch is bad, they sell their fish at a market in Bay. Because her husband seldom goes out to fish, Femia must travel to San Pablo City early in the morning to obtain fish to sell. A few other similarly situated vendors also make the same journey on the same specially hired jeep. While on the jeep she is startled by others to liven up an otherwise dull trip virtually every day. In the market, especially during slack periods when the customers are few and the vendors are bored, she is also repetitively startled and commanded to do things. Watching interactions in the market, we once saw her intentionally startled by others three times in the space of 2 hours.

Although some *mali-mali*s seem to enjoy the attention that episodes of *mali-mali* elicit, many convincingly told of their unhappiness about being vulnerable to sudden startles and prolonged teasing by virtually anyone. *Mali-mali*s sometimes said that they felt angry, embarrassed, nervous, or demeaned after being startled and teased, and sometimes they retaliated by throwing objects, cursing, or even spitting at those who had made fun of them. Several of the episodes we witnessed involving Femia seemed anything but pleasant for her, and her distress appeared genuine. She has sought unsuccessfully for a cure.[12]

When I wanted to see a *mali-mali*, I was frequently told that there was one selling such and such at such and such a market, and market women are said to be more often *mali-mali* than others. As no epidemiological data are available, one might easily have a biased sample since market women with *mali-mali* would be more widely known than persons leading more sequestered lives. Yet in a small town like Bay, the presence of anyone with such an amusing and durable handicap is not easily overlooked.

Even in the absence of epidemiological data, I believe that there is probably a higher incidence of *mali-mali* in market women than in the general population. By their very presence in open markets, market women, the small stall-holders and traders of a single commodity, are more socially exposed to the potential for startle-teasing than those whose lives are largely spent at home or in more socially protected environments. In addition, because marketing is both a social and a commercial activity, market women live lives especially rich in the subtle nuances of interpersonal relationships. From which vendor with virtually identical trays of fish will one buy? And when there are many vendors, one must look sharp to sell. Femia's fish are neatly stacked or attractively sprawled over ice. They are repeatedly freshened by being sprinkled with water, and after each sale the remainder are rearranged. When a potential customer enters the fish stall aisle, Femia stands and takes the weighing basket from off the scale. She and the other vendors attempt to make eye contact with the potential purchaser. They look alert, attentive, and respectful; they monitor themselves and others constantly. It is a situation in which the potential for startle is high.

As is true of most forms of hyperstartling, *mali-mali* can at times be interactionally useful. One *mali-mali* with problems in her marriage told us that her condition was helpful in her dealings with her husband.

> When I talk to him now, it's as if I'm nothing to him, but I serve him very well so that we don't have to fight each other. I'm very patient. No matter what he does to me I'm patient. He's very tight, and he watches my grocery money carefully. He teases me as a *bal-atong*. He makes me jump and say things. It's not different from what other people do, and it puts him in a better mood.
>
> No, he doesn't get upset when other people do it to me; it makes him laugh. People are a little careful around him. They tease me, but they don't make me lift up my dress if he's there. But he knows that they do it. He scolds me some for it, but not that much.

She told us that her children sometimes protected her, and that she rather liked it when her children teased her in this way:

> When other people are doing it to me, sometimes my children stop them and sometimes they take me away. . . . But the children do it too. Sometimes they pretend they're going to tickle me. I really don't mind that—that's kind of nice.

Most of the townspeople we interviewed said they found episodes of *mali-mali* funny and entertaining. A few told us that episodes were danger-ous, or that they found them unpleasant to watch. Those interviewed also varied in their opinions about the state of mental health of *mali-mali* sub-jects, some saying that they believed *mali-mali*s to be in as good mental health as anyone else. Others considered them mentally ill.

CULTURE EXPLAINS DISTRIBUTION; BIOLOGY EXPLAINS FORM

Where startle-matching syndromes occur and who manifests them are determined by the kinds of social interactions (chiefly but not exclusively teasing and victimizing behaviors) practiced by small interacting social groups. Cultural factors, which may be highly local or highly generalized (the culture of a specific shop floor or the major culture of a nation-state), account for the spacial/temporal distribution of startle-matching syn-dromes, the frequency of their occurrence, and, in part, the selection of spe-cific victims. How an instance of startle-matching is understood, what moral values are attributed to the victim and to his tormenters, and what role each plays in the life of the small society that is the setting for the teasing interactions are by definition cultural considerations.

Those who originally reported startle-matching in countries other than Malaysia and Indonesia often noted the resemblance of their observations to *latah*, the first-described and best-known of the startle-matching syndromes, and several referred to their cases as cases of *latah*. This use of the term "*latah*" to refer to startle-matching syndromes outside of Malaysia and Indonesia generated some rather pointless arguments about whether such cases were "really" *latah*, since they did not share important cultural features with the Malaysian and Indonesian cases. Of course they were not "*latah*," but rather were forms of the syndrome elaborated in other culture-typical ways. In the hope of circumventing this unenlightening debate, I originally suggested the use of uppercase "*Latah*" to refer to the Malay and Indonesian form and lowercase "*latah*" for the condition when referred to generically (Simons, 1980). This proved to be unworkable; for one thing, it made it impossible to refer to the general case at the beginning of a sentence. I now use the term "startle-matching syndromes" for the general case and the local name to refer to each specific version of it. (Simons & Hughes, 1985, p. 41)

The thesis of this chapter is that all the individually named startle-matching syndromes are local culture-specific variants of a single syndrome whose form is determined by the properties of an exaggerated startle-reflex and the capture of attention it may engender. This would scarcely seem to be worth saying were it not for the fact that there is a considerable body of recent literature asserting that the resemblance between the syndromes found in various places is merely coincidental.[13] Indeed, I think it would be fair to say that the prevailing opinion in contemporary American anthropology is that "the notion [*sic*] that culture-bound syndromes share underlying common disease forms is rejected" (Carr, 1978, p. 269). When resemblances between the individually named startle-matching syndromes are grudgingly acknowledged to exist, they are often referred to as "superficial" (e.g., Kenny, 1983, p. 166) or "uninteresting" (e.g., Winzeler, 1984, p. 101). I believe that this position is untenable. There are an inordinate number of similarities among the reports:

Similarities among the Startle-Matching Syndromes
  1. The subjects are all hyperstartlers; they startle readily and violently to stimuli that others find innocuous.
  2. The condition usually begins in adulthood, never or virtually never before adolescence.
  3. Once the condition begins, it is virtually always permanent. I know of only one convincing account of anyone either having spontaneously lost or having been cured of the condition.[14]
  4. In all accounts the same or similar stimuli elicit the phenomenon. These include sudden, loud, unexpected noises, being poked (especially in the ribs or on the buttocks), unexpected and phobic objects

(snakes, scorpions, spiders, etc.), and culturally or idiosyncratically significant objects.[15]

5. In all accounts various stimuli produce the same range of effects on any given subject.

6. In all accounts the same responses are described. In virtually all there is a mild form in which the response behaviors are those associated with hyperstartling itself—exaggerated movements and vocalizations, naughty talk, throwing or dropping objects—and also a more extreme form, which includes matching, disorganized behavior, and usually obedience.

7. In all cultures onsets tend to occur during periods of anxiety, depression, or worry or in a situation in which a person finds himself (herself) wary. Because stories so often tell of the first episode having occurred after being deliberately startled by another person, one suspects that some of the time the potential victims were already known to be hyperstartlers. Culture-typical differences in stories of onset are discussed below.

8. In all accounts, once a subject is seen to respond in the way typical of those with the startle-matching syndrome, he or she is expected to fill the culturally defined role of a *latah, jumper, mali-mali*, etc. This role has culture-typical rights and expectations.

9. In all cultures lower-status persons are more likely to receive startle-teasing than those of higher status.

10. People vary in their attitudes about, and in their social responses to, being identified as hyperstartlers. All degrees of acceptance and resistance to the role occur, including a frequent pattern of differential acceptance: It is all right under certain circumstances (often festive social occasions), all right when done by certain persons (especially one's own children), alright when done in a loving way but distressing when done at most other times.

Because so much is similar across cultures, the pattern of dissimilarities is also revealing.

Differences among the Syndromes

1. The proportion of men and women affected varies from place to place. Though in most groups studied it is women who preponderantly manifest the syndrome, in some it is mostly men. I know of no society in which either sex is entirely immune. Among the Ainu the ratio of men to women with *imu* differs markedly among communities (Ohnuki-Tierney, 1980), as it does for *latah* among Malay communities (Winzeler, 1988). It seems to vary with the game being played. In Maine where it was the lumberjacks who watched for jumpiness in others of their number and repetitively teased the jumpy, those who developed the syndrome were virtually all male. In settings in which it is less personally consequential to tease women, it is they who are disproportionately startled and they who develop the syndrome.

2. Stimulus preferences vary somewhat from place to place. There are local styles of startling.

3. Not all elements of the startle-matching syndrome occur in all sites. Obedience, for example, is only present when commanding just startled hyperstartlers is part of the cultural repertoire. When an aspect of the syndrome is not used by a culture, it may be because of specific superordinate factors having nothing to do with startle per se. Differences in how societies treat stigmatized persons is such a superordinate factor. Although startle responses are always "odd," the extent to which they are seen as sick, bad, or funny varies in ways determined by superordinate cultural constructs. These superordinate constructs are not primarily about startle but rather define social worlds generally—for example, whether status and gender differences are emphasized or minimized, how personal space is defined, how important it is always to appear unperturbed, alert, and ready to respond, and how stigmatized persons are treated.

4. The indigenous social and cultural significance of the syndrome of course varies, as does its relationship to other social roles. Ohnuki-Tierney (1980), for example, reported that in some but not all of the Ainu villages she studied shamans appeared to have *imu* with disproportionate frequency. The startle-matching syndrome is notably prevalent among homosexual transvestite males in Malaysia and Indonesia but not, so far as I was able to discern, in the parallel population in the Philippines.

5. Beliefs about the condition's cause also vary considerably from site to site, though there is often some notion of soul-loss or possession. Such beliefs are reasonable hypotheses, used in many belief systems to explain a variety of aberrant mind states and behaviors.

6. Besides containing elements common to many sites, stories of onset have elements that are culture-typical. When people are asked how the startle-matching began, in a number of sites they recount culture-typical occurrences with a relatively abrupt onset. In my sample this was especially the case in the town of Bay in the Philippines, where I often heard a story of being startled in the presence of a corpse. This was not the case in Guagua, also in the Philippines, or in Malaysia, where stories of onset varied greatly. Though stories of onset vary from site to site, in any given setting they include elements congruent with local beliefs about startling.

In a few of the places where the syndrome is found, stories of onset may include significant dreams, often dreams with startle-related elements such as snakes, other scary things, spooky places, and genitals (Chiu, Tong, & Schmidt, 1972; Kenny, 1978). Because the significance of this observation has been the subject of contention in the scholarly literature, the hypothesis that dreams are important in the genesis of the startle-matching syndrome merits some discussion.

I believe there is good evidence that dreams are not significant in the syndrome's genesis. Evidence for this includes the observation that dreams are believed to be important in the etiology of the syndrome in only a few of the places in which the syndrome is found. More significant is the fact that even in places where the local culture-typical belief is that the syndrome begins with a certain sort of dream, most persons with the syndrome deny having had such a dream, even when specifically interrogated on this point by an investigator who believes that dreams are important in the syndrome's etiology.

Chiu et al. (1972) report that in Sarawak, East Malaysia, among the Sarawak Malays "the initial attack is believed to be the results of a dream during which the *Latah* antu or spirit enters the subject and that dreams maintain the condition" (p. 158). In their study, Chiu et al. (1972) asked all of their sample of 50 *latah*s to describe (1) "any dream which recurred frequently over about five years" and (2) "any dream which immediately preceded the onset of *latah*" (p. 158). They found that despite both the subjects' and the investigators' belief in the etiologic significance of dreams only 12 of the 37 Malay subjects and only 4 of the 13 Iban subjects admitted to having had a relevant pre-onset dream. In spite of the locally prevalent belief, two-thirds of the Malay subjects and slightly more than two-thirds of the Iban subjects denied having had one (see Simons, 1983b). I believe that stories of special dreams at onset are much like other culture-typical stories of how statuses change—for example, stories many Yukatecan midwives tell about how their calling came to them in a dream (Jordan, 1989).

The distribution of the startle-matching syndromes is largely due to the fact that the kind of repeated, prolonged, and unwelcome teasing of stigmatized and handicapped persons generating and perpetuating the syndrome is vastly more acceptable in some cultural contexts than in others. The syndrome is relatively infrequent in cultures in which such teasing is frowned upon or has stringent limits, which is the case in much of the West. It is also infrequent in cultures such as those discussed in Chapter 4 in which it is believed that serious and long-lasting negative effects may result from being startled, a belief widespread in Latin America and in Africa. In such cultures the play with startle so characteristic of cultures in which the startle-matching syndrome is prevalent is not socially acceptable.

When a specific element of the syndrome has not been reported from a particular site, one cannot at present conclude that it does not occur there. It may simply not have been reported. It would be possible to investigate the separate forms of the syndrome, making more systematic point-by-point comparisons, but this is work that has yet to be done. This caveat aside, the resemblance of the stories from different places to one another is so great that the conclusion that all are culture-typical elaborations of the same set of phenomena seems to me inescapable.

NOTES

1. Hildred Geertz, for example, who believed that the behaviors which *latah*s perform are determined by specific elements of Javanese culture, recognized that to anyone who held this belief, the existence of virtually identical syndromes elsewhere in the world was paradoxical (1968).

2. I suspect that there may be a more descriptive literature on *miryachit* in various Russian languages, which yet need to be searched.

3. This account, like several of the accounts of other startle-matching syndromes that follow, tells of a sudden and specific onset. As hyperstartling has been documented to develop after a single severe trauma in the posttraumatic stress syndrome, I believe this is possible. However, in many of the accounts I believe that what is being described is the first instance of matching, obedience, or otherwise notably erratic behavior in someone who previously only considered herself or himself to be "rather jumpy." Stories of onset are discussed later in this chapter.

4. This account, like a scattering of others, tells not only of startling subjects but also of "tickling" them to achieve the desired state. Tickling may indeed be an effective stimulus, but there is another possibility. The repetitive poking by a single person, sometimes at intervals of as little as a second, which I saw and recorded on film in Malaysia and the Philippines and which is shown in films and videotapes provided to me by others from Thailand and Japan, could easily be called "tickling." It is not exactly what most Westerners mean by the word.

5. Named and elaborated startle-matching syndromes appear to be especially widespread in Southeast Asia. I have been reliably informed that there is a Vietnamese startle-matching syndrome called *noi mai*, which is similar to *latah* in most respects, but I have no other information about it. I suspect there are Laotian and Cambodian forms as well.

6. The paper excerpted below was translated from the original Italian for me by Ms. Maria Rosaria.

7. "Negative automatic obedience" (standing when commanded to sit, approaching when commanded to depart, etc.) remains a puzzling behavior. I never witnessed it myself, either in Malaysia or in the Philippines. In addition to its mention in this and the next report, it is shown nicely in the film of *imu* collected by Professor Uchimura in 1936 in the course of what appears to be a "role" performance. Whether it may sometimes be a special manifestation of attention-capture and whether it occurs elsewhere is not known.

8. The film of *imu* collected by Uchimura in 1936 shows a very nice "Get-It-Off-Me!" response. I suspect that this is what is described here.

9. It is interesting that the objects introduced by the Japanese, which were reported to precipitate episodes of *imu*, were not only unfamiliar but also shiny, potentially startling and potentially attention-capturing, like a neon sign and bright metal or, in the case of the cat, a small carnivorous predator. Other items introduced by the Japanese, such as yukatas, futons, and scrolls were not reported to precipitate episodes. (See Chapter 1, note 2.)

10. Dr. Gutmann also participated in the writing of this section dealing with *mali-mali*.

11. The same word as in Malay. Although the cultures are in most respects quite different, the Malays being Islamic and most Filipinos in these areas Roman Catholic, the languages are related.

12. In parts of the Philippines it is believed that *mali-mali* may be cured by

whispering to a corpse the request to take the condition back with it to the grave. Femia has tried this and she has also consulted local healers.

13. For example, see Geertz (1968), Karp (1985), Kenny (1978, 1983), Lee (1981), and Winzeler (1984).

14. This was a report of a case of startle-matching in the Netherlands in which the treating psychiatrist claims to have achieved a lasting cure. If this report is accurate, it deserves close study as it is unique (see Jenner, 1990).

15. Even small details about the stimuli and their presentation are similar across cultures—for example, the fact that words like "snake!" and "crocodile!" may precipitate an episode, that commands won't work unless they are issued in a framed and forceful manner, etc.

REFERENCES

Bah-tsche

Suwanlert, S. (1972). Psychiatric study of *bah tsche (latah)*. Paper presented at the 26th Annual meeting of the Division of Mental Hospital, Department of Medical Services Surat Thani, Suan Saranromya Hospital, Thailand.

Imu

Anonymous. (1937/1938). The syndrome of *imu* in the Ainu race. *American Journal of Psychiatry, 94*, 1467–1469.

Kumasaka, Y. (1964). A culturally-determined mental reaction among the Ainu. *Psychiatric Quarterly, 38*, 733–739.

Ohnuki-Tierney, E. (1980). Shamans and *Imu*: Among two Ainu groups: Toward a cross-cultural model of interpretation. *Ethos, 8*, 204–228.

Ohnuki-Tierney, E. (1981). *Illness & healing among the Sakhalin Ainu: A symbolic interpretation* (pp. 175–178, 198–203). Cambridge: Cambridge University Press.

Uchimura, Y. (1935). *Imu*: A malady of the Ainu. *Lancet, 1*, 1272–1273.

Winiarz, W., & Wielawski, J. (1936). *Imu*—a psychoneurosis occurring among Ainus. *Psychoanalytic Review, 23*, 181–186.

Jumping

Beard, G.M. (1878). Verbal communication. *Proceedings of the American Neurological Association*, 525–526.

Beard, G.M. (1880a). Experiments with the Jumpers or Jumping Frenchmen of Maine. *Journal of Nervous and Mental Diseases, 7*, 487–490.

Beard, G.M. (1880b). Experiments with the "Jumpers" of Maine. *Popular Science Monthly, 18*, 170–178.

Day, H.F. (1902). *Pine tree ballads: Rhymed stories of unplanned human natur' up in Maine* (pp. 251–253). Boston: Small, Maynard & Co.

Kunkle, E.C. (1967). The "Jumpers" of Maine: A reappraisal. *Archives of Internal Medicine, 119*, 355–358.

Kunkle, E.C. (1965). The "Jumpers" of Maine: Past history and present status. *Journal of the Maine Medical Association, 56*, 191–193.

Moss, G.E. (1968). The "Jumpers" of Maine: A sociological appraisal. *Journal of the Maine Medical Association, 59,* 117–121.

Rabinovitch, R. (1965). An exaggerated startle reflex resembling a kicking horse. *Canadian Medical Association Journal, 93,* 130.

Saint-Hilaire, M. (1986). Jumping Frenchmen of Maine. *Neurology, 36,* 1269–1271.

Stevens, H. (1965). Jumping Frenchmen of Maine. *Archives of Neurology, 12,* 311–314.

Lapp Panic

Collinder, B. (1949). *The Lapps* (pp. 151–152). New York: Greenwood.

Mali-mali

Musgrave, W.E. (1910). *Mali-mali*: A mimic psychosis in the Philippine Islands: A preliminary report. *Philippine Journal of Science, V-B,* 335–339.

Miryachit

Aberle, D.F. (1952). Arctic hysteria and *Latah* in Mongolia. *Transactions of New York Academy of Sciences, 14,* 291–297.

Czaplicka, M.A. (1914). *Aboriginal Siberia: A study in social anthropology* (pp. 307–324). Oxford: Clarendon Press.

Grygier, T. (1947/48). Psychiatric observations in the Arctic. *British Journal of Psychology, 38,* 84–96.

Hammond, W.A. (1884). *Miryachit,* a newly described disease of the nervous system and its analogues. *New York Medical Journal, 39,* 191–192.

Shirokogoroff, S.M. (1935). Psychological conditions of groups investigated. In S.M. Shirokogoroff (Ed.), *Psychomental complex of the Tungus* (pp. 241–260). London: Kegan Paul.

Nekzah

Natoli, A. (1937). *Latah* in natives of Bengasi. *Giornale Italiano di Clinica Tropicale, 1,* 20–24.

Penso, G. (1934). Il *"Latah"* nella Somalia Italiana. *Archivio Italiano di Scienze Mediche Coloniali, 12,* 364–367.

Sarnelli, T. (1924). La malattia del *Latah* in Tripolitania. *Giornale di Medicina Militaire, 72,* 104–106.

Sarnelli, T. (1934). Primi casi di *"Latah"* osservati nell' Alto Yemen (Arabia S.O.). *Archivio Italiano di Scienze Mediche Coloniali, 12,* 750–759.

Young-Dah-hte

Still, R.M.L. (1940). Remarks on the aetiology and symptoms of *young-Dah-hte* with a report on four cases and its medico-legal significance. *The Indian Medical Gazette, 75,* 88–91.

Other

Carr, J.E. (1978). Ethnobehaviorism and the culture-bound syndromes: The case of *Amok*. *Culture, Medicine, and Psychiatry, 2,* 269.

Chiu, T.L., Tong, J.E., & Schmidt, K. E. (1972). A clinical survey of *Latah* in Sarawak, Malaysia. *Psychological Medicine, 2,* 155–165.

Geertz, H. (1968). *Latah* in Java: A theoretical paradox. *Indonesia, 3,* 93–104.

Jenner, J.A. (1990). *Latah* as coping. *International Journal of Social Psychiatry, 36,* 194–199.

Jordan, B. (1989). Cosmopolitan obstetrics. *Social Science and Medicine, 28,* 935.

Karp, I. (1985). Deconstructing culture-bound syndromes. *Social Science and Medicine, 21,* 221–228.

Kenney, M. (1978). *Latah*: The symbolism of a putative mental disorder. *Culture, Medicine and Psychiatry, 2,* 209–231.

Kenney, M. (1983). Paradox lost: The *Latah* problem revisited. *Journal of Nervous and Mental Disease, 171,* 159–167.

Lee, R.L.M. (1981). Structure and anti-structure in the culture-bound Syndromes: The Malay case. *Culture, Medicine and Psychiatry, 5,* 233–248.

Pfeiffer, W. (1971). Die *Latah*-artigen reaktionen. In *Transkulturelle psychiatrie* (pp. 80–125). Stuttgart: Thieme.

Pfeiffer, W. (1986). Personal observations of *Latah* in Java (unpublished interview).

Simons, R.C. (1980). The resolution of the *Latah* paradox. *Journal of Nervous and Mental Disease, 168*(4), 195–206.

Simons, R.C. (1983a). *Latah* II—Problems with a purely symbolic interpretation. *Journal of Nervous and Mental Disease, 171,* 168–171.

Simons, R.C. (1983b). *Latah* III—How compelling is the evidence for a psychoanalytic interpretation? *Journal of Nervous and Mental Disease, 171,* 178–181.

Simons, R.C., & Hughes, C.C. (Eds.). (1985). *The culture-bound syndromes.* Dordrecht: D. Reidel.

Winzeler, R. (1984). The study of Malayan *Latah*. *Indonesia, 37,* 77–104.

Winzeler, R. (1988). *Malaysian conceptions of Latah and healing.* Prepared for Symposium on Cultural Dimensions of Healing in S.E. Asia. Association for Asian Studies meeting, San Fransisco.

Winzeler, R. (1991). *Latah* in Sarawak, with special reference to the Iban. In V. Sutlive & G.N. Appell (Eds.), *Female and male in Borneo: Contributions and challenges to gender studies* (pp. 317–333). Williamsburg, VA: Borneo Research Council Monograph Series.

11

CULTURE, BIOLOGY, AND INDIVIDUAL EXPERIENCE

For "human nature" is far from being a constant parameter of cultural events; indeed, the biological mechanism upon which culture depends is exquisitely variable in response to genetic and ecological processes that, in part, are radically independent of culture per se.

Anthony F. C. Wallace, *Culture and Personality*, 1970, p. 244

If biological and cultural variables are seen within the context of a single process, then we shall be able to draw freely upon data from all the subdisciplines of anthropology.

Alexander Alland, *Adaptation in Cultural Evolution*, 1970, p. 42

This book has presented a curious assemblage of material: a description and analysis of the startle-reflex and attention-capture; stories from the lives of people living in a variety of cultures; a discussion of fright illnesses; excerpts from novels, plays, poems, and newspapers; descriptive and historical discussions of *latah*; and briefer descriptions and discussions of a number of other culture-bound syndromes. Each of the pieces of data presented might have been analyzed in many different ways, but here the emphasis has been on what they have in common. Each is an example of the ways people in a variety of times and places have dealt with one readily identifiable bit of evolved biology—the startle reflex. The heterogenous materials that this book has examined are held together by only this single common thread, the startle reflex and how it is experienced and culturally elaborated.

The thesis that has been presented is that behaviors and experiences are shaped in specifiable ways by evolved neurophysiology, that the startle reflex is a resource for cultural elaboration, and that the constituent elements of the reflex have provided the raw material for its social uses. I have argued that, although the constituent elements do not in themselves determine the interpretations that people make of them, the nature of those constituent elements biases interpretations.

The culture-typical references to, depictions of, and practices concerning startle that each person is exposed to profoundly influence his or her startle-related behaviors and the ways in which his or her own startles and the startles of others are experienced. However, one's personal experience of startle and of the discontinuity in experience and behavior that startles induce also has elements that do not have to be learned from others. Although particular uses of the reflex can plausibly be explained without reference to the elements of its physiology, it is possible to discern patterns of social and cultural usage and interpretation that are shaped by physiology and thus appear recurrently across disparate cultural contexts.

The reasoning employed can be summarized as follows:

THE STARTLE REFLEX

A. Startle is an evolved, programmed response to an as yet unassessed danger.

B. Both stimulus and response elements of the reflex are concerned with protecting the startled person from a suddenly appearing threat or danger.

C. The most usual immediate response to being startled consists of defensive withdrawal, often coupled with a vocalization and unfocused aggression.

D. After the immediate response, unreflecting mechanisms for refocusing attention scan the environment for the startle elicitor.

E. This scan is tuned to search for whatever feature of the perceptual field is most strongly demarcated from the perceptual background.

F. This demarcation may be the result of intrinsic properties of the feature, such as size, color, and motion, or may result from its associational significance.

G. The associational significance may be personal and idiosyncratic or widely held and culture-typical.

H. When an environmental feature has been selected, attention is focused on it, and the search ceases.

I. The feature selected is not necessarily the source of the startling stimulus.

J. All of the above hold across cultural contexts, and all therefore provide themes for culture-typical exploitation and interpretation.

INDIVIDUAL VARIABILITY AND HYPERSTARTLING

A. Individuals vary considerably in their readiness to startle and in the violence of their startles.

B. Because inputs from higher brain centers modulate the startle response, how a person responds at any given time depends in part on his or her past experience and on his or her current state.

C. People intently monitoring their thoughts or sensations or their external environments (i.e., who are hypervigilant) startle readily and violently.

D. Neurophysiological, psychological, sociological, and demographic variables associated with intense internal or environmental monitoring are therefore also associated with ready and violent startles.

E. Being frequently startled most often leads to increasingly ready and violent startling.

F. Other individual factors, including innate temperamental ones, may also be associated with ready and violent startles.

G. All of the above hold across cultural contexts, and all provide themes for culture-typical exploitation and interpretation.

STARTLING OTHER PEOPLE

A. Startle is an altered state of consciousness that one person can readily induce in another.

B. In many cultural contexts, people intentionally startle others for a wide variety of purposes, often but not always for the amusement of onlookers.

C. In a wide variety of cultures, people known to startle especially readily and violently are preferentially selected for startle-teasing.

D. Rules about who may startle whom in what circumstances and how one behaves toward a just-startled person are specific to cultures.

E. Social status and gender are the major relevant considerations in determining who may be intentionally startled. Lower-status persons are more subject to startle-teasing in all cultures. Women, who in many cultures have lower social status than men, are intentionally startled more than men in most cultures.

F. The meanings and values with which startle-teasing is associated are specific to specific cultures. However, the nature of the experience of being startled and the kinds of behaviors associated with being startled suggest recurrent themes that can be found in historically unrelated cultures.

COMMON USES OF THE REFLEX IN THE WEST

A. Accounts and depictions of persons being startled and metaphoric references to being startled are frequent in British and American culture, where they are used for a variety of expository and explanatory purposes.

B. Culture-typical accounts, explanations, and metaphoric references make use of small and specific features intrinsic to the nature of the reflex.

C. Parallel uses of startle's many small and specific features can be found over great stretches of historical time in the West and in at least some non-Western cultures—for example, Japan.

ATTENTION-CAPTURE AND THE STARTLE-MATCHING SYNDROME

A. Persons who hyperstartle may find their attention locked onto or captured by a strongly demarcated environmental feature.

B. Members of societies in which the startle-matching syndrome is found become expert at providing vulnerable just-startled others with intentionally selected and strongly demarcated stimuli likely to capture attention.

C. This expertise is learned in childhood from frequent observations of people interacting in this way.

D. Capture of attention is sometimes followed by matching, completion of model-initiated actions, and automatic obedience.

E. The association of hyperstartling, attention capture, matching, and obedience may be referred to as the "startle-matching syndrome."

F. Because the startle-matching syndrome results from pan-human physiological variables combined with cultural variables of frequent occurrence, its form is similar even in culturally disparate settings.

G. Cultural and social factors account for the syndrome's geographic distribution.

LATAH

A. *Latah* is the name of the startle-matching syndrome found in Malaysia and Indonesia.

B. Three distinguishable types of behavior are indigenously referred to as *latah*:

1. Immediate-response *latah*, which consists of strong responses to startle found amusing by others (violent body movements; assumption of habitual defensive postures; striking out; throwing or dropping held objects; shouting; repeating of words just said, thought, or attended to; naughty talk).

2. Attention-capture *latah*, which consists of matching, "automatic obedience," and completion of other-initiated actions (all of these involving bodily activity, speech, or both).

3. Role-*latah*, which consists of behaviors selected from the above two categories and elaborated idiosyncratically into intentionally amusing performances.

C. Explanations of *latah* necessarily must take into account the syndrome's minute and specific features. When this is done, it is readily apparent that *latah* is a culture-typical elaboration of features inherent in the startle reflex and attention-capture.

THE STARTLE-MATCHING SYNDROME IN OTHER CULTURES

A. In a number of societies hyperstartlers and those who exhibit the startle-matching syndrome have named and elaborated roles.
B. These roles are comfortably accepted by some but are unacceptable to others.
C. If the role is comfortably accepted, a hyperstartler will integrate the role into his or her "life story." If it is unacceptable, the hyperstartler will shun occasions where startle is likely, seek cures, and deny his or her hyperstartling status.
D. In many societies the role of hyperstartler is more congruent with other aspects of the roles of women than with those of men.
E. In these societies, the role of hyperstartler will in general be more acceptable to women than to men.
 F. Hyperstartlers who find the role gratifying may perform behaviors more or less typical of those elicited by startles even in the absence of physiologically adequate stimulation.
G. Behaviors homologous with those of immediate-response *latah* may be found in any society.
H. Behaviors homologous with those of attention-capture *latah* may also be found, albeit infrequently and only in special circumstances, in any society.
 I. Behaviors homologous with those of role-*latah* occur only in those societies in which the role of a teased hyperstartler is acceptable to some people.

THE FRIGHT-ILLNESSES

A. In many historically unrelated cultures, a heterogenous assortment of illnesses are commonly explained as the result of having been previously startled. Sometimes, the explanation is that someone closely associated with the ill person was previously startled.
B. The association of startle with illness is suggested by properties intrinsic to the reflex: the fact that being startled results in involuntary attentional changes and loss of self-control and the reflex's association with danger, wariness, trauma, and debility.
C. In cultures in which having been startled is believed to cause illness, the actual illnesses attributed to having been startled are many and varied, having to do with locally prevalent diseases rather than elements specific to the startle reflex itself.

D. In such cultures, startle is usually only one of a set of experiences believed to cause illness. Others include extreme fear, the receipt of bad news, and significant reversal in personal fortunes.

E. In such cultures, frequent and prolonged startle-teasing of vulnerable persons is limited, and the startle-matching syndrome is absent or rare.

THE GENERAL CASE

A. In the most diverse social contexts, in cultures widely separated in time and space, the inescapable physiology of the startle reflex both shapes the experience of startle and biases the social usages to which the reflex is put.

B. Studies of the startle reflex illuminate a more general problem: how one's experience of being in the world is shaped by one's physiology and how it is shaped by one's prior experiences, beliefs, values, and social condition.

C. The raw material for cultural elaboration is human experience, and significant aspects of that experience are species-typical.

D. Specific and specifiable bits of evolved human neurophysiology shape experience and meaning.

EXPLANATIONS AND ACADEMIC DISCIPLINES

As Michael Kenny once pointed out,

Fundamental differences of view exist between authors who advocate a fusion of biological, psychological and cultural explanations of culture-bound syndromes, and those who construe these syndromes [exclusively] in symbolic and sociological terms. (1985, p. 163)

This dichotomy is much debated in current anthropological thought. Because conflicting explanations of even as esoteric a subject as *latah* are conflicting explanations of the nature of reality, there are strong partisans on both sides. Each scholar sees certain concepts as the relevant and therefore necessary elements of an adequate explanation, and each scholar's preferred level of abstraction is the level that he or she knows best.

In contemporary scholarly anthropological writing, debates about the interpretation of a behavior or experience are often not about empirical evidence but rather are about the most appropriate level of analysis with which to conceptualize the problem. It is useful to differentiate those critiques that challenge the accuracy of a set of observations from those that argue against their relevance on general theoretical grounds. Restricting relevancies in this way may be a useful rhetorical strategy, but it is not useful in the search for understanding. The interpretation of *latah* and the other startle-matching syndromes presented in this book has been challenged not on the accuracy of the observations adduced in support of the interpretation offered but rather on the relevance of the kind of data offered to support the interpretation.

However, the understanding of any event must begin with accurate and detailed description. If the question is one of the nature of *latah*, the answer must begin with an exhaustive description of *latah* behavior and the experiences of *latahs*. Observational data must take precedence over inferred but not observed variables. Observations must be accounted for; descriptive data cannot be ignored, even if inconvenient. Although data other than data descriptive of a behavior are always relevant to its understanding, the relevance of any particular set of such data needs to be demonstrated. However, data describing the experience or behavior are necessarily relevant and must always be accounted for in explanatory formulations.

Robert Hahn has written of how biology circumscribes and constrains human thought and activity:

> Human physiology, psyche and culture operate conjointly. What can be learned is circumscribed by the physiological properties of the person's body by which learning takes place. Our cultures may prescribe our actions, but our capacities are also physically constrained. While culture shapes physiological reactions, its development is in turn affected in profound ways by our bodies and our environment. (Hahn, 1985, p. 171)

The fact that biology provides constraints to human behavior is usually conceded even by the strongest proponents of an exclusively cultural approach. But it is the thesis of this book that our bodies do more than circumscribe and constrain. In addition, they provide resources for cultural elaboration. At least in the case of the startle reflex, the minute and specific features of the reflex are precisely what meanings and practices are built of and are about. Physiology is just as much a resource for cultural elaboration as is the local ecology. Because that which cultural anthropologists attempt to explain is the experience and behavior of actual persons, physiology *ought* to be of significant interest in many contexts.

A good explanation of the startle-matching syndrome, or of any other set of human behaviors, must suggest how the cited data are related, how they produce the behaviors observed, and what is experienced by the individuals involved. What is desired is not mere assemblages of relevant considerations or factors but rather actual causal chains: This circumstance induces that circumstance which induces the next circumstance. The elements of such causal chains may lie in the territories of different intellectual disciplines. The causal chains that generate observed and experienced behaviors include biological, psychological, social, and cultural components that are intertwined in situationally specific ways. The discipline-specific strands of cause and effect cross and recross each other, join, and diverge.

"Culture," it must be remembered, is an analytic construct, not a functional one. Culture is not a disembodied entity existing somewhere out in the world doing things to people; there are no mysterious "cultural forces." Although for many purposes the analytic or synthetic creation of cultural categories is both useful and necessary, the categories thus created do not exist as functioning entities in the real world. The functioning entities, the units on which forces act and which respond to them, are individual persons.[1]

It is customary in much contemporary anthropological writing and discourse to deal with human experience as if it were infinitely plastic. At least in the case of startle, however, many of the ways in which people experience the reflex appear to transcend cultural boundaries, to have at least as much to do with what it is like to be human per se as it is to be a member of a particular cultural group. Just as physiology shapes experience, experience shapes culture. The stimuli that elicit startles, the responses people make when startled, the states and settings in which they startle readily and excessively, and the potential for habituation and sensitization—in short, all of the major features of the reflex listed in Table 1.2—transcend cultural boundaries. That startle is an altered state of consciousness which one person can readily induce in another is true everywhere. The fact that not only the physical properties but also the significance of stimuli may startle provides considerable scope for cultural variability, but even this variability has some striking consistencies embedded within it.

In Chapter 1, startle was suggested as a model system, which if traced through a wide variety of times and places would make certain aspects of the relationship among physiology, experience, and culture especially apparent. Because it is easily identified and traced, startle permits a comparison of quite disparate types of data, but it is necessary to look for the constancies that underlie apparently disparate presentations.

Much controversy in the anthropological literature consists of disagreements as to whether the practices of persons in different cultural settings can validly or usefully be considered members of a single class. For example, everyone knows how varied are fashions in dress and how culture-specific are notions of male and of female modesty. The theme of who may properly show what to whom is played out in quite different ways between the sexes in different times and places, and we smile at the swimsuit fashions of even our own elders. However, one cannot conclude from this evidence that there are only differences, for abstracted at another level there is also a great similarity. How one deals with genitals is always specified; how one deals with breasts, the most prominent secondary sexual female characteristic, is usually specified as well. Rules are most strictly prescribed and most strictly enforced among those of reproductive age.

How widespread such rules are is quite extraordinary. Napoleon

Chagnon, for example, reports that the Yanomami Indians of Venezuela, whom we think of as going naked, have quite definite rules about covering genitalia—one, for example, being the rule requiring women to sit in a posture in which the perineum is shielded from gaze by the heel of one foot. Men must wear a string that holds up the penis; if it dangles, one is considered indecently naked. Once Chagnon's cameraman, Timothy Asch, removed his shorts to keep them from snagging on a bush: "At this point everybody screamed, and the five Yanomami women that were with us jumped into the bushes and hid. 'What's the matter?' I asked. The Yanomami pointed, 'You're naked!'" (Asch, 1979, p. 44). He was not wearing a penis string.

Our rules and practices dictating modesty are different from those of the Yanomami, but there are striking similarities as well. Why is this so, and why are such rules and practices so widespread? Do they reflect something basic not just to being Yanomami or American, but to being human? Similarities are not invalidated by the demonstration of difference; similarities and differences coexist quite comfortably.

The startle reflex is used, experienced, and understood both similarly and differently in the wide diversity of cultural contexts presented in this book. Both the commonalities and the differences reveal much about the relationship of neurophysiology to experience and to culture. It is the pattern that is most revealing. For example, a person who observes a hyperstartler for a long time and has many opportunities to startle him or her can become especially expert at it. Such a person may become the one chosen to elicit hyperstartling performances in situations in which such a performance is desired. Vreeland noted that Goosey Gus "responded most readily to a buddy of his, about his own age, who had been with him the longest in the shop. . . . This man knew just where to poke or grab him for the best effect" (H. Vreeland, 1953, personal communication).

Among the Ainu, who expect *imu* behavior at certain festive and ceremonial occasions, the role of this expert friend is culturally elaborated and has a name, "*Imu-yara.*" Obviously, Gus's buddy did not perform all of the features of the *Imu-yara*'s role, certainly not those associated with specifically Ainu practices and beliefs. Nevertheless, the fact that someone long observing reactions and testing them out over time can become especially expert at it, that this person is likely to be someone with a prior special relationship to the hyperstartler, and that this person will therefore often be called on as a preferred elicitor is a set of conditions that is likely to be present in many cultural and subcultural settings. It is not surprising to find it culturally exploited.

THE CENTRAL ROLE OF INDIVIDUAL EXPERIENCE

Unni Wikan has recently argued for an anthropology based on a more direct and concerted examination of the nature of human experience and against a perspective focused exclusively on meanings and values:

[I]t is inadequate for an anthropological analysis to focus only on the realm of "concepts within which a people's experience moves," so long as we are given no notion of what that experience in fact is. The scrutiny of an assemblage of such concepts may lead to the construction of an "ethos" that is very wide of the mark. Rather, we need to see how an actual range of events, and the specific interpretations imposed upon them, together create the experience that makes up a socially and culturally mediated "reality." (Wikan, 1987, p. 363)

Individual experience is the key. The route from the physiology of startle to its cultural elaborations lies through personal experience—direct experience of what being startled is like, observation of the startled behavior of others, and the experience of being raised as a participant in a particular culture.

A useful model for the way in which the experience of a physiological state and its interpretation may operate in concert was suggested in a paper by Gazzinaga on the organization of the human brain. Gazzinaga points out that when a physiological event produces a deeply felt experience, the person who has that experience will seek to interpret it. The interpretation he or she adopts will then color subsequent episodes of the same physiological event.

These observations have led to insights into the nature of a variety of psychological disturbances that are initially produced by endogenous errors in cerebral metabolism, such as those known to be associated with panic attacks. Such biologically driven events produced a different felt state, which in turn must be interpreted. Each individual's interpretation, unique to their own past and present psychological history, is then stored in memory and becomes powerfully determinant in the content of an individual's ongoing consciousness. (Gazzinaga, 1989, p. 951)

This passage speaks to the uniqueness of each individual's interpretation, but of course here is precisely where the role of culture lies. Each individual's interpretation of any felt state is determined not only by unique factors in his or her idiosyncratic psychological history, but also by factors shared with other members of the same culture. By virtue of belonging to a given culture, a person has access to a range of interpretations, readily available to make sense of the biological event when it occurs.

Everywhere being startled is both felt and observed to be a discontinuity in ongoing experience and in the smooth flow of behavior and social interaction. This discontinuity is a fact of human life that transcends cultural boundaries, and the range of ways in which it may be considered and dealt with is not infinitely great. There are in general two main themes. The discontinuity may be considered amusing and something to play with, or it may be considered dangerous and something to be avoided if at all possible. Because discontinuity is integral to the experience of the reflex, it is always culturally marked. The special and specific properties of startle always inform and color the way people understand it, wherever they may happen to live.

SUGGESTED RESEARCH

The ultimate test of any explanation of phenomena in the real world must be its ability to generate testable hypotheses, to suggest lines of evidence that would confirm it or cause it to be rejected. Startle-matching being nowhere a national scourge, there is no Startle-Matching Institute, and funding for research has come only in driblets. But if funding were to become available, it would not be hard to lay out a master program for investigation. Although this book has examined startle in quite a few contexts, it must be obvious that the surface of the subject has barely been scratched. How much better our understanding might be with quantified distributional data, with the neurophysiologic understanding of 10 years hence, with detailed data from more cultures!

The work done so far on startle, hyperstartle, and the startle-matching syndromes raises almost as many questions as it answers, questions requiring answers from both field and laboratory investigations. What follows is a brief description of some lines of research that could answer many questions about the human experience of startle and its many culture-typical elaborations.

Test the Major Hypothesis: Hyperstartling and the Startle-Matching Syndrome Result from Variant Physiology

Whether or not a hypothesized neurophysiological variant pattern operates in any context can be determined only by empirical investigation focused on this point. Such a question cannot be definitively answered by reasoning alone. Whether there is a physiological abnormality that recruits people into the cohort of those whom their peers class as *latahs* is ultimately an empirical question. No one who manifests any of the startle-matching syndromes has yet been subjected to systematic neurophysiological testing, yet I believe that the evidence from the detailed analysis of such behavior is overwhelmingly convincing that a physiological abnormality exists.

However, direct testing of this hypothesis is not only desirable; ultimately it is necessary. Here is the hypothesis as I would like to see it tested.

I have hypothesized that American hyperstartlers, *latahs*, and those with other startle-matching syndromes share a common physiological peculiarity that differentiates them from their normally startling peers. Comparison of reports of the syndrome from various cultures strongly suggests that this physiological peculiarity transcends cultural boundaries. Does this physiological peculiarity exist?

If a physiological peculiarity exists, what is it? As noted in Chapter 1, work done so far with American hyperstartlers suggests that one characteristic of hyperstartling persons that differentiates them from others may be a failure to habituate to startling stimuli. A second may be the inability to moderate their response to an anticipated stimulus (Ekman, Friesen, & Simons, 1985). Tests of these measures with a larger sample of American hyperstartlers, *latahs*, and persons who manifest the startle-matching syndrome in other cultural settings need to be done. The difficulty in habituation suggested by field observations and self-reports raises a second question: Do hyperstartlers also habituate more slowly than control subjects to stimuli other than those which startle? If the suggested differences are found, studies aimed at discovering the physiological mechanisms involved need to be undertaken.

Test the Corollary Hypothesis: The Physiological Variant Includes an Alteration in the Physiology of Attention

I have also hypothesized that one relevant physiological peculiarity lies somewhere in the neurological mechanisms serving attention. The reasoning behind this hypothesis is that aberrant functioning of this one neurophysiological system would account for many of the observations of behavior and reports of experience that we now have. Attention is important in the normal startle reflex, hyperstartling, and the startle-matching syndromes in two logically distinct ways:

1. Before a startle occurs:
    a. People startle especially readily and violently when they are in states in which there is some alteration in usual attentional mechanisms: when attention is intently focused on some task, when deeply engaged in introspective thought, when intensely monitoring the environment, and when drowsy or falling asleep.
    b. Situations in which hyperstartling occurs are disproportionally those in which hypermonitoring of the environment might be expected.
    c. People who manifest the startle-matching syndrome are disproportionally those who, for a variety of disparate reasons, habitually hypermonitor their environments.
    d. Ready and violent startles have been demonstrated to be associated with hypervigilance in the posttraumatic stress syndrome.
2. After a startle occurs:
    a. Many of the normal responses to being startled include striking alterations in attention.
    b. Many of the behavioral manifestations of *latah* and the other startle-matching syndromes follow the locking of attention onto some salient environmental feature.

Attentional abnormalities including attention-capture have long been known to be associated with brain injuries. When a person's brain is injured in a variety of ways, both day-to-day behavior and behavior on neuropsychological tests become much more susceptible to the influence of external stimuli. As early as 1948, Kurt Goldstein observed that

> As a result of the loss of structure . . . we also observe in the seemingly inattentive patients . . . a morbidly exaggerated attentiveness. It works like this: The patient is attracted by anything that may appear in his environment, his attention flitting from one object to another. Suddenly he fixates on one thing, and then he can be gotten away from it only with difficulty. (Goldstein, 1948, pp. 86–87)

This susceptibility follows a great variety of injuries to a great variety of sites in the brain. The usual deduction from this is that increased susceptibility is not directly elicited by the injury but rather is the result of the activities of brain structures no longer held in check by the portion of the brain that was injured.

A series of experiments in which normal and hyperstartling subjects are startled while attentional parameters (e.g., number of visual loci to be monitored) are systematically varied would be especially revealing. Dependent variables should include magnitude and quality (e.g., directionality) of motor response, magnitude and quality of psychological response (including the amount and nature of the disruption of an ongoing assigned task), and magnitude and quality of physiological responses, both in the central nervous system (e.g., evoked potential) and in other physiological systems associated with arousal. One could systematically modify attentional parameters in volunteer subjects and measure the following:

1. Magnitude of physical response
2. Magnitude of psychological disruption
3. Magnitude of (various parameters of) physiological response
4. Magnitude of task disruption
5. Lag time for responses to both physical and symbolic stimuli.

Study Speech Anomalies

The involuntary spontaneous verbalizations that follow being startled are commonly attributed to emotionality pure and simple.[2] However, because its elements include both "indecent," often sexual references and references to culturally appropriate deities, the common denominator appears to be the uttering of words usually sequestered from normal speech. Neither the startled speech of persons with *latah* (or any of the other startle-matching syndromes) nor the startled speech of American hyperstartlers have yet been studied with sophisticated linguistic techniques. How can the apparent consistencies across linguistic groups be best described and explained?

Collect Epidemiological and Genetic Data

How is hyperstartling distributed? Are the strength and the ease of elicitation of startle distributed bimodally or are hyperstartlers merely at the high end of a normal distribution of responses? Though there are hints that hyperstartling and *latah* sometimes run in families, data so far gathered are inconclusive. Questions that could usefully be investigated include:

1. Is there a smooth continuum of strength and ease of elicitation of startle responses or is the distribution bimodal, with hyperstartlers being a distinct group? Evidence previously cited suggests that the latter may be the case.
2. *Latah* appears to run in families. Genetic data should be collected systematically. Is there a genetic marker—that is, does the presence or absence of *latah* correlate with any genetically determined feature?
3. What is the reason for the high prevalence of the startle-matching syndrome in Southeast Asia? I have hypothesized social and cultural factors having to do with the ways stigmatized others are treated, especially patterns of startle-teasing. But is some genetic predisposition also a factor?[3]

Collect Further Phenomenological Data

If Malay villagers could see a film of *imu* as it is found in Ainu villages, would they consider it a form of *latah*? Conversely, how would Ainu villagers describe a film of *latah*? Cross-cultural analyses such as these would be very useful in pinpointing subtle ways in which the syndromes are alike and how they differ. Films of other startle-matching syndromes (e.g., the Maine *Jumpers*) could also be collected, systematically compared, and shown for comment to members of other societies in which other startle-matching syndromes are prevalent.

Study Coexisting Syndromes

I have suggested that startle-matching syndromes are unlikely in places where fright-illnesses occur. One might expect that where people believe that startling someone may have serious negative health consequences, social sanctions would prevent persons from intentionally startling others with the frequency necessary to generate and maintain the syndrome. In general, this suggestion is consistent with what has been found and would explain the absence of the syndrome from Latin America and from most of Africa. However, two anomalous reports provide the opportunity to learn more about the ways in which culturally held beliefs and values and social practices are related to the syndrome.

Mali-mali, a startle-matching syndrome, has been reported from many other areas of the Philippines, but so far not from the Visayan Islands, from which Donn Hart described the fright-illness, *lanti*. Is there indeed no startle-matching syndrome in the places where *lanti* is found, or do the two conditions somehow coexist? If both conditions coexist in the Visayans, discovering how they are considered and managed there would be revealing.

Similarly, Unni Wikan has reported a fright-illness, *kesambet*, from northern Bali, where a local form of *latah* occurs. Discovering how the system works in northern Bali would be especially informative. I believe it likely that the answer is that *kesambet* and *latah* are believed to affect different age and sex classes of persons, so that those startle-teased are not those believed to be susceptible to falling ill as a result of being startled. This, however, is only a guess; direct ethnological investigation of this question is highly desirable.

Investigate the Relationship Between the Startle-Matching and Gilles de la Tourette Syndromes

In his famous paper of 1885, Gilles de la Tourette considered *latah* and the syndrome that now bears his name to be one and the same. Comparison of detailed descriptions and of films and videotapes of persons with both conditions show that this clearly is not the case. There are many features, however, which characterize both conditions—too many to be purely coincidental.

At times, people with both conditions match the behaviors of others, involuntarily utter normally prohibited speech, and fling held objects. Although these behaviors are not preceded by startles when performed by those with Tourette's syndrome, individuals with the syndrome suffer from frequent strong spontaneous convulsive tics. People with Tourette's syndrome need no special stimulation to elicit their symptoms. Instead, they often describe an intermittent awareness of an increasing urge to throw something, to match a movement or bit of speech, or to utter a normally prohibited word or phrase. With conscious effort, the urge may be resisted for a time, but if this is done, the pressure to perform the act grows. In contrast, people with *latah* and the other startle-matching syndromes are unremarkable in their behavior and thought except when startled or when attention is otherwise captured.

The large number of overlapping features suggests that when the neurophysiology of Tourette's syndrome is better understood, much of what is found will be helpful in understanding the startle-matching syndromes. Similarly, better comprehension of the neurophysiology underlying the startle-matching syndromes should be helpful in understanding the mechanism of Tourette's syndrome.

Investigate the Relationship Between the Hyperstartling of *Latahs* and Hereditary Hyperexplexia

Hereditary hyperexplexia (sometimes spelled "hyperekplexia") is a neurological condition present from birth. Infants with this condition display an exaggerated startle reflex and severe muscle rigidity, which may cause death if they startle and choke when the exaggerated tone of the muscles associated with respiration makes breathing impossible. If these infants survive to adulthood, muscular hyper-rigidity decreases, but they continue to startle violently, and muscular rigidity recurs whenever they are startled. It has been known for a considerable time that the amino acid, glycine, exerts a tonic inhibitory inflence on acoustic startle. (Kehne, Gallager, & Davis, 1981, p. 177) Recent research has shown that hereditary hyperexplexia is caused by a single genetic alteration affecting glycine receptors in the brain and spinal cord that normally moderate startles (Ivinson, 1993, p. 488; Shiang, Ryna, Zhu, & Hahn, 1993, p. 351).

Hyperexplexia is not *latah*, but the finding that it is caused by an abnormality in neurological pathways that use the neurotransmitter glycine raises the question of whether some variant in the usual metabolism of glycine occurs genetically or is induced by repetitive startling in those individuals who become *latahs*.

Provide Treatment to *Latahs* Requesting It

Latah is not merely a historical phenomenon; it is a contemporary one. Because it is contemporary, investigators have a moral responsibility to include as part of their work some assessment of the wants and needs of the *latahs* they are investigating. The scholarly debate about the nature of *latah* has an ethical and moral dimension because interpretations may affect the lives of actual living persons.

The most obvious application of what is now understood about *latah* and other forms of hyperstartling, of course, is in the medical treatment of *latahs* and other hyperstartlers. Although it is true that for some persons to be a *latah* is to live out an acceptable social role, it is equally true that for others it is a great misery. Many people find their vulnerability to hyperstartling a great handicap both socially and in the workplace, and they experience the frequent intentional startles they receive as humiliating. Treatment both with and without medication should be offered to those desiring it. Because *latah* is more often regarded as a handicap by Malaysian men than by Malaysian women, I hypothesize that in Malaysia men would seek treatment more often than would women and that men would both report and show more benefit from treatment than would women.

If medication is to be used, which medication in what dose range would suppress excessive startle with a minimum of side effects? Clonidine, which is known to suppress startle in low doses, might be the first medication tried.[4] Clonazepam, which has successfully been used in the treatment of people suffering from hyperexplexia (Ivinson, 1993, p. 488), is another possibility.

The physiological effect of treatment could be monitored by having *latah* volunteers wear startle-recording devices for a period before and after treatment to determine whether treatment actually reduces the frequency and intensity of startles. In addition to the effect of drug treatment on the startle reflex itself, would there be any change in poststartle attentional effects?

Of even more practical importance, what effect would efficacious treatment have on hyperstartlers' life experiences and social roles? This question could best be studied with the standard anthropological technique of participant observation. It would be especially revealing in places such as Malaysia where culture-typical beliefs and practices surround and color hyperstartlers' lives. In Malaysia, interviews with *latahs* and their neighbors could be conducted before and after treatment, and the social and other effects of treatment could be studied by participant observers.

Other Questions and Applications

1. In cultures in which the startle-matching syndrome is endemic, is the posttraumatic stress syndrome indigenously considered to be a manifestation of the startle-matching syndrome, or is a distinction made between the two conditions? In such cultures are the attention-capture phenomena characteristic of startle-matching syndromes shown by those who suffer from posttraumatic stress disorder? The prediction is that this will be the case, since their hyperstartling may lead to their being assigned the status of *latahs*, (or *mali-malis*, etc.) and to their being so treated by other members of their societies.

2. Claims of posttraumatic stress injury are often contested by third parties responsible for compensation in cases of injury. Could testing for altered startle responses be used to provide objective evidence for injury or lack thereof?

3. Does what we already know about startle and attention-capture have practical implications with regard to emergency alarms and response devices? Data already available suggest that in situations in which people need to respond quickly to a continuous loud alarm signal, the apparatus for response (a fire extinguisher, for example) should be located immediately adjacent to the alarm. This is because the attention of a significant number of persons may be captured by the signal itself, making it difficult for them to respond promptly when a response devise is located at a distance from it. Does positioning the response device close to the alarm generally reduce response time? Is an intermittent alarm signal less likely to produce attention-capture paralysis than a continuous signal?

EPILOGUE

When I began this work, I did not anticipate how often I would find startles either prominent in people's lives or elaborated in their cultures. It turns out there are a lot of startles and a lot of thinking about startles. Why startles and their elaborated uses and meanings are so frequent and ubiquitous was itself puzzling at first. Gradually, the reason became clear: The startle reflex is everywhere reflected on and culturally elaborated because it is the response of body and soul to an overwhelming existential reality. Injury and death wait just around the corner; there are no safe times or places; life is a bubble.

In many of the world's religions this truth is taught in stories. Hinduism tells of Hiranyakasipu, a demon king who had been promised by Brahma that he could not be killed by day or by night, in his house or outside it, by man, beast, or god. Hiranyakasipu believed that he was safe.

To rid the world of this demon, the god Vishnu transformed himself into Narasinha, a terrifying creature, half-man and half-lion. One evening at twilight, a time that is neither day nor night, Narasinha, who was neither man, beast, nor god but an amalgam of all three, stepped out of a pillar, and in the doorway, which was neither inside nor outside Hiranyakasipu's house, seized and disemboweled him.

Picture the scene. It is growing dark. Suddenly there looms a giant figure with the head and torso of an angry lion—out of the growing dusk, death in that awesome shape. Do you not think that Hiranyakasipu startled?

NOTES

1. David Hufford points out that "many scholars have lost sight of the fact that group constructs can never be more than a rough aggregation of information about individuals. . . . [For these scholars] individual data is seen merely as exemplifying the aggregate, rather than the aggregate being a description of commonalities derived from specific individual cases" (1994, personal communication).

2. "[Expressive or emotional speech] is a part of the totality of expressive movements and arises simultaneously with emotions. It is involuntary rather than intentional. This form of speech corresponds to a more simple cerebral functioning. Thus, it may be relatively well-preserved in spite of cerebral damage and in all events it suffers less severely than representational speech" (H. Jackson, cited in Goldstein, 1948, p. 165).

3. One piece of data suggesting that this may be the case is the recent report of the presence of a startle-matching syndrome in certain individuals—the "*Rajin' Cajuns*" of Louisiana—who share a common ancestry with the *Jumpers* of Maine but who are culturally quite distinct from them (McFarling, 1988, p. 361).

4. Suggested by Michael Davis (personal communication).

REFERENCES

Alland, A. (1970). *Adaptation in cultural evolution*. New York: Columbia University Press.

Asch, T. (1979). Making a film record of the Yanomami Indians of southern Venezuela. *Perspectives on Film, 2,* 44.

Ekman, P., Friesen, W.V., & Simons, R.C. (1985). Is the startle reaction an emotion? *Journal of Personality and Social Psychology, 49,* 1416–1426.

Gazzinaga, M.S. (1989). Organization of the human brain. *Science, 245,* 947–952.

Goldstein, K. (1948). *After-effects of brain injuries in war*. New York: Grune & Stratton.

Hahn, R. (1985). Culture-bound syndromes unbound. *Social Science and Medicine*, *21*, 165–171.

Ivinson, A.J. (1993). Inhibition and over-reaction. *Nature*, *366*, 488.

Kehne, J.H., Gallager, D.W., & Davis, M. (1981). Strychnine: Brainstem and spinal mediation of excitatory effects on acoustic startle. *European Journal of Pharmacology*, *76*, 177–186.

Kenny, M. (1985). Introduction: New approaches to mental disorders. *Social Science and Medicine*, *21*, 163.

McFarling, D.A. (1988). *Rajin' Cajuns*: The Jumping Frenchmen of Louisiana. *Neurology*, *38 (Suppl. 1)*, 361.

Shiang, R., Ryan, S.G., Zhu, Y.Z., Hahn, A.F. (1993). Mutations in the Alpha 1 subunit of the inhibitory glycine receptor cause the dominant neurologic disorder, hyperekplexia. *Nature*, *366*, 351–358.

Simons, R.C. (1988). Round three. *Culture, Medicine & Psychiatry*, *12*, 525–529.

Tourette, G. de la (1885). Étude sur une affection nerveuse caractérisée par de l'incoordination motrice accompagnée d'echolalie et de coprolalie. *Archives de Neurologie*, *9*, 19–42, 153–156.

Wallace, A.F.C. (1970). *Culture and personality*. New York: Random House.

Wikan, U. (1987). Public grace and private fears: Gaiety, offence, and sorcery in northern Bali. *Ethos*, *15*, 363.

APPENDIX

LIST OF TOPICS DISCUSSED WITH *LATAHS*

In addition to both identifying and demographic data,[1] interviews of *latahs* covered some selection from the following list of questions:

1. Do you consider yourself to be *latah*?
2. Why/why not?
3. When was the very first time you were *latah*?
4. What were the circumstances?
5. Why do you think you became *latah*?
6. Is it a little *latah* or strongly *latah*?
7. Has it changed at all over time?
8. What kinds of stimuli will make you startle?
9. What else?
10. Do you startle more easily at some times than at other times?
11. If yes, please explain.
12. What kinds of stimuli will make you *latah*?
13. What else?
14. Are you *latah* every time you're startled?
15. Can you be *latah* even if you're not startled?
16. Are there some times when you're especially likely to become *latah*?
17. Please explain in more detail.
18. Have you ever become *latah* after a sudden touch?
19. After a sudden loud noise?

20. When your foot slipped?
21. When you were tickled?
22. When someone made as if to tickle you?
23. Have you ever been startled by a snake? (If yes) Tell me about it.
24. From just being in front of someone important (without even being startled)?
25. From just being in front of many people (without even being startled)?
26. What else has made you become *latah*?
27. Does it make any difference if you're thinking very intently about something before the *latah* stimulus occurs?
28. What happens when you're startled?
29. What else?
30. What do you say?
31. Do you always say the same thing?
32. Tell me what you do.
33. Anything else?
34. Do you ever imitate what other people are doing?
35. Do you ever obey what they order you to do?
36. Tell me about some particular time you were *latah*.
37. What do other people do to make you *latah*?
38. What do they do then?
39. When you're *latah*, how does it stop?
40. When you're *latah*, what do you feel in your body?
41. Your heart?
42. Your breathing?
43. Your arms?
44. Your legs?
45. Your head?
46. In your mind? [Be sure to ask about awareness.]
47. Has your being *latah* affected your relationships with other people?
48. Who most often tries to make you *latah*?
49. Who else?
50. Is there anyone who never does?
51. How has being *latah* affected your life?
52. How would your life be different if *latah* were gone?
53. Do you think it is a kind of illness?
54. Have you ever tried to be cured?
55. How? Explain.
56. If there were a medicine that would stop you from being *latah*, would you want to take it? (Understand that at present there is no such medicine—this is only hypothetical.)
57. What is the most embarrassing incident that ever happened to you while *latah*?
58. Does it ever happen while you're alone—for example, when a coconut leaf falls?

59. Does it make any difference if there are important people around?
60. [If relevant] Does it make any difference what day it is in your monthly cycle?
61. Is anyone else in your family *latah*?
62. Tell me about it.
63. Does anyone else in your family have nervous or mental trouble?
64. Tell me about it.
65. How has your general health been?
66. Do you see a medical doctor regularly for any illness?
67. Do you take any medicine regularly?
68. What for?
69. Do you have headaches?
70. Dizzy spells?
71. Fainting spells?
72. Mental trouble?
73. Are you more shy than most people? (If yes) Were you before you became *latah*?
74. Are there some things you can do more easily with you left hand that most people do more easily with their right? Was that ever the case with you? (If yes) Tell me about it.
75. I've asked you many questions, and you've been very patient to answer them all. What else that we haven't talked about have you noticed about being *latah*?

NOTE

1. Name, Address [village/city of (number) persons], How long there, Previous residence (if above is short), Contact person, Age, Sex, Ethnic group, Principal language, Other languages spoken, Marital status, Number of children, Occupation, Principal source of income, Household Income (approximate per month), Position in family of origin, Father's occupation.

LIST OF TOPICS DISCUSSED WITH MALAYSIAN NON-*LATAH* INFORMANTS

In interviews with non-*latah* informants I especially asked about the following topics:

1. Tell me about the *latahs* in this Kampung.
2. Tell me about some especially memorable incidents of *latah*.
3. What kinds of things do *latahs* do?
4. When do you say that a person is a *latah*?
5. If you want to see a *latah* dance or pretend to play the violin or throw something away, what do you do?
6. Do *latahs* ever do things that are dangerous?
7. Do *latahs* ever do things that are embarrassing?
8. What makes a *latah* get into a *latah* state?

9. Why are some people *latah* and not others?
10. Is *latah* a kind of sickness?
11. Is it rude to startle or tease a *latah*?
12. What makes a *latah* different from an ordinary person?
13. Everyone can be startled. How are *latahs* different from ordinary people?
14. Do some people ever just pretend to be in a *latah* state?
15. (If so) Why should they want to do that?
16. Are *latahs* responsible for what they do while in a *latah* state?
17. In what kinds of situations is one most likely to see *latah* behavior?
18. Why are most *latahs* women?
19. Is *latah* or a tendency to *latah* inherited?

LATAH STORIES REPORTING FORM

This is the form that my assistants and I distributed to collect descriptions of latah *incidents systematically. In retrospect, one can see how subtly and not so subtly the wording of the form biased responses in the direction of good stories. This form was distributed in both Malay and English versions. Literacy in the study area is well nigh universal.*

Please tell me about some incidents of *latah* that you know of. Use as many pages for each story as you need, and start each new story on a new page. Many people can tell five or six *latah* stories. Some may know many more. If you like, you may fill the entire notebook and use extra paper.

When you tell each story be sure to include.

1. A brief description of the *latah* giving at least sex, ethnic group, and approximate age. Examples:

"This *latah* was a Malay woman of about 40. She is a *bidan* in the next *kampung*."

"This happened to a *Baba* Chinese sergeant in the Army. He must have been about 30 when the incident I'm telling took place. "

2. What it was that started the incident going; what someone did to the *latah* to start him/her off or whatever else it was that started things.
3. What the *latah* said and did.
4. Who was there to see it.
5. How people reacted to what the *latah* said and did.
6. How did the incident end?
7. Was it funny? Was it dangerous? (If so, to whom?) How else might you describe it?
8. Did you see the incident yourself? If so, approximately how old were you then? If not, how did you learn of this story?

Please tell me just a little about yourself

Name:
Address:
Age: Sex:
Ethnic group: Education:
What do *you* think is the cause of *latah*?

Is it an illness, or what kind of thing is it do you think?

Have you ever known anyone who was *latah* at one time and then later got over being *latah*?

If so, please tell me what you can about it.

Perhaps as you wrote these stories and filled out this questionnaire you had some other memories or ideas about *latah* that you could tell me. If so, please write them down using as much paper as you wish.

Many, many thanks for your careful help.

Ronald C. Simons, M.D.
Jaafar bin Omar
Institut Penyelidikan Perubatan
Jalan Pahang
Kuala Lumpur 02-14, Malaysia

SCRIPT OF THE FILM:

Latah: A Culture-Specific Elaboration of the Startle Reflex

SCRIPT AND NARRATION BY RONALD C. SIMONS © 1983

Distributor: Indiana Audio-Visual Center, Bloomington, Indiana 47405-5901 USA

Subtitle: The village of Padang Kemunting,

Melaka State, West Malaysia, 1978

Title: Producer, Director, Ethnographer

Ronald C. Simons, M.D., M.A.

Title: Film Maker

Gunter Pfaff

Title: Location Sound Recordist

Betsy Shipley

NARRATOR: Everyone startles, some of us very readily and very strongly.

NARRATOR: This is Cik Rahamah Kamis.

NARRATOR: This is Cik Maimun Hussin.

NARRATOR: In Malaysia, persons who startle readily and strongly like Cik Rahamah and Cik Mun are called "*latahs*." "*Latah*" is also the name of the behavior complex built around hyperstartling.

NARRATOR: The woman facing us is Hajjah Misah Bani. She's a *latah*.

NARRATOR: She's 70 years old. Her *latah* began when she was 62.

HAJJAH MISAH BINTI BANI: Speak!

RCS: How long have you been like this?

HAJJAH MISAH BINTI BANI: A long time—eight years now.

HAJJAH MISAH BINTI BANI: It began when my mother died. I was very sad. I was sitting quietly like this, thinking my mother is gone. Someone came from behind. He grabbed me and said, "What's up?" I was startled! My body trembled like this. My mind went blank. When my body stopped trembling, he teased me again. I picked up a stick and hit him. I couldn't think—what could I know? Later, wherever I went people liked to watch me. They thought I was just pretending. They poked me in the ribs over and over until I became ill.

NARRATOR: The man in the suit is Pawang Lumun, an indigenous healer. His wife, Cik Layut Ali, is a *latah*.

LAYUT BINTI ALI: At first one is merely startled. One sees a centipede, or a snake, or a coconut leaf falls, and one is startled. Then someone sees that happen. Later when he sees me again, perhaps he'll poke me in the ribs. After a while something can happen. Take an ordinary person like Betsy here—if she's startled. Whenever you see her you poke her in the ribs. After a while she'll get very flustered! She'll say whatever comes out. If you tell her to dance, she'll dance. If you poke her in the ribs whenever you see her, she'll do this too. That's what it's like.

NARRATOR: This is Sidang Hussain Dalip. He's the village headman.

RCS: If someone poked you in the ribs every day, would you become a *latah* or not?

SIDANG HUSSAIN BIN DALIP: If it were done face-to-face like this, I think not. But if it were done from behind, and over and over, I think I'd become a *latah* too. But not if I caught sight of the person doing it. But if a person is *latah*, one can put her into a *latah* state even from the front.

RCS: Because they're so easily startled?

SIDANG HUSSAIN BIN DALIP: Yes, they're easily startled.

PAWANG LUMUN: If we don't poke them in the ribs, they don't become *latahs*. If we keep poking a normal person like that he'll become a *latah*. It doesn't take long. Five days poking over and over, little by little by little, a person gets quite flustered.

LAYUT BINTI ALI: Not everyone is a *latah*, right? Only certain ones. Like me, I'm a *latah*. Like Cik Mah—she's a *latah*. In the village here, only certain ones. Not everyone—no! If everyone were like that, it would be like the whole world was crazy!

NARRATOR: As Cik Layut points out, not everyone becomes a *latah*. Many of the villagers think that a tendency to *latah* runs in families. Nenek Kamsiah Ngah thinks so, but she's not quite sure.

NENEK KAMSIAH BINTI NGAH: Once it starts, it becomes hereditary. If a mother is *latah*, her children will be too. Still, my mother was *latah* and I and my children aren't. Sometimes a mother is *latah* and her children are too. Grandmother is *latah* and Auntie Jenah, too. My mother was *latah* but I'm not. My brothers and sisters aren't either.

NARRATOR: The role of heredity in *latah*, if any, is uncertain. One thing that is certain is that the overwhelming majority of *latahs* are women. Villagers say this is because women have less *semangat*, or soul-substance, than men. They also point out that it's safer to startle women.

Subtitle: Cik Aspah binti Sidek

ASPAH BINTI SIDEK: Many more women than men are *latahs*.

ASPAH BINTI SIDEK: Women's *semangat* is a bit weaker than men's. Men have rather stronger *semangat*.

ASPAH BINTI SIDEK: Men's *semangat* is a bit stronger. Because even their physical strength is greater than women's.

SIDANG HUSSAIN BIN DALIP: Because if a man becomes *latah*, when people poke him suddenly in the ribs, he might become strong. So people fear his striking back. But people don't fear women much because they're weaker.

ASPAH BINTI SIDEK: People are afraid to poke and startle men. Even other men don't like to do it to each other. It's women who like to poke each other. When they're sitting around, someone pokes someone, someone else pokes someone else. Women are shy about poking men.

RCS: Shy or afraid?

ASPAH BINTI SIDEK: Shy; well, shy and afraid too.

NARRATOR: 'Tok Mohamad Hasan Rahmat is the only man in the village who admits to being *latah*, though the villagers told us of two others. Ever since he was young 'Tok Mohamad Hasan has been teaching *bersilat*, the Malay art of self-defense. When he's startled, he assumes *bersilat* poses.

NARRATOR: When startled, both ordinary persons and *latahs* sometimes hit out. In this case the woman hitting out is a *latah*, Cik Ara Leman.

NARRATOR: When startled, both ordinary persons and *latahs* often blurt out something that they normally wouldn't say, usually something silly, or holy, or obscene.

RCS: Is it always that Mak Cik can be startled so easily?

RAHAMA BINTI KAMIS: Oh, black and blue prick!

RCS: What just happened?

RAHAMA BINTI KAMIS: A boy poked me!

RCS: What was it that Mak Cik said after that?

RAHAMA BINTI KAMIS: What did I say?

RAHAMA BINTI KAMIS: I said, "Black and blue prick!"

RAHAMA BINTI KAMIS: Black and blue prick!

RAHAMA BINTI KAMIS: No. Prick!

NARRATOR: What Cik Rahama said is indecent by Malay standards, and she'd never say it in ordinary speech. However, she's just been startled, so it's excused. It's just considered part of *latah* and "funny."

NARRATOR: Sometimes when a *latah* is poked over and over, she becomes so flustered that her speech gets very scrambled.

ARA BINTI LEHMAN: Paint, paint, make small, small flowers. Growing make small, small flowers. Like the food cover—take it near the kitchen, kitchen. Below, below—go and take, go and take it—go and take the food cover. Like this—like this, like this—then paint it. Go and take it near the rice—kitchen door—there isn't any!

Subtitle: Cik Mah binti Kamis

NARRATOR: After being startled, *latahs* become highly aroused. Though her friends try to quiet her, it's hard for Cik Mah to settle down.

NENEK GAYAH BINTI MOHAMAD DIN: Quiet! Quiet, it's finished!

NARRATOR: Notice how intently Cik Ara watches me. When someone is startled and highly aroused, his or her attention is focused narrowly.

NARRATOR: This narrowed attention tends to be caught by prominent or unusual objects, like our shotgun microphone and our camera.

NARRATOR: After a *latah* is startled, movements may also capture her attention, and often she will match them.

YOUNG FISHERMAN: You can make her dance.

NARRATOR: Aroused and with attention narrowed and fixed, some *latahs* not only match movements but also do what others order them to do if they're flustered enough and if they're commanded forcefully enough.

Subtitle: Cik Alimah binti Mamad.

ALIMAH BINTI MAMAD: When she's sitting quietly we can take a piece of wood and bang it, or we can poke her in the ribs over and over and she'll become *latah*. She gets startled! Then if we order her to hit or dance, she'll hit or dance. And she'll do whatever we tell her to do with what she's holding. Whoever is in front of her will be hit. That's what a *latah* does!

RAHAMA BINTI KAMIS: If someone pokes and startles me and orders me to do something, I won't know what I'm doing. I might even take off my clothes!

Subtitle: Encik Yusof bin Kecut (husband)

YUSOF BIN KECUT: She only gets flustered if she's poked and startled.

YUSOF BIN KECUT: If we were just to tell her normally to take off her clothes, she wouldn't do it. But if she were poked and startled first, she might.

NARRATOR: Spouses and other family members can't do much to protect *latahs*; *latahs* are considered fair game.

YUSUF BIN KECUT: I don't believe there's anything we can do. We can't scold much because this kind of teasing is considered acceptable. But if it's too extreme, we can scold a little.

Subtitle: Cik Asmah binti Leman

ASMAH BINTI LEHMAN: It happened to my sister at a wedding. People kept startling her with pokes in the ribs, over and over. After she became *latah*, they ordered her to eat and she ate, they ordered her to dance and she danced. They ordered her to do all sorts of things and she did whatever they ordered.

Finally, someone ordered her to take her clothes off, and she did that too. She didn't know what was happening so she just stripped off. When she took her clothes off, the people around her were embarrassed, and her children were embarrassed too. One of her children got very angry. He gave her a stick and told her to hit the person teasing her. But instead of hitting him, she smashed all the dishes and plates. Her children were furious, and they took her home. When she came to her senses, she was ashamed.

It wasn't right or fair to do what they did to her, ordering her to strip! Startling her should have been enough. When she's that flustered, she doesn't know what she's doing. Whatever they ordered she did. Like a person without shame.

NARRATOR: Although they may be embarrassed, *latahs* are not considered either morally or legally responsible for what they do after being startled.

Subtitle: 'Tok Ahmad bin Ngah.

'TOK AHMAD BIN NGAH: A long time ago I heard a story. It happened when the British governed here. When the British were here there was a court in Pengkalan Balak. Major Bawal was the judge. He was responsible for sentencing.

One time a *latah* was holding a knife when someone came up from behind, startled her with a poke, and ordered "Stab!" Right away she stabbed, and she stabbed a man to death! When the victim died, she was arrested by the police.

A while later when the time for the trial came, she was taken to court. During the hearing the judge asked, "Why did you kill that man?" She said, "I didn't know what I was doing. When I killed him I didn't know anything! I'm a *latah*, and someone poked me and startled me. I didn't intend to kill anybody. I lost my reason because I was startled by a poke in the ribs, and when I was ordered to stab, right away I stabbed. Because of that I plead not guilty. "

About a week later came the trial. To prepare for it, the judge ordered a plank to be studded with nails, about ten nails. Then the plank was positioned with the point of the nails facing up. The judge said, "Now we'll test whether you're a real *latah*. " A policeman came up behind the *latah* and poked her in the ribs, and he shouted, "Slap those nails!" Right away the old lady slapped down on those nails. When she slapped down on the nails, blood began to gush from her hand.

The judge had to agree. "Truly, this woman is a real *latah*. This old woman is not guilty, the guilty one is the person who poked her. " So the woman who poked the *latah* was the one who was sentenced to be hanged.

NARRATOR: Sometimes *latahs* are teased for a very long time, even if they're obviously exhausted. Watch how Cik Ara is not permitted to escape, and notice how tired she appears.

NARRATOR: *Latahs* are startled and teased like this over and over and over again. One way to cope is to accept the role of a *latah* and play it for all it's worth. After all, a *latah* is not considered responsible for anything she does after being startled.

NARRATOR: It's clear that Cik Mun enjoys the clowning that the *latah* role permits.

NARRATOR: Notice the "Eh!" sound Cik Mun repeatedly makes. It functions as a kind of self-startle, and by signifying that she's been startled, it justifies what she does. *Latahs* say "Eh!" only when performing and then only when others aren't startling them enough.

NARRATOR: Heterosexual men who are *latah* strongly resist entering the *latah* state. They don't voluntarily clown or perform. In contrast, homosexual male transvestites, who are frequently *latahs*, usually accept the *latah* role. This young man is not from our village but from a neighboring city.

NARRATOR: Hajjah Misah, who earlier described how her *latah* began, is a dignified woman, so at first becoming fair game for startle teasing wasn't easy for her. But she's learned to cope and even to use the role of being a *latah* for some teasing of her own. After being interviewed she offered to let us film a *latah* performance. The couple you'll see playing with her are her neighbors. Notice how they shape and modulate what she does.

HAJJAH MISAH BANI[1]: When I chew betel, it's very "good," sir! Bump you off! I'll betel you! On the ground it pushes through; here it's strong as wood. Bump you off, Mat! Really meticulous! Really meticulous! Bump you off! Isn't this "good," sir? More. This is very fine, sir! I'm fed up, Mat! Want to watch? Come! I'm fed up, betel is finished, gone to sea. Die Mat! Bump you off! Put here, here it pushes through. This is fine wood, this is. Ah. Pushed through. Fine wood, finished, topsy-turvy, bumped off. Ah. . .I'm fed up again. I'm tired. I've gone to sea. You betrayed me, wasn't it you! Why did you bring me here, Mat? You ordered me to tell a story, ordered me to talk. Pushing it through here is fine! Enough pushing through. You betrayed me, wasn't it you? Bump you off, turn you upside down. A frog! What is it? Good Heavens! So many different kinds of things he brought here for me: a frog, a spade, anything you want, like, like. I've finished doing anything. Only a little left. Enough. Finished. I'm fed up now. I've also wanted to go to sea. Forget it. Why don't you just be quiet! I'm going to go to sleep!

NARRATOR: Everyone startles, and everywhere some people startle more readily and more strongly than others.

Subtitle: East Lansing, Michigan, U. S. A.

NARRATOR: In this composite film of a laboratory experiment, the two guns behind the women will fire simultaneously. Try to watch both women.

NARRATOR: The woman on the left is teased by her family and friends. Sometimes they startle her intentionally too, just to see what she'll do. But she's not intentionally startled often, or in public, or by casual acquaintances. I believe that if she were a Malay villager, she would be made into a *latah*.

NARRATOR: However, Malaysia is not the only place where startling readily and strongly has been elaborated in a culture-specific way. The island of Hokkaido in northern Japan where the Ainu people live is another. Here are excerpts from a film collected there in 1936.

Subtitle: Imu, a Psycho-reactive Manifestation of Ainu Women

NARRATOR: The Ainu people shown are not related either ethnically or culturally to the Malays. You'll see hyperstartling, flustered behavior, hitting, matching, dancing on command and sexually explicit gestures in this culture-specific elaboration too.

Subtitle: SNAKE!

NARRATOR: Behavior complexes much like *latah* have been reported from many parts of the world. Wherever hyperstartling persons are startled often and teased, the same behaviors are seen: hitting, matching, obedience, and saying vulgar words. However, the details of what happens, who may startle whom, how the audience modulates what happens, and how it all is understood—these are always shaped by a particular cultural setting. *Latah* as we've been seeing it in this film is specific to Malay culture. It's a Malay way of dealing with hyperstartling persons.

NARRATOR: At weddings and at dances, in this case at our research project's farewell dance, Malay villagers play with their *latah* neighbors. Hyperstartling is a psychological state, but *latah* is an interactive process; it's a culture-specific elaboration of the startle reflex.

Tail Credits:

(Stationary)—Translating voice
Cik Rashidah Shuib

(Roll)—Support for the research illustrated
by this film came from the

Harry Frank Guggenheim Foundation
and an NIH Biomedical
Research Support Grant to
Michigan State University

Institutional sponsors
Institut Penyelidikan Perubatan
Kuala Lumpur, Malaysia
The Departments of
Psychiatry and Anthropology
The Medical Anthropology Program
The College of Human Medicine
Michigan State University
The University of California
International Center for
Medical Research

Thanks to
Encik Jaafar Omar, Sidang Hussain Dalip,
Encik Ahmad bin Ngah, Richard Schmidt,
Bob Wilks, Encik Mohamad Md. Yusoff
The Sri Kenangan Joget Band
The *latahs* and other villagers of
Kampung Padang Kemunting
and surrounding area, Melaka State,
West Malaysia

The Ainu sequences were
provided through the courtesy of
Professor Uchimura Yoshi
University of Tokyo.

NOTE

1. This is a rough translation of Hajjah Misah's longest speech in this sequence, given here to suggest the flavor of the performance. The sequence is untranslated in the film. The need to hear Hajjah Misah's unusual vocal tone made voice-over translation inappropriate, and our severely limited budget made the subtitles we originally hoped to provide impossible. The "scrambled" nature of *latah* speech makes this an approximate translation only.

INDEX

n = note

acoustic startle, defined 11. *See also* loud noises

action, release of 117–118. *See also* motion

actual startles 62, 103–104, 108, 112–113. *See also* startle reflex

adolescents 105

advertisements 68, 82, 83, 92n10

aesthetic sensitivity 75

Africa, view of startle in 225, 243

age differences, perceived for startle 77

Ainu. *See* imu

alarms 68, 246

American presidency 80

animals. *See also* birds; creepy crawlies; primates; snakes
  experiencing startle 134–136
  as models 7

anticipation 126–127. *See also* startle reflex, states inducing

approach, with attention-capture 147–148

art
  conveying cultural meaning 60–61, 94–95, 136–137
  startle as device in 61, 63–91, 103, 108, 112–113, 124–127, 129–130, 136–137, 232–233

attention. *See also* attention-capture; hypervigilance
  neurophysiology of 127, 241–242
  prior to startle 105, 127, 129, 241
  redirection of 8–9, 43, 65–66, 105, 231, 241–242
  social 80, 184

attention-capture 81, 116–117, 143–152. *See also* approach; learning; metaphor; startle-matching syndrome; startle stimuli
  for *latahs* 161, 162, 174, 191, 234
  linked with startle-matching 206, 222, 233, 242
  neurophysiology of 206, 241–242

automatic obedience 124, 150, 152–156. *See also* commands;

INDEX OF CITATIONS

n = note